The Three-Dimensional Leader: Negotiating Your Mission, Resources and Context provides a unique, scalable paradigm and interviews of business and organizational leaders, who successfully have put these principles into practice. Leaders within corporations, small and medium sized companies, and not-for-profits will benefit from Earl C. Wallace's original concepts and illustrations that answer the question: "What is a leader supposed to do?"

What do the following people have in common?

- A military general who trained subordinates to understand "the art of leadership," who now heads up a growing national veterans' organization and oversees developing work and business opportunities for homeless veterans

- The head of a convenience store chain who shares ownership with employees and has grown the business to 325 stores throughout three states and achieves a billion dollars in annual sales

- The director of a not-for-profit city housing corporation who receives foreclosure notices on his third day on the job and who must overcome challenges hidden by the previous director

- The owner of a trailer supply distributorship who provided such amazing customer service that even when competitors tried to undersell him, his business continued to grow

- An entrepreneur who expands into a new territory only to find that cutthroat competition makes it impossible for him to succeed in the new venture, jeopardizing his businesses. As bankruptcy looms, he takes the lead in taking pay cuts and gives the employees the opportunity to rally around the mission in hopes the company and their jobs can survive

- A route manager whose product quality and income are being undermined by decisions made by a new crop of inexperienced leaders from a remote corporate location

Each are three-dimensional leaders who know that "mission matters most," that "people provide potential," and how to "convert within the context!" The Three-Dimensional Leader: Negotiating Your Mission, Resources, and Context unfolds their stories to show how these concepts apply in real-life case studies. The Three-Dimensional Leader will take you on insightful journeys you do not want to miss!

Whether tasked to organize a group effort, steer a project team, perform as a shift supervisor, run a plant, steer a division, or oversee an entire corporation, the three-dimensional leadership paradigm can assist you to develop your leadership profile and maximize your potential.

The Three-Dimensional Leader

The Three-Dimensional Leader

Negotiating Your Mission
Resources and Context

Earl C. Wallace

TATE PUBLISHING & *Enterprises*

Published by Tate Publishing & Enterprises, LLC
127 E. Trade Center Terrace | Mustang, Oklahoma 73064 USA
1.888.361.9473 | www.tatepublishing.com

Tate Publishing is committed to excellence in the publishing industry. The company reflects the philosophy established by the founders, based on Psalm 68:11,
"The Lord gave the word and great was the company of those who published it."

Book design copyright © 2009 by Tate Publishing, LLC. All rights reserved.
Cover design by Joey Garrett
Interior design by Stefanie Rooney
Edited by Kylie Lyons

Published in the United States of America
ISBN: 978-1-60696-883-3
1. Business & Economics, Leadership
2. Business & Economics, Motivational
09.05.14

Acknowledgments

Thanks to my wife, Pamela, a brilliant leader who discerns the context, has turned me on to many great leadership materials and resources, and who continues to turn me on. Thanks to my daughter Deb, who understands the most important mission in life is family, and whose three children, my grandchildren, Daina, Danielle, and Jamie, have given me great insight into the challenges organizations—like families—face. Their unwavering dedication to the mission of play actually gave me the title of this book, as they frequently operate in their own dimensions, seeking to entertain themselves. Thanks to my son, Tim, who is a great manager who always sees what needs to be done and then works within his local context to achieve it. Thanks to my daughter Carrie, who is a naturally born leader on the road to discovering where that gift will take her.

I thank the leaders who took time out of their busy lives to be interviewed for this book, so others would have the benefit of their experiences. Thank you to the proofreaders, Kathleen, Salvatore, and Deanna, who paid exquisite attention to detail, and whose comments and suggestions made this a much, much better product.

If you are reading this book, I trust you are interested in growing as a leader. Thank you for taking time from your life to review my work here. May your dimensions and capacity as a leader be expanded as you do so.

Table of Contents

Part One

The Three Dimensions

Introduction

This book puts forth a leadership template that addresses what leaders are supposed to do. Throughout my life I moved in and out of leadership positions, sometimes feeling I was doing a good job and other times feeling I was not doing so good a job. I did not have a manual that explained what I was supposed to be focusing on. I did not have a paradigm to provide a frame of reference for comparison or a template to evaluate what I was doing. This book provides that paradigm.

As I continued being promoted in my own career, I tried learning leadership by observing the leaders around me. This left me lacking, however, because while some of them did some things very well, they also seemed to have huge blind spots and did other things that frustrated workers and partners, and they missed key opportunities to lead and conduct themselves in ways that inspired employees to serve with pride and enthusiasm. As I pursued my MBA and studied organizational failures and successes, I found some great materials but still could not find a template that provided a gauge to guide leaders regardless of the circumstances they are in or the type of organizations they manage and oversee.

In the immediate years following completion of business school, I began developing my own template, which I tested and honed as I got opportunities to work with leaders in different types of organizations in the private, not-for-profit, and government sectors. In the following pages I set forth the answers I have found to my question: "What are leaders supposed to do?" I believe this template can assist leaders to achieve a fresh and clear perspective on their roles and responsibilities that will enable them to revitalize their management of the people they oversee to accomplish the missions entrusted to them. My paradigm provides a scalable template to rate leadership effectiveness.

Whether tasked to organize a group effort, steer a project team, perform as a shift supervisor, run a plant, steer a division, or oversee an entire corporation, this paradigm can help you. Every leader's abilities can be improved through learning and development. Leadership can be augmented by proper exercise, just as muscle groups are developed. This book is a training aid to develop your personal leadership profile. It seeks to strengthen your performance by providing a new leadership mind-set. It provides a new perspective on what to do as you lead. Most importantly, it will help you make the most of your experience as you develop your maximum potential as a leader.

What do the following people have in common?

- A military general who trained subordinates to understand "the art of leadership," who now heads up a growing national veterans' organization and oversees developing work and business opportunities for homeless veterans

- The head of a convenience store chain who shares ownership with employees and has grown the business to 325 stores throughout three states and achieves a billion dollars in annual sales

- The director of a not-for-profit city housing corporation who receives foreclosure notices on his third day on the job and who must overcome challenges hidden by the previous director

- The owner of a trailer supply distributorship who provided such amazing customer service that even when competitors tried to undersell him, his business continued to grow

- An entrepreneur who expands into a new territory only to find that cutthroat competition makes it impossible for him to succeed in the new venture, jeopardizing his corporation. As bankruptcy looms, he presents employees with the opportunity to rally around the mission by taking pay cuts in hopes the company and their jobs can survive

- A route manager whose product quality and income are being undermined by decisions made by a new crop of inexperienced leaders from a remote corporate location

Each are three-dimensional leaders who know that "mission matters most," that "people provide potential," and how to "convert within the context!" *The Three-Dimensional Leader: Negotiating Your Mission, Resources, and Context* unfolds their stories to show how these concepts apply in real-life case studies.

My three-dimensional leadership concepts will revolutionize your perspective on your business and organizational challenges that have to be negotiated to effectively deploy and manage people and other resources to accomplish your missions within the changing contexts in which they unfold.

Here is a brief list of my own leadership accomplishments achieved in education and government services by deploying the Three-Dimensional principles in my book:

- As a high school English teacher, ninety-two to ninety-four percent of my students passed the New York State Regents exams each year I taught. By comparison, most teachers in the State average between fifty to seventy-six percent.

- As a State Veterans Benefits Counselor, I won the largest retroactive VA settlement in New York State history (and possibly in federal history). The claim provided a previously disenfranchised female veteran with retroactive disability compensation from 1954–1994, plus ongoing monthly entitlements.

- As a State Department of Labor Veterans Program Administrator, within nine months I reinvigorated the organization to meet its federal performance standards for the first time, and by my fourth and fifth quarters at the helm, employees exceeded those standards by ten to fifteen percent.

- As a business consultant, I assisted entrepreneurs to understand my MRC—mission, resources, and context—

concepts to determine where the synergies exist around which their businesses should be organized, and how to obtain resources and deploy them within the operational and competitive contexts to achieve business and organizational success.

These accomplishments were achieved as I deployed and fine-tuned the principles in this book. Read on to discover what I mean by "mission matters most, people provide potential, and how to convert within the context." When you discover how to apply these concepts in your personal, business, and organizational life, the people around you, clients, customers, employees, and bosses will notice positive results.

Background

Like Peter Drucker, who, since the 1940s, has defined the human element's role in managing organizational achievement, Jim Collins's work in *Good to Great* struck a chord within me and helped me solidify my ideas of what outlook, attitudes, and actions characterize an effective leader, and I strategically applied them within the organizations where I exercised leadership. Collins's work is a study of why comparable companies in all kinds of industries succeeded while their counterparts failed, primarily due to the quality of leadership, which he identified as consisting of five levels. Some of Collins's levels, however, are determined by the actual position one has within an organization. My work deals strictly with issues related to the leader's character and the way he or she views the world.

I realized there were three things God required of leaders in the book of Judges in the Bible, and those leaders provide excellent models of both positive and negative leadership behaviors. I formulated my template when I realized that leaders need to be concerned about three operational elements: mission, resources, and context.

There are three dimensions in which a leader can operate. Three-dimensional leadership is the most desirable and effective and encompasses what Jim Collins describes as his level-five leader, who selflessly pursues organizational objectives. A one-dimensional leader does not care about the organizational mission but is egocentric and uses his/her leadership position to pursue personal agendas. A two-dimensional leader may understand the mission and may grasp to some extent how the resources are supposed to accomplish it but fails to see the organizational "big picture." The three-dimensional leader is conscious of all three operational elements and is distinguished by an ability to get an objective ten-thousand-foot view of the "context" to see how available resources are deployed strategically within the arena in which the mission unfolds. An organization achieves an enduring legacy by repeating the leadership principles outlined in this book, over and over again, through the succession of many leaders.

Below I explain what leaders are supposed to do and how they are to go about doing it. Though I explain the answer in simple terms, the application is not simplistic. In the following pages, sophisticated principles are presented so that leaders of varying degrees of experience and position readily can grasp and apply them to their specific circumstances, whether on a school or professional sports team, organizing a military operation, overseeing government services, developing and pursing strategy in a retail or manufacturing operation, or from a corporate boardroom. Our leadership performance is determined by how we process the elements of this template to demystify the complexities around us to bring structure to ambiguity, which enables us to pursue rational strategies for organizational achievement.

The behavioral aspects that govern our responses and who we are as leaders are a matter of our maturity and character development. Great leadership, in my opinion, is about passion for a mission and a calculated, reasoned approach to deploy resources appropriately, so the mission is achieved effectively within a particular context. If the heart (character) is right, the head can be right. If the heart is wrong, regardless of what is in the head, we probably will respond emotionally in a way that undermines or thwarts our effectiveness in pursing the mission. Companies that have been graced with mission-focused three-dimensional leaders historically have progressed to outperform their peers and achieve the status of greatness. This book unpacks what mission-focused leadership is and does. Any organization led by it has the greatest potential to fulfill its purpose for being.

Chapter One

Leadership Is a Blend of Behavioral Science and Art

Effective leadership is a blend of the science of observing the physical elements of mission, resources, and context with the art of how to deploy those resources strategically into the changing context to fulfill that mission. Leadership is the social science of how to work with people. It is understanding what needs to be accomplished, with what and with whom it must be accomplished, and into what circumstances people and other resources are to be deployed to accomplish it. Leadership is about understanding how we go about deploying resources and working with others in such a way as to efficiently and effectively accomplish the mission within the particular circumstances in which it must unfold.

A few years ago, all my leadership and managerial studies solidified, and I was able to conceptualize a basic template through which to perceive and analyze how leaders ought to think and behave. I have been fortunate to see how implementing these principles can have a dramatic impact on organizational performance. By deploying them, I led more than a hundred professional employees in a government program, spread throughout a large state, to achieve their performance standards for the first time and then to exceed them by ten to fifteen percent within five quarters of my tenure there. The environment negotiated to accomplish this achievement was characterized by "politics as usual" at the federal, state, county, and local levels. Employees also strategically pursued their mission in offices where consolidations caused them to coordinate with others who were paid through varying funding streams, each of which was governed by laws and overseen by bureaucratic policies that limit employees to fulfilling certain functions and not other rationally related functions.

I found that the principles in this book resonated with my employees, so they focused on their mission and how to accomplish it within that complex context. The best employees intuitively discern their environment, and they negotiate it well. Because of their intellectual discernment and their heartfelt mission focus, they understand how to efficiently fulfill program requirements for their roles and responsibilities in a way that complies with all the needs of the larger, complex, and diverse organization. If the principles I lay out in this book can be beneficial to improving employee performance and productivity in that environment, they can be used to help leaders understand how their workforces can achieve their missions in other environments and industries where multiple partner, supplier, manufacturing, and support operations must be coordinated to succeed.

In *The Seven Habits of Highly Successful People,* Stephen Covey quotes Aristotle: "We are what we repeatedly do. Excellence is not an act but a habit." May this book set us on a path of repeatedly doing what excellent leaders do. May the concepts in this book help leaders everywhere make a habit of identifying their organization's principle mission, available resources, and the relevant context in which operations must unfold, so they can cut through the noise and the immediate daily pressures to continually be able to focus on the issues upon which their long-term success ultimately depends.

Learning How to Lead Requires Learning How to Learn

Leadership can be taught, and we can learn to be better leaders. The primary step is learning how to learn. To grow you must recognize that there is something to learn about how to lead. Even though we may not know specifically what there is to be learned, a willingness to learn is essential, and acknowledging "I don't know what I don't know" is a great beginning. We sever ourselves from potential growth by saying, "I don't need to know whatever it is that I don't know."

You grow as a leader by taking on a leadership role that provides the opportunity to bear more responsibility for an organization's mission and its related job processes. Though it is apparent that some of us naturally are more disposed to directing others, good leadership ability is not an inborn trait that some have and others lack. People can study and grow to be great leaders. The learning process can be both formal and informal. Just as you learn the technical aspects of your job, you can learn and develop into a better leader of that job.

I believe over time people who had no desire or intention of becoming a leader find that they grow to a place where they can see their job in a larger dimension to understand the employer's mission, and how and why the company's product or services are valuable to customers. These employees understand the value proposition of why customers choose to do business with the company, and they strive to make the organization better at delivering what those customers value. Those with leadership potential also learn how meaningful the relationships with suppliers are to the parent company, and they learn what drives the organization's partners to fulfill their responsibilities in the mutual mission that is spelled out in its agreements and contracts.

If we think of leaders functioning in different dimensions in terms of how well they see and are successful at steering an organization to fulfill its mission, those who rank the highest understand how to trigger the motivation of internal workers and external partners so they come together to perform their individual assignments effectively to fulfill their mutual reasons for existing in the organization and partnership.

Leadership is serving others so they can work in an organized, systematic, and efficient way. Leadership is negotiating to arrange a set of circumstances that are favorable for others to succeed at their jobs. Leadership is respecting your company by organizing, focusing, and empowering the people it has hired to commendably do the jobs it wants them to accomplish. Great leaders serve their organizations and the people within them with unwavering dedication to the mission. To springboard from what Patrick Lencioni says in his book, *The Five Dysfunctions of a Team,* great leaders organize and serve employees and volunteers with an indefatigable mission focus that fosters an exceptional team spirit that accomplishes far more than any mere collection of individuals can. To understand leadership and its applications, it will help us to review some models of both good and poor examples.

Leadership principles are timeless because human nature has not changed over the centuries. The three-dimensional (III-D) leadership behaviors that motivate people today to collectively achieve outstanding results are the same that motivated people yesterday. The one-dimensional (I-D) and two-dimensional (II-D) leadership pitfalls that contribute to an organization's underperformance yesterday are what cause them to fail today.

Because leading involves people, leadership can be thought of as "the study of human behavior within an organizational context." The concept of "context" and accomplishing a mission within a context that I introduce in this book is central to being an effective leader who will successfully accomplish the mission in any organization of any type and size.

Great leadership is a set of human behaviors to which people tend to respond well and will rally around to accomplish the purposes and outcomes that both the followers and the leader have been hired or placed within the organization to achieve. The leadership principles to which people positively respond apply to all types of organizations, whether they are for-profit or not-for-profit and whether they pay salaries that are above or below average or if they operate primarily with volunteers.

Good and poor leadership is found in all kinds of organizations, including privately held companies and publicly traded corporations, government, churches, and civic and volunteer organizations. The behavioral traits that make for effective leadership in organizations that achieve their missions primarily with volunteers are the same ones that make for effective leadership in the for-profit workplace.

Those in leadership roles make, break, or stagnate an organization. There are many leaders who are like the Bible's Samson, who have great personal gifts but never pull off the organizational mission. There also are many leaders who find themselves in the challenging (and possibly frustrating) middle-management or transitional circumstances similar to those in which Samuel operated. There are many of us who can thank God that we have been led by a leader who demonstrated the three-dimensional characteristics that Deborah did.

I could have called this book *Three Dimensions of Employee Behavior*, because regardless of where one is within an organization's hierarchical structure, one can have a I-, II-, or III-D perspective. I do not want readers to tune out the message here because they do not perceive themselves as leaders.

A friend of mine, Michael Martinez, who has studied Albert Einstein extensively, says that "Einstein's contribution was not so much that he was a mathematician, but that he gave us a way to look at the world." Einstein is not renowned for inventing anything but for showing a profound understanding of the relationship between the elements within the context of what he studied. Just as Einstein's Theory of Relativity provides a template for looking at the universe in terms of how different phenomena are related to each other, my aim is to provide a clear and compelling understanding of the relationship between the leader's focus and behaviors and organizational success. One cannot disassociate leadership, however, from the responses the leader gets from followers. Great leaders have great followers. If the leader violates basic principles related to how humans get along with each other in organizational settings and behaviors that facilitate them trusting and working well with each other, that leader will tend to fail in the mission he or she is tasked to lead to accomplish.

In his inaugural address to the Prussian Academy of Sciences in 1914, Albert Einstein said,

> The theorist's method involves his using as his foundation general postulates or "principles" from which he can deduce conclusions. He must first discover his principles and then draw conclusions which follow from them ... the scientist has to worm these general principles out of nature by perceiving certain general features which permit of precise formulation, amidst large and complexes of empirical facts.[1]

The paradigm I outline for the three dimensions of leadership provides valid principles to the degree that it satisfactorily corresponds to the reality of human interaction within organizational settings. I briefly illustrate the three-dimensional leadership paradigm through three biblical characters—the strong man Samson, the wise man Samuel, and the astute, courageous, and sensitive Deborah—and then expand upon those principles with interviews and stories of some great contemporary leaders that glean from them leadership values that illustrate how the principles in this book have helped them achieve outstanding results at accomplishing their missions. I believe the stories will resonate with you because they illuminate and reflect experiences many of us share and are powerful tools to educate and encourage us.

As Einstein culminated years of study by giving the world the precise, accurate formula of $E=MC^2$, which ushered the world into the nuclear age, I aim to provide a precise and simple template to help leaders everywhere to accomplish their missions by negotiating a set of circumstances that is most conducive to employees successfully doing their jobs, whether they are selling, manufacturing, distributing, or providing services. To be effective, leaders must accurately perceive and act within both the internal and external contexts that must be negotiated to provide for circumstances wherein employees can be successful. They provide simplified processes and instructions to managers, who in turn provide easily comprehensible direction to subordinates who readily understand the process steps to accomplish their jobs. Thus the organization "converts within the context" to achieve its mission.

Great leadership brings structure where ambiguity exists by providing straightforward and simplified approaches to explaining and handling the various elements within a context, which can seem so daunting. Leaders only can do what they know, and they only know what they have been willing to learn. While it may make us feel important to go around and tell everyone that our jobs are complicated, difficult, and tough, we need to understand that great leadership demystifies complexities to provide simple, actionable direction to subordinates. In his book *Good to Great,* Jim Collins explains that brilliance provides simplifications of complex concepts, so that the complexities are handled in bite-size, actionable chunks. He illustrates this concept through the life of Albert Einstein as follows:

> Albert Einstein did not try to impress the world with the complexity of thought it took for him to develop the theory of relativity, which was a gigantic intellectual leap that opened the door to the nuclear age. He did not try to impress the world by displaying the parking lots that he could have paved with the papers full of equations that it took for him to develop the concepts and mathematically compute them over more than the decade it took to develop them. Once he grasped this amazingly voluminous concept and mulled it over and lectured on it repeatedly and analyzed it time and again with the other mathematicians and scientists, the concepts became clearer and clearer to him and he was able to take the highly complex and make it simple for people to understand. Rather than impress us, Albert Einstein, who was a lover of God and a believer in scripture, gave the world an amazingly actable formula that was as beautiful in its simplicity as it was intellectually deep: $E=MC^2$.

I hope you find this book the $E=MC^2$ of leadership that provides concepts in a simple, practical guide that demystifies some rather complex issues and dynamics. I hope the distinctions and definitions of the three dimensions of leadership provide examples most of us can identify and relate to and see the steps we immediately can take to manifest a higher dimension of leadership in our current situations. I also hope that the templates of leadership in this book will be frameworks that support us to provide three-dimensional leadership behaviors in all our organizational interactions, whether within our families, our businesses, our workplaces, our churches, and our volunteer situations.

Chapter Two

The Role of Mission, Vision, and Values in Strategic Planning

Here is how mission, vision, and values relate to organizational direction and achievement. A strategic plan explains how an organization intends to use what it has to accomplish what it desires or is required to do. A strategic plan says, "We will use these resources to accomplish this mission that will get us to our vision as we pursue it with these values." People implement strategic plans by living out values when dealing with coworkers, partners, suppliers, and customers. When employees are mission focused, they will deploy resources to fulfill the mission. If the mission is achieved successfully over time, the organization's vision becomes reality. I once heard the relationship between mission, vision, and values explained this way: Dr. Martin Luther King, Jr.'s mission was equality. His vision was expressed beautifully in his "I Have a Dream" speech. And his values were nonviolence.

Mission

As a leader, Dr. Martin Luther King, Jr. successfully rallied people to the mission of equality. The values of nonviolence fueled the operational engine that propelled the people of his organization to persevere by focusing on achieving the vision of nonviolent revolution. Once volunteers rallied to the cause, Dr. King focused them on the organization's values—so much so that his marchers faced violent and murderous opposition in the most hostile environments, yet they persevered in carrying out the organization's mission with the values of nonviolence.

Dr. Martin Luther King, Jr. embodied three-dimensional leadership. He understood the mission, and he passionately articulated a vision to achieve it. King stated his mission and vision so clearly that it was easy for people to follow him, to see what he was talking about, and to believe that if he could do it, they also could. He organized people resources around a set of values that they consistently lived and applied. King helped his followers negotiate the hostile context as a team that often locked arms together and sang "We Shall Overcome"! The America we live in today is in large part the fruition of the vision—the Dream, which was the focus of Dr. King's life.

Vision

Vision is the future state of the world or your organization that will exist if you use your resources appropriately to fulfill your mission. There are two primary mistakes when it comes to vision: the first is not having any; the second is having the wrong one. Proverbs 29:18 states, "Where there is no vision, the people perish." Where there is no revelation, the people cast off restraint; but blessed is he who keeps the law (KJV). In this case, let's say that the law stands for the mission. Revelation refers to the strategy to do the work of the mission that, if successful, leads to the vision. "Casting off restraint" is another term for losing focus and straying from the mission path.

If leaders lack vision to articulate your organization's mission, it can drift like a rudderless ship, or languish, stagnate, and die. An appropriate vision is one that is consistent with the reasons why the organization exists. An appropriate vision resonates within the hearts and minds of followers, as it is consistent with why they signed up to join the company in the first place, so they rally to pursue it and devote themselves to work hard to see it come to fruition. The lack of an appropriate vision results in lackadaisical followers and organizations that meander about with no sense of determination to consistently achieve a mission.

Vision mistake number two is to strike out in the wrong direction, to pursue the wrong goal, or to reach for the wrong prize. Proverbs 19:2 says, "It is not good to have zeal without knowledge, nor to be hasty and miss the way" (NIV). When leaders are objective in their mission focus, they may make a mistake and catch the wind of the wrong initiative and set sail down a course that is wrong for their organizational vessel to negotiate, but their ship will not sail that course for very long. A friend of mine named Lou refers to certain types of leaders as "pirates," because they are always saying, "Aye, aye, aye"—meaning, "I, I, I." Pirates get into leadership and sincerely believe that their egotistical desire for personal recognition and getting their name and picture in the newspaper is good for the organization. They sincerely are wrong.

Great leadership works toward developing and organizing a favorable set of circumstances that gives employees the opportunity to succeed at their jobs. Pirates never stop to think that the energy they expend trying to get their name mentioned is time and energy taken away from doing the jobs for which they were really hired. Great leadership is not making a name for ourselves by touting initiatives that will get us noticed; it is designing processes so that those at the front end are successful with their clients, equipment repairs, manufacturing, service delivery, et cetera . . .

Pirate leaders have a vision to see their name up in lights and their picture taken with the "right people." Pirates hijack the organization's mission and sacrifice the organization's resources for the sake of "I, I, I." They may say they are trying to bring name recognition to the "organization" or "the program," but those words ring hollow—especially when they demand that everyone around them stop doing their real jobs to continually work on one project or another that is designed only to get the leader into the limelight, at the front of the ceremony, or at the head table of events—even those that are unrelated to the organization's mission.

By contrast, III-D leaders keep the organizational ship on course with its overarching long-term vision. Even in a crisis they respond by keeping their eye on the long-term goals, so that everything they do to get through the challenge is done as consistently as possible with the course they planned the organization to travel in the first place.

Vision casting shapes the mission and inspires people to fulfill it within the context that the organization functions. Bill Hybels, pastor of Willow Creek Church in South Barrington (near Chicago), Illinois, says, "Vision is the fuel that leaders run on. Vision is the energy that creates action; the fire that ignites the passion of followers; the clear call that sustains focused effort year after year, decade after decade, as people offer consistent and sacrificial service."[2] A vision of what can be accomplished brings the mission into focus.

Without vision people lose the vitality that keeps their energy directed toward the right efforts. Hybels says that when a group or team is discouraged, it needs the vision of an encourager who can see the process steps and encourage them to take the next one and then the one after that. When the context seems chaotic and disorganized, the team needs the vision of a gifted administrator who can provide direction that shapes order out of ambiguity. When negative circumstances have overcome us and we are hurting from a setback, we need the vision of a leader who provides understanding, forgiveness, and healing.

Henry Ford had an appropriate vision for an auto-manufacturing and sales company. He envisioned a Ford in every driveway. Dr. Martin Luther King, Jr. had an appropriate vision for a nation without prejudice, where children of different races could play together without concern about their individual skin colors. Billy Graham envisioned tens of thousands of people in stadiums gathered together to hear the Gospel. Steve Jobs has a vision that the Apple computer is an extension of what people do. He wants every kid in school to have access to one. Mission fulfillment starts with someone in leadership envisioning what can be.

Effective leaders cast compelling visions to which their followers can pledge wholehearted allegiance. Vision casting involves stating the organization's main purpose and reason for its existence in a slogan-like statement that will wear nicely on a T-shirt. At every appropriate opportunity, leaders continually restate that vision to keep it in focus.

Vision compels conscientious commitment, increases the seasoned veteran's sense of ownership, and provides focused parameters for the members of the organization. Vision equips employees with the value system to choose only those activities that are in line with the mission. When the appropriate vision is cast effectively and consistently, succession planning is intuitive, as there are multi-levels of employees and volunteers who can articulate it, are passionate about it, and who are available to step up into leadership to fulfill it and pass it on to others.

To achieve a vision involves setting goals. A BHAG, says Jim Collins, is a big, hairy, audacious goal. For a BHAG to be rational and become reality, it must be attainable by doing the mission in a way that is consistent with the organization's values. If people have pledged allegiance to the organization's vision, working toward a BHAG that is consistent with it inspires and motivates them.

Three-dimensional leaders are guided by the appropriate vision to grasp and properly negotiate the three operational elements of mission, resources, and context. Two-dimensional leadership grasps and properly negotiates only one or two of the operational factors. One-dimensional leadership fails to grasp any of the three operational components. If leaders consistently focus on the mission and can get people at all levels of the organization to do likewise, and if leaders effectively negotiate the context appropriately to deploy resources and continually align them so employees can succeed at their jobs, their organizations have a high potential to succeed and see their visions come to fruition.

Values

Many organizations spend lots and lots of time on vision and mission statements and, as an afterthought, issue a values statement as a series of nouns like "honesty, integrity, continuous learning..." which never amount to anything more than a series of platitudes. This may be an indication that leaders are uncertain of the mission. If you do not know the mission, you certainly cannot link it to any action words or values. Worse yet is that some organizations never get around to articulating a set of values. I believe that most people find accountability uncomfortable, and, once articulated and spelled out, values become the mirror that anyone at any level in the organization can hold up to leaders and pretty much make a determination as to whether or not their actions and behaviors reflect or deflect the organization's stated values. People do not necessarily like holding others accountable and do not like being held accountable. We tend to avoid, therefore, the issue of organizational values.

Values are best captured and articulated once the organization has well defined the culture it wants to hold up as both its internal heart and public face. To have one culture when dealing with the public and another one for internal company policy confuses employees and is asking for trouble. Conflict is bound to emerge over the tension between the two. When employees act in accordance with the internal values, they can be placing themselves in conflict with external public laws and statutes. Inconsistency in the application of values is "hypocrisy." One-dimensional leaders all too often leave followers and constituents scratching their heads because their personal behavior within the organization is markedly inconsistent with the stated organizational values. People grow disinterested at best, and outright resentful at worst, by leadership that acts out "Do what I say, not what I do."

Perceptions of institutionalized hypocrisy breeds public distrust and resentment. Contrast the public attitude about the tobacco industry, where internal memos indicated that they knew they were selling a product harmful to humans, and the Johnson and Johnson Company's reaction to the Tylenol scare of 1982. Companies whose internal values are in sync with their public personae quickly will own up to accidents, challenges, and mistakes. They, therefore, will cycle through the trauma more rapidly and efficiently to transition through any possible red ink to more quickly get back into the public confidence and achieve black ink. Those companies that dissemble and attempt to deflect responsibility will spend a lot of time, effort, and money doing so. Long-term beneficial results, including enduring stockholder value, are achieved by those who live their values both within the home office as well as in the public forum.

Johnson and Johnson took effective action to safeguard the public by living out its values in the face of unprecedented adversity. It is believed the company recalled 31 million bottles of Tylenol with a retail value at that time of over $100 million. The company offered to exchange solid tablets for any and all capsules already purchased by consumers. Johnson and Johnson's conscientious, aggressive, values-driven action, coupled with its ability to negotiate the new context posed by the threat of product tampering, resulted in an amazing product rebound less than a year later. About a month after the recall, it reintroduced new, triple-sealed capsules, and over the next several years, Tylenol was effectively priced and advertised to become the most popular over-the-counter pain medicine in the nation. By contrast, tobacco companies face ongoing lawsuits and are targeted today in negative TV ads by special-interest groups and routinely are summoned before government officials.

Values articulate the heart and motives that drive actions. To be intentional about the behaviors organizations desire, they should be clear, concise, and consistent about the values espoused. An organization forges its culture by rewarding behaviors that are consistent with its values and discouraging those that are not.

Chapter Three

Three Dimensions of Leaders: Samson, Samuel, and Deborah

The Old Testament, and the book of Judges in particular, provide us with crisp, terse examples of the challenges organizations face and rely upon leaders to address. The book provides clear patterns of behaviors leaders engage in that demonstrate the three dimensions of leadership. Our role as leaders today parallels that of an Old Testament judge. Leaders must negotiate three operational elements of mission, resources, and context:

1. In the Old Testament, leaders were to follow God in personal integrity and discern his mission. Today's leaders must walk in integrity to honorably focus on the missions they are hired to achieve that will make their organizations successful.

2. Today, as in the Old Testament, leaders must rally and organize resources to maximize their effectiveness for achieving these missions.

3. In both the Old Testament and today, leaders must deploy resources and empower people to use them to convert within the context or situation unfolding before them to accomplish the mission.

Wherever you see three-dimensional leadership in the book of Judges, there is peace in the land for forty years or more! Wherever you see III-D leadership in today's organizations, there is mission fulfillment, organizational success, economic prosperity, and social stability.

Once we are familiar with the three dimensions of leadership, we can analyze to determine how well leaders focus on the mission; how well they rally their resources to that mission; and how effectively they deploy and empower those resources to convert within the context of the specific challenges unfolding.

Samson is a I-D leader. Samuel is a II-D. Deborah is a III-D leader.

Samson's story is found in Judges 13:24–16:31. Samuel was the last judge, and the story of his succession begins in 1 Samuel 8. Deborah's story runs from Judges 4:4–5:31 and ends with peace in the land for forty years.

The One-Dimensional Samson

Samson is the strong man of the Old Testament. Reading his story in the book of Judges reveals that, like many I-D leaders, he had tremendous personal abilities. Samson had a winning personality and could go into enemy territory and entertain hostile crowds with riddles and jokes while he enticed their women. Samson killed one thousand men at one time, so he was a great warrior. Over his lifetime, he personally defeated perhaps as many as eight thousand to ten thousand enemy troops, so he had great personal gifts. Samson was a terrible leader, however, and never rallied resources to the mission. Had he done so, the team might have overcome tens of thousands of the enemy, as happened in Judges 1, where two tribes form a team and destroy that many enemy troops in a day.

Samson made a mess of his personal life and failed at following the worthy mission of personal integrity. He consorted with women who were manipulated by his enemies, and his downfall resulted from those self-inflicted wounds. He never elevated the mission to rallying-cry status. Had he tried, because of his poor behaviors, few would have paid attention because his rallying cry would have been, "They took my girlfriend whom I was not supposed to have in the first place!" People will attach themselves to a worthy cause and will rally to a suitable mission, but they won't rally to your personal mess. Samson failed at leadership, and the organization never experienced the social stability and prosperity that was possible had he perceived a dimension beyond his personal whims and performed at a higher level.

One-dimensional (I-D) leaders, like Samson, act as if they believe that being in leadership makes them above the rules. Instead of working to achieve the organization's mission, they operate from a perspective of "What really matters is *my will* for the organization or *my will* for God," which is quite a bit different than actually doing God's will and operating within the organization's prescribed methods and procedures. These are the misguided hallmarks of I-D leadership. Samson never did what was necessary to gain the confidence of his people so he could be the leader they needed. The people willingly would have rallied to anyone with Samson's great personal gifts, who also showed that he cared for what they cared for, believed in what they believed in, and would stand for what they stood for. Samson squandered whatever leadership potential he may have had. Soon afterward, he was betrayed by a woman who sold him into the hands of his enemies because they threatened her family.

There are many I-D leaders like Sampson who cannot see the larger mission because they are so focused on their own personal wants and whims. Because these leaders have great personal gifts, however, they are sought out for positions of leadership. But because they cannot see the larger picture, they are oblivious to the context that should be negotiated from their leadership perch. Samson forfeited the strong coalition he could have forged with the leaders of his own people who could have overcome organizational difficulties and imposing challenges and thus secured peace and prosperity for Samson's corporate generation.

The Two-Dimensional Samuel

Samuel the Prophet was the last judge of Israel. Throughout his career, Samuel was an outstanding, strong leader and moral force for the organization. Samuel, however, failed to select appropriate resources and strategies for succession. When Samuel retired, he bequeathed leadership to his two corrupt sons (1 Samuel 8:1–5). Because the sons were so evil, the people cried out for a human king. The corruption of Samuel's sons made the people look for a bureaucratic solution to their trials. Samuel never should have placed his corrupt sons in power as priests to succeed him. They were not the right resources for the priestly leadership mission.

Incompetence and corruption (real or imagined) causes people to crave bureaucracy. Bureaucracy tends to drain resources and focus away from the mission. Some bureaucracy or administration is necessary to run all organizations, so bureaucracy in and of itself is not bad. What is detrimental is having one-dimensional (I-D) and two-dimensional (II-D) people in your bureaucracy, because I-D's and II-D's are problem creators who will develop red tape, hassles, and hurdles that stifle people who, unfettered, would work more efficiently. Both I-D's and II-D's have a tendency to build the wrong types of bureaucracy. I-D's hire people not to fulfill organizational processes, but rather their own agendas. This is why I-D's think it is perfectly rational to hire into leadership roles people who have no verifiable record of accomplishing anything remotely related to overseeing an organization's front-line mission. If a I-D wants to hire an employee, the personnel department should prevent it at all costs. II-D's, on the other hand, do not hire people to fulfill processes that serve the entire organization, but rather their specific pet units or favorite projects. Neither of these types of bureaucracy building aligns operations to support the main mission of meeting the needs of internal and external customers.

Samuel warns that an earthly king tends to want too much bureaucracy and would take the best of the land and fields and food that grows. You practically will become his slaves! The people saw the bureaucracy of a king as an alternative to the corrupt leadership under which they were suffering, and they cried out for a king anyway. They got one and the bureaucracy that accompanies it (1 Samuel 8:11–17).

I have been involved with boards and organizations that responded to financial challenges or alleged incidents of impropriety by wanting to add bureaucracies and administrative oversight committees. A trap that many organizations all too readily fall into is to create levels of bureaucracy for which there is little or no front-end mission focus, and each position created drains resources away from a focus on the core mission because it requires more reporting, meetings, and justifications. The results of many I-D and II-D hiring practices are unnecessary layers of approval authorities and levels of communication that make it difficult for an organization to be fluid and adaptable to fulfill the mission to meet customer needs. Too many layers characterize poorly performing organizations.

Sometimes organizations add on people because the ones they previously hired are not performing up to par. It is costly to an organization when more and more people are hired to do what the first hires were supposed to accomplish yet still is not being done. Even when other people are hired, the I-D's in the system often perform to undermine the synergy the organization could achieve. People who are mis-hired make work that justifies their existence in their own minds while they fail to do what they are hired to do and, unfortunately, leave others throughout the organization to pick up their slack.

In manufacturing and in some service organizations, it can be relatively easy to determine the number of employees needed to produce so many units or to complete so many oil changes. In human service and administrative environments that process paperwork, however, the number of employees needed can be more challenging to determine. It's easier to skew the bureaucracy and weigh it down with too many positions that are not mission focused.

If the leaders are not focused on the front-end mission,

bureaucratic processes become a mission unto themselves. People end up passing pieces of paperwork between themselves that less frequently are related to what the organization ultimately produces and the services it provides at the organization's front end. The bureaucratic paperwork is not directly related to sales, production, operations, or delivery of a service or product—all of which generate income or the outcomes the organization exists to achieve.

The Two-Dimensional Samuel Twice Failed at Negotiating the Context

Samuel failed twice at negotiating the context. He knew enough about the mission to anoint Saul as king, and then he discerned enough to anoint David as king. But Samuel never negotiated a succession or transition plan between the two. In some ways Samuel sabotaged his own retirement because when his corrupt sons were disqualified, he had to keep working. I wonder how many contemporary leaders get themselves in a similar pickle, trying to bequeath corporate leadership to offspring who just don't understand what roles and responsibilities their new positions require?

The challenges Samuel faced included some role confusion on the part of headstrong Saul, who was the first king. As king, there were certain things Saul could not do without Samuel's approval. As a prophet, Samuel had special knowledge and resources to interpret some ambiguous information and to provide definitive direction on strategic matters. Saul had authority as the military general. So Samuel had responsibility to advise when and where the organization would go into battle, and Saul determined how the campaign would be conducted on the battlefield.

As king, Saul was the chief operating officer (COO) overseeing the day-to-day operations of his court and the administration of the kingdom. Samuel was vizier, a highly trusted consultant, who provided oversight for the COO much like a chief executive officer (CEO) oversees a COO or president in today's corporations.

Saul kept stepping out of his role, and Samuel, passively at times, seemed more like a middle manager who could not surmount the challenge to negotiate between Saul, the supreme leader, and David, the subordinate up-and-coming anointed successor. The people below a middle manager frequently hope he understands the mission and can get the leadership above him to do what the employees need to be able to accomplish their jobs and succeed in the context. I bet there were people who wished Samuel would get Saul to stop pursing David and focus on successfully operating the kingdom.

If the senior managers or senior executives are III-D leaders, they will expect the manager to transfer to them information directly from the front-line staff, so they can act upon it appropriately to channel it down throughout the organization with directives that facilitate efficient and effective processes.

We have no record, however, of Samuel negotiating between Saul and David to make a succession plan to appropriately transfer authority (or share power). Samuel seems oblivious to what results, which is that one leader runs around trying to kill the other. Saul continually focuses on killing David, while enemy Philistines continue to oppress the nation. Like many I- and II-D leaders, Saul causes internal turmoil, which detracts from an organization's ability to meet and solve its most pressing external challenges. Although there is no guarantee that Saul would have listened to Samuel anyway, the latter is the only person the former ever listened to and respected. The mid-level manager always should try to get executive leaders to understand the mission and what the front-end resources need to make it happen.

Perhaps Samuel felt uncomfortable with confrontation. He failed to confront his sons in a way that got them to change their poor behavior, and he failed to confront Saul when it became apparent that he had no interest in succeeding his leadership role. Although Saul ultimately is responsible for the turmoil within his kingdom's internal context, it is easy to see how Samuel might have exercised some influence over the situation. Many executive leaders today also fail at confronting what they should. Do you have leaders within your organization trying to assassinate each other? If so, confront them to bring about reconciliation before your organization is thrown into turmoil.

The Three-Dimensional Deborah

In the book of Judges, Deborah demonstrates III-D leadership. She understands the mission and rallies the resources to it. She ensured those resources reached their potential by empowering Barak, the main human resource, to use his talents and gifts to lead the army his way. When Barak says, "I will not go into battle unless you come with me," Deborah does not belittle him for his request. Neither does she undermine his authority by pirating the battlefield and playing general. Thus she converts within the context of Barak's request while not micromanaging. Micromanaging imposes one's lack of expertise over another person's expertise. Deborah did not make this I-D mistake.

Three-dimensional leadership, in contrast to the other two, effectively deploys resources within each particular context so the mission gets fulfilled. Deborah's successful leadership included the people skills to effectively work with Barak and the organization's human capital to derive synergy from the acumen of all the team players. The most effective and potent leadership is that which rallies people with diverse skills and backgrounds to focus upon a common mission. "Teamwork," says Patrick Lencioni, "is the ultimate competitive advantage, both because it is so powerful and so rare!"[3]

Deborah's recorded tenure ends with her organization basking in "love," "sun," and "strength." The peace her leadership brought to the land is the foundation for the social tranquility in which people can lead productive and prosperous lives.

One-dimensional leadership is "all about me"—not the mission. Two-dimensional leaders understand and can negotiate one or two of the three operational factors of mission, resources, and context. Three-dimensional leaders selflessly pursue negotiating the three operational elements for the good of the organization, and they understand the available resources and how to deploy them within a changing context to fulfill the mission.

Three-dimensional leaders have an enterprise perspective and understand that people are the most complicated and sophisticated resource but also provide the most potential to achieve the mission. The context is the environment that has to be negotiated to accomplish the mission. III-D's focus upon the mission and well manage, utilize, and deploy the resources by negotiating the context to fulfill the organization's vision. People can exercise III-D leadership regardless of what position they hold or at what stratum they are serving within an organization.

Great People Can Be Lousy Leaders

Many people can be commended for their faith, courage, and heart but can fail miserably at leading others to accomplish collectively what the organization needs. As we examine leadership ability, we only are looking at one area of a person's life. How one performs in the area of leadership does not take away from their other amazing personal achievements. In terms of organizational success, however, we will see that nothing is more important than the leader's ability to negotiate the three operational elements.

A great leader must see beyond his or her self-interests. To be III-D leaders requires us to get out of our comfort zone to learn the traits necessary for us to effectively handle our resources, inspire and support followers, and be tough-minded enough to negotiate a set of circumstances that are favorable for them to succeed at their jobs.

Chapter Four

One-Dimensional Leadership Characteristics: Self-Centered Traits Leave Leaders Lacking What It Takes

One-dimensional behaviors leave followers scratching their heads, wondering what the leaders are thinking, because they do not make sense in terms of the organization's mission. The I-D leader is thinking only about his or her own wants or desires and is unconcerned about what the organization needs. One-dimensional leaders come in a variety of packages, including the Dictatorial I-D, the Passive-Aggressive I-D, and the blatantly Self-Serving I-D. This list is not exhaustive. Regardless of their personal styles, I-D's consistently demonstrate that they care more about themselves than the mission.

One-dimensional leaders destroy or stifle group and team synergy because they will not let you do what they do not know. Since no one can know everything, and I-D's are not learners, the organization gets limited to what they know. Dictatorial, autocratic, overbearing, and domineering I-D's operate as if they believe, "My style preferences are the only ones that matter." There is no support or tolerance of other's opinions. Their perspective is, "I do things this way because I am the leader and you are not!" I-D's communicate, "It's my way or the highway!" II-D's communicate, "It's my team's way or the highway." III-D's communicate, "It's the organization's mission way or the highway."

Passive-aggressive I-D's appear quiet and acquiescent yet fail to cooperate either because they do not care about or are incapable of doing what the mission requires. I have served under leaders who never would voice opposition to what the board desired but passive-aggressively kept doing their own thing, never furthering organizational directives. Passive-aggressive I-D's will not be open and tell you they disagree with the organization's direction or that they believe the focus should be on another mission. Their behaviors, however, reveal that they are not going to do what is expected. Talk is cheap! Even if these leaders talk about your organization's mission and say they want to make things better for the mission to be adequately accomplished, their actions belie their empty words.

One-dimensional leaders do not intend to serve the operation or the employees it relies upon to accomplish the work. The Bible, in Matthew 23:11, says, "The ... greatest among you must be your servant." By contrast, I-D's use their leadership positions so the organization can cater to their desires and whims. I-D's resist accountability and do not want to submit to anyone or anything, including mission requirements. I-D's demand all the perks of leadership. They want the best seat that says, "I'm the boss!" Their main preoccupation is gaining name recognition and getting credit. They are not going to share recognition for what they perceive as "glory" with the team of other employees— especially those they see as "rivals" to the attention they seek for themselves.

One-dimensional leaders are over-controlling, micromanaging, poorly delegating "Try to Do it Alls." The operative word in the last phrase is "try," because no one can do it all. I-D's often try to do everything themselves, because empowering others means sharing credit, and I-D's do not want to do that. Guiding others through the process of handling responsibility is what builds the leadership character that organizations need to succeed at their missions for multiple generations. One-dimensional leaders cannot accomplish success for the long term.

Dictators in particular generally cannot take their leadership directives beyond their tenure or lifetimes. This partially is because their insecure and controlling natures prevent them from building a robust team and deep bench of competent successors. A contributing factor to the short lifespan of dictatorial regimes is that their policies narrowly are focused to serve the supreme one-dimensional leader's whims, and they do not have broad-based community, corporate, or political support. They, more or less, are forced upon the populace. Thus when the leader is removed or dies, the initiatives die along with him.

Dictatorships are one-dimensional in their essence. Dictators crave power. They may say they are after power because that is a way to serve the people or the nation or the corporation. But their I-D behaviors reveal that power is an end in itself. Because one-dimensional leaders attract one-dimensional followers, the government ranks within communist, dictatorial, and totalitarian regimes have layer upon layer of self-aggrandizing people. Even if such governments facilitate noble initiatives, like educational or food-relief programs, their I-D officials and employees abscond much or most of the resources provided for it. The people who are victims of those governments continue to suffer as if the aid never had been given.

When I-D's have control of corporations for long periods of time, the same dynamics take place. People tend to hire people who are like them. One-dimensional leaders, therefore, tend to establish organizational cultures that gravitate away from the mission the organization actually exists to fulfill.

I-D's can be gifted people who personally can do a good job at some things yet fail to empower the team to accomplish collective greatness. Jim Collins notes that the I-D leader makes productive contributions using his or her own personal gifts and talents, technical skills and abilities, good work habits, winning and strong personality. Despite the I-D's personal charming attributes, their organizations suffer because they cannot get work or mission achievements beyond what they personally can accomplish. They cannot lead a team to accomplish more than they can alone.

If a person does not or cannot act well in a team setting, he or she should be identified as a I-D participant who is not ready for leadership. The following one-dimensional behaviors preclude one from being an effective leader who can motivate people-resources to work from their hearts to collectively achieve an organization's mission.

Several I- and II-D leaders I have known routinely managed through emotional outbursts that demanded everyone's attention and took the focus away from completing assigned projects to deal with the leader's "mania of the moment." Everyone responds to the outbursts either to get it to stop or to alleviate the perceived "suffering" of the one being emotional. Leaders must safeguard their teams against "emotional control freaks" who try to "hold hostage" the team process with their outbursts that prevent rational discussion to take appropriate actions in situations. Some I-D's believe their emotion is what validates them, so they frequently look to react to circumstances by getting into a frenetic "crisis mode." They think that having emotional reactions signifies their importance or indicates they are involved in really important tasks, events, or processes. Emotion can be like a narcotic rush that gives one a jolt of exhilaration. The challenge is that when we are under the influence of hyper and excited emotions, we tend not to make the best decisions.

Rude and abusive behavior to those in subordinate roles is an I-D trait that creates needless tension in organizations, because employees never know which assignment, discussion, or interaction will include what is repugnant and obnoxious to them. Few people believe that leaders who are abusive to them have them or the organization's best interest at heart. Rudeness causes people to spend time trying to figure out how to avoid or deal with the leader instead of focusing on their missions. Organizational synergy dissipates as a result.

If a leader in your organization persists in poor behavior, decisive steps should be taken to remove them as soon as possible from an authoritative role. To allow them to remain in place sends demoralizing signals throughout your organization. Others will interpret that either you are not astute enough to recognize the poor performance or that you do not care enough about them and others who routinely suffer under the abuse. Failure to deal with poor leadership discourages and dilutes the effectiveness of perhaps dozens or more dedicated and gifted employees.

Even the greatest leaders can stumble and degenerate to one-dimensional behaviors. A classic leadership trap is growing wise in your own eyes, which we are prone to do following some success. Because of the emotional euphoria that can accompany success, we can be lured into believing that the accomplishments have been all about us. We can forget the team that contributed to it, and we can forget about the mission focus that guided it. We can forget about the rules that provide the safeguards that have encouraged partners, investors, and customers to contribute resources. Getting proud and becoming arrogant can lead us to ignore rules and to run through safety signals and headlong into disaster. This has been the case with many corporate failures.

In Jim Collins's book, *Good to Great,* he relates how the Chrysler Corporation, after a great turnaround, was led into trouble by its gifted leader, who had a soft spot for Italians. First, he purchased an Italian villa. Then he purchased an Italian sports car company, Maserati, which drained significant resources ($200 million) from Chrysler.[4] Leaders who engage in self-aggrandizement and lose mission focus make decisions that drag their organizations into trouble.

Chapter Five

Two-Dimensional Leadership Characteristics

A two-dimensional (II-D) leader generally only understands and successfully negotiates just one or two of the three operational elements. A II-D may see the mission but generally cannot see the big picture to determine how it must be accomplished by strategically deploying available resources within the given context. II-D leaders may be able to talk about the mission in impassioned terms, but because they do not understand the context in which the mission unfolds, they mishandle the resources available to accomplish it. A II-D leader may understand the mission but may lack an essential people-skill ingredient to lead an effective team. Thus the leader fails to encourage the human resources to rally to effectively undertake the mission.

Kouzes and Posner, who wrote *The Leadership Challenge*,[5] surveyed twenty thousand people who said the number-one trait they appreciate in a leader they respect is character—meaning someone who has integrity and who tells the truth. These character traits are synonymous with uprightness, honesty, reliability, honorableness, and morality. A leader who articulates the mission but who treats the people around them poorly fails to understand how to negotiate the organization's inner context to gain employee respect and cooperation, so they willingly bring heartfelt devotion and passion to their jobs. If employees respect the leader, they will take to heart messages coming from that leader. Many two-dimensional leaders think they are making progress by being aggressive and abrasive and berating the people around them. This behavior is a poor motivator and often builds resentment and fosters within employees a desire to see the leader fail or removed. Because those behaviors undermine employee confidence and respect, leaders who practice them actually jeopardize the effectiveness of their roles and positions within their organizations.

II-D's tend to fail to motivate people to achieve what is required for success. Leaders rarely can succeed without impassioned followers. If II-D's really had foresight and specific insight for how the team must move forward given a particular set of changing conditions and varying circumstances, they would know that it is the employees who ultimately will carry the day. It is the front-end employees who daily must make the nimble adjustments that provide outstanding customer service that make or break the organization. Thus leaders should do what communicates to those employees that they are the most valuable players the organization needs to succeed at mission fulfillment.

Like I-D's, II-D's can have good personal and work habits, skills, and abilities. They fail, however, at leading by negotiating the context to work equally well with all the various departments. Too many II-D leaders are dictatorial, and thus they border upon being one-dimensional and slightly more effective than them. II-D's are the kind of people who like the purchasing department, because when they call and ask if they can order a particular item, they are told, "Yes, that item is on the approved menu of supplies and materials you can obtain." The II-D's like this news, but they bad-mouth the finance department when they are told, "You cannot order that at this time because you are over budget." The II-D's fails to see within the larger organizational context that the finance department has instructions from senior executives who are being overseen by a Board of Directors, both of whom must ensure that units work within their budget allocations.

The 2008 Fannie Mae and Freddie Mac crisis, which ripples throughout our financial sector, came about by II-D decision makers who fulfilled the mission to help people achieve the American dream of owning a home by leveraging the easing of credit restrictions to make commissions on sub-prime loans (for people who were poor credit risks) that provided short-term profits that have jeopardized the organizations' long-term missions. The lack of long-term mission focus also has undermined many, many institutions that held stock in those companies.

II-D's can't lead in varying situations. They don't understand how to motivate and deploy the resources to accomplish the mission within various contexts. A II-D will deploy the same strategy and style regardless of the situation. II-D's may have tunnel vision or may lack trust or the circumspection to see all the options available in the context. I wonder how many Freddie Mac and Fannie Mae employees were scratching their heads, wondering what their leaders were doing.

Two-dimensional leaders fail to franchise the organization so it can be succeeded to others who will keep the mission going. Thus we saw how, in the Old Testament, Samuel's succession failure led to a breakdown of his simple but, up to that time, effective organizational structure.

Chapter Six

Three-Dimensional Leadership Characteristics

Three-dimensional leadership is so potent because it works well with and obtains synergy from others in the team environment. It is the type of leadership that transforms human capital by funneling individual potential into a dynamic team effort that accomplishes far more than a loosely associated group of individuals who happen to work in the same company or unit.

By contrast, I-D leaders pursue self-interest at the expense of the overall mission, which forfeits the team's success. I-D's will pick their child to be the team captain, even though that communicates favoritism to the other players, which undermines team dynamics. This especially is true when the coach's child lacks any of the gifts or talents for which great coaches pick their captains. Other times a I-D coach will pick a captain who has something in common with the coach. The coach's interaction with the captain will communicate to the other team members that the one in the leadership role was not picked for gifts or abilities that will help the team fulfill its mission, but because he or she is the "coach's pet." These situations communicate that the coach's style preferences are more important than the mission of achieving team success. It leaves players who see the big picture scratching their heads, wondering how the decision fits in with a team strategy to win games by molding the members into a cohesive, well-focused unit.

Two-dimensional leaders may not make these types of I-D assignment mistakes but will fail to rotate players into different positions, even when the context is screaming to do something differently with them because everything they have tried is not working, and the team is losing badly. In basketball, if their point guard can't stop a much taller opposing point guard from scoring, II-D's do not assign the smallest and quickest of the forwards to that point guard—especially in a clutch situation when there is little time in the game.

Legendary Texas A&M's and University of Alabama's Crimson Tide coach, Bear Bryant, once was substituting a player to stop a short pass play, and the player said, "I'll do my best, Coach!" Bryant directed the player to go back to the bench, saying, "Heck, just let the other player stay out there. He's already doing his best. I need someone who is going to get the job done!" Results mattered most to Bryant, not players' names, who they were related to, and what status they had. As Texas A&M coach, Bryant's first training camp became a cornerstone of the legend he forged. He took his "Junction Boys" to a small Texas town about two hundred miles from the university and conducted a boot camp, during which about two-thirds of the players quit. Bryant said, "I don't want ordinary people. I want people who are willing to sacrifice and do without a lot of those things ordinary students get to do. That's what it takes to win." Players within his "team-based, mission-focused" system could not expect to be team captain just because they were related to one of the coaches. Players had to earn their way within the established team system.

A coworker of mine coached a little league baseball team, and a first-year player, who was a bit smaller than the other players and had not been given an opportunity to demonstrate a lot of ability, kept asking to play first base. The idea was rejected by the other coaches, and even players voiced their opinions in protest—as if "the little new guy" had no right to even ask to play the key position. My coworker, the head coach, however, was looking for an opportunity to give the kid a chance without creating mutiny amongst his coaching staff. As he prepared the team for a game, he knew the first-string first-base player was not available to play, so he announced that the new player would start at first base. From the first ball thrown to first base, it was obvious that the young man had come to play. He caught every ball thrown at him. Each time at bat he hit and got on base, and he even stole a base. My theory is that when young people ask to do something, it means they are ready to do it or they are ready to learn to do it. Someone just needs to give them a chance when they ask. Someone has to say, "I believe you can do this, and I am going to coach you and give you the chance to show what you can do."

Coach Bear Bryant's only losing season was when the Aggies were 1–9 in 1954, following that first training camp, which started with 111 players and ended with thirty-five on the team after only ten days! Bryant refined his system and coaching methods, established the culture to achieve it, and then attracted players who were compatible with it. Two years later they won the Southwest Conference championship by achieving a record of 9–0–1.

In terms of building team dynamics and toughness, Bear Bryant was unrelenting. It is said that no one could meet a group of players, mold them into a cohesive unit, define their singular mission and purpose, rally them to it, and then drive them to collectively accomplish it better than Coach Bear Bryant. He did this in part by creating team toughness—a sense that they would rise and fall together. Players whom Bryant coached say there were no superstars on the team, no favorites; everyone served under the high expectations of the coaching system.

Bryant's consistency can be seen in how he suspended star players for breaking "team rules." Bryant suspended legendary quarterback Ken Stabler during the 1967 season, following Stabler leading the team to an 11–0 1966 season, and he suspended the superb Joe Namath during his 1963 junior year season, after he already had led the team to an 8–0 start, and the suspension meant the star quarterback would miss the Sugar Bowl!

Three-dimensional leaders cheer and coach others to achieve the mission, which they value more than individual name recognition and taking personal credit for achievement. The players on their teams are more prepared for position changes and adjustments, because the coach has acclimated them to doing whatever is necessary for the team to win. Cohesive teams like the New England Patriots, under Coach Bill Belichick, consistently accomplish far more than those teams that merely cater to their superstars and thus foster an organization of loosely associated individuals with little or no team-mission focus.

The long-term, enduring benefit of III-D leadership to the health and viability of an organization is that it provides the context in which strong teams flourish, and each individual on it gets developed, so there exists a deep bench of individuals throughout all levels of the organization who understand the mission and are living the values that make it operationally viable in the team—human-interactive settings throughout the company.

In one sense, regardless of how personally dynamic and charismatic a III-D leader is, he or she should prepare to lead with an anonymity born of subordination to the organizational good. To state it another way, III-D leaders should lead in such a way so that the organization is the dominant force—so much so that the organization is almost personified in the leader's mind. I believe this type of anonymity characterizes Fortune-500 giants like Proctor & Gamble and 3M. Both have been dominant companies since before the turn of the last century, selling many beneficial products that we use daily and take for granted. Though the products are commonplace, they literally have revolutionized how modern people live!

Think what our households would be like today without one of Procter & Gamble's cleaning products. How would your office function if the personnel did not have 3M's Post-it Notes? These products save us time, add convenience to our lives, and are so pervasive that we take their existence for granted. Though we recognize each individual product by its brand name, we forget the name of the company producing them. The organizational values and work life within those companies is mission focused and producing product quality that has prospered those organizations for more than a century.

How many of us can name the CEO of either organization, even though Proctor & Gamble's Alan George (A.G.) Lafley was Chief Executive Magazine's 2006 CEO of the year? CEO Lafley is renowned for "leading Proctor & Gamble to its strongest performance in more than two decades by growing the company's core businesses and turning its Beauty, Health and Personal Care and developing-market businesses into strong growth engines. Equally important, Lafley has set a clear vision for future growth with the most diversified, balanced portfolio in the consumer products industry. The acquisitions of Clairol in 2001, Wella in 2003, and Gillette in 2005 have been critical steps toward balancing P&G's portfolio—and have helped make P&G a 'mega-cap' company, ranking it among the 10 most valuable companies in the world."[6]

Yet the fact that Lafley nor his 3M counterpart, George W. Buckley, have not intentionally used their positions to further their individual name recognition, prestige, or public prominence has not deterred the companies from achieving decades of outstanding results. Perhaps anonymity comes with being the head of an organization that is involved in making commodity products, any one of which is not noticeably exciting. Often the organization is the casualty, however, when leaders use their positions to pursue paths that parallel their personal interests as opposed to what objectively is good for the mission.

Below are two examples of people who had great personal gifts but made great one-dimensional leadership mistakes. The University of Kentucky (UK) Web site[7] has a tribute to Dr. Joseph C. Boyd, who earned a Bachelor of Science in 1946 and Master of Science in 1949 in electrical engineering from that institution. He held a position on the UK faculty while working on his graduate degree, and he received his Ph.D. in 1954 from the University of Michigan. Dr. Boyd entered the electronic industry in 1962, when he joined Radiation Incorporated, a company with a market-leadership position in pulse-code telemetry. He was named president of Radiation in 1963. He became executive vice president and a board director of the parent company upon the merger of Harris-Intertype Corporation and Radiation.

In 1974 Harris-Intertype became Harris Corporation and moved its corporate headquarters to Melbourne, Florida, in 1978. The same year Dr. Boyd was elected chief executive officer and chairman of the board. At the time of the Web site posting, Harris had worldwide sales of more than $3 billion and is focused on four major businesses: advanced electronic systems, communications, semiconductors, and an office-equipment distributions network. Dr. Boyd retired from Harris in 1987 and was inducted into the College of Engineering Hall of Distinction in 1993. Dr. Boyd fills his retirement years, in part, with golfing and fishing.

It is interesting to point out that Joseph Boyd is pursing his passion of fishing during his retirement. Perhaps he used his promotion at Harris Corporation as an opportunity to start enjoying his retirement early and take advantage of corporate perks while he did so. For the board of Harris Corporation to allow what is explained below, it must have placed great faith in Dr. Boyd and treated him as a superstar whom they hoped singlehandedly would transform the franchise. They were wrong.

Let's review the leadership story of Dr. Boyd's career at Harris Corporation in an analysis provided by author Jim Collins. In his classic work, *Good To Great: Why Some Companies Make the Leap and Others Don't*, in a section entitled "Leaders Who Stop the Flywheel," Collins tells of the "frequently observed doom loop pattern ... of new leaders who stepped in, stopped an already spinning flywheel, and threw it in an entirely new direction."

Collins's flywheel concept is how corporations achieve greatness by pursuing the one or two activities or products they can be better at providing than almost anyone else in the world. Break-through to greatness comes, says Collins, not with a "single defin-ing action, no grand program, no one killer innovation, no solitary lucky break, no miracle moment. Rather the process resembled relentlessly pushing a giant heavy flywheel in one direction, turn upon turn, building momentum until a point of breakthrough and beyond."[8]

Two previous Harris Corporation leaders understood it "could be best in the world at applying technology to printing and com-munications. Although it did not adhere to this concept with perfect discipline ... the company did make enough progress to produce significant results. It looked like a promising candidate for a good-to-great transformation, hitting breakthrough in 1975. Then the flywheel came to a grinding halt." Collins tells how, in his opinion, Boyd's leadership stopped it:

> In 1978, Joseph Boyd became chief executive. Boyd had previ-ously been with Radiation, Inc., a corporation acquired by Har-ris years earlier. His first key decision as CEO was to move the company headquarters from Cleveland, Ohio, to Melbourne, Florida—Radiation's hometown, and the location of Boyd's house and forty-seven-foot powerboat, the *Lazy Rascal*.

> In 1983, Boyd threw a giant wrench into the flywheel by divest-ing the printing business. At that time, Harris was the number one producer of printing equipment in the world. The printing business was one of the most profitable parts of the company, generating nearly a third of total operating profits. What did Boyd do with the proceeds from selling off this corporate gem? He threw the company headlong into the office automation business.

> ... Horrendous software-development problems delayed intro-duction of Harris' first workstation as the company stumbled onto the battlefield to confront IBM, DEC and Wang. Then in an attempt to jump right to a new breakthrough, Harris spent one third of its entire corporate net worth to buy Lanier Business Products, a company in the low-end word process-

ing business. Computerworld magazine wrote, 'Boyd targeted the automated office as a key ... Unfortunately for Harris, the company had everything but an office product. The attempt to design and market a word processing system met with dismal failure ... out of tune with the market, and had to be scrapped before introduction.'

... From the end of 1973 to the end of 1978 Harris beat [outperformed] the stock market by more than five times. But [during Boyd's reign] from the end of 1978 to the end of 1983, Harris [Corporation's performance] fell 39 percent behind the market, and by 1988 it had fallen 70 percent behind.[9]

Today, Harris Corporation currently is focused on its communications products and systems. In 2007, Harris reported annual revenue of more than $5 billion and had sixteen thousand employees—including nearly seven thousand engineers and scientists. Harris's niche now is providing communications and information technology to government and commercial clients in more than 150 countries. The company remains headquartered in Melbourne, Florida.

Here is a more contemporary story of a leader whose personal style overshadowed the company with negative results:

Henry C. Yuen, credited with helping to invent the VCR Plus technology that assists users to program their VCRs, continued generating patents and later became CEO of Gemstar-TV Guide. While relatively few people used VCR Plus, Gemstar's fortune resulted from Yuen's personal ability to convince publishers of TV listings like Rupert Murdoch's *TVGuide* and technology hardware makers to pay license fees for it. The aggressive Yuen was said to exhibit a certain swagger about his technology, and, armed with a Ph.D. in math and a law degree, he became known as a "patent terrorist" due to relentlessly pursuing patent infringement suits against potential partners and competitors. Among his targets were EchoStar (DISH), TiVo (TIVO), Thompson Electronics, and Time Warner.

Yuen's plan was to make Gemstar's interactive program guide

the portal to negotiating TV's thousands of channels, much like America Online Inc. (AOL) or MSN greets you as you log on to the Internet. Revenues were to come from a "pay-per-click" strategy through your cable bill each time someone clicked on the guide and from the advertisers who want to reach those users. Gemstar's light burned out, however, when its stock collapsed from forty-one dollars to three dollars per share following disclosure that Yuen committed securities fraud to manipulate the inflation of stock values by between $240 million to $330 million from 1999–2002.

Yuen, a martial artist, was known as feisty and even rude and, prior to Gemstar's stock collapse, had never lost a lawsuit. An April 2006 *New York Times* report noted that at Gemstar, Yuen "was abrupt and secretive as a chief executive, and former colleagues say his only confidant was Elsie M. Leung, Gemstar's longtime chief financial officer. Three Gemstar employees said during meetings with other executives Mr. Yuen would suddenly turn to Ms. Leung and begin speaking with her in Cantonese." [10] Even partners who signed deals with Gemstar reportedly did so only after bruising negotiations.

Henry C. Yuen was heralded for his prior successes and considered one of America's most successful Asian entrepreneurs. Perhaps it was the embracing of his celebrity status and believing the press about his ingenuity and genius that compelled him to overreach and think he was above the law. The Gemstar Company may rise again, but only after it is long disassociated from its former enigmatic leader.

Being mission focused and working in a way that is for the good of the organization does not confine one to the mundane. Colin Powell said, "Leadership is the art of accomplishing more than the science of management says is possible."

Chapter Seven

Three-Dimensionals Delegate, so the Organization's Performance Inflates

One-dimensional and many two-dimensional leaders often become the "context" the employees and organization have to negotiate. Two-dimensional leaders talk about the mission very well and with passion. They fail to see the larger organizational picture in relation to partners, suppliers, distributors, and the other entities with which coordination is necessary. I-D and II-D leaders ultimately impose their backgrounds, past experiences, insignificant pet peeves, and personal preferences inappropriately into the process. For instance, a manager who is competent in leading a particular program gets appointed over a division that has numerous operations, including the one the new divisional director is from. A common dimension-two mistake is to try to get all the other units to mirror the divisional director's former program, even though those operations involve widely varying elements and different contexts to negotiate.

The much-too-narrow focus of two-dimensional leaders makes them poor stewards and delegators of mission responsibilities that are necessary for the other departments to run effectively. They insinuate themselves so prominently into processes that nothing can be accomplished because the "It's All about Me and My Preferences, Friends, and Department" II-D's keep you preoccupied with their dysfunctional agendas. Here is an example of what I mean: A government II-D leader once compelled a subordinate to write a wage subsidy to encourage contractors to hire subcontractors who are military veterans. The challenge with the concept is that for six months it artificially would inflate the income of those hired and then would pull the financial rug out from under them, when the wage subsidy would end. The subordinate, who had done some business-development work in the private sector, tried talking senior leaders out of the proposal by stating "the proposed added government-sponsored income would encourage recipients to purchase vehicles and tools to start businesses, but within six months their income would drop by 30 percent, leaving them without the ability to continue making payments on those high-ticket items. It is highly improbable that a sub-contractor's income would rise thirty percent in such a short period of time." Senior leaders compelled the employee to write the program anyway, stating that within six months the subcontractors' incomes indeed would go up, and they would be able to keep up with their business expenses. Thankfully, the law necessary to implement the program was not passed. The employee later found out that the department was losing a program the senior leader used to head. The II-D leader had hoped to obtain funding for the veterans' subcontractor initiative and then have those funds administered by the program that was scheduled to be relocated to another department, in hope of anchoring it in place.

This logic was shortsighted and skewed, because not only would it have set up veterans for business failure, but even if the program was approved, the funding could have been administered from the program scheduled for departure, regardless of what department or building it was located. The subordinate felt ill used in the process because the ill-fated scheme drained time and capacity away from other pressing issues.

One- and two-dimensional leaders do not see themselves as being in partnership with their subordinates, though they may at first give subordinates the impression that that is what they want. The others learn pretty quickly that "it is all about the leader." The management team cannot accomplish the mission because the I-D or II-D is not where the team needs him to be, or the leader comes late and then insists that the project goes the way he wants—regardless of how many issues have been negotiated with other parties to move forward a previously agreed-upon strategy.

In a like manner, many two-dimensional leaders think they validate their leadership by undermining the confidence and leadership abilities of others, so that when the II-D is not present, things fall apart. Others recognize the poor leadership, however, and prefer the leader would delegate and empower. The II-D continually communicates to others, "You can't make decisions, and your ideas and contributions never will be accepted because I am the boss." Thus when a II-D is temporarily away, the self-fulfilling prophesy of failure they have scripted unfolds, and followers feel unsure and awkward. To the detriment of the organization, the II-D has bred dependency by stifling the initiative of others.

I spoke to a retail store manager whose corporation headquarters provides templates for how each of its hundreds of stores must arrange their stock rooms. The challenge with this centralized planning scheme is that it assumes each store has the same shelving and space, which is not true. The reality is that stores within the same district actually vary in size of square footage and in the amount of storage space available, and their shelving varies in depth and length. A district manager liked the in-store organization and inventory retrieval system one store had developed. That store also was outperforming every other store in the district over a period of several quarters. The district manager advised another store manager to visit and see how the higher-performing store looked neater and was more efficient in retrieving and restocking products. When the second store's manager visited the higher-performing store, he noted that that store's system was not following the corporate template, and he called the corporation's headquarters and reported this. The corporation's headquarters ordered the district manager to make the store manager make his stock room match the template sent from corporation headquarters, even though that particular stock room was twenty-five percent smaller than the stores the template was designed for.

The manager explained to me that they sell a particular product that provides a better-than-average profit margin in steady, predictable volumes. Because their local inventory system was disrupted, they thought they were out of that product and ordered more but could not get any of it for almost thirty days. About a month after they got some, they found several cases of the item in the stock room, buried beneath other items that do not sell nearly as well in their local market.

Think of all the scenarios that can unfold in a situation, operation, store, or a classroom or in a section of the building or department where we cannot always be with our subordinates who need the authority to make on-the-spot adjustments to keep things flowing smoothly. To the degree that we do not give them authority to problem solve is the degree to which we have set them up to fail and our customers to be frustrated. Do we want our volunteers and employees merely to be button pushers or people who have a full spectrum of training to operate machinery with the skills to handle and resolve any problems that may arise? Whatever skill sets and authority your followers lack reflects poorly upon you as a leader, because part of the leader's role is to ensure people properly are equipped and trained.

I know a II-D leader who types and prints instructions to his assistants. Then he reads them verbatim, tying up both his and their time. What should happen is that he sends the instructions in an e-mail and communicates, "If you have any questions or concerns, let me know how I can help you with these assignments." He then efficiently can move on to coordinate and direct other activities instead of treating his staff like first-graders and trying to micromanage their tasks. The II-D leader may think he's being helpful, but the staff sees the time wasted by these frequent exercises.

Delegation is the downward assignment of formal authority from superior to subordinate, so the employees or volunteers are empowered to act for the good of the organization. Effective leaders function in the 3-D: Do, Delete, and Delegate.

- *Do* what essentially needs to be done.

- *Delete* those tasks that really are not necessary, but which you end up doing in a compulsive, non-productive way.

- *Delegate* those tasks that can be done reasonably well by someone else. Use the eighty percent principle for delegation. If someone can do something eighty percent as well as you, empower and encourage him/her to do it. But follow the delegation principles in the following section.

Two-dimensional leaders try not to delegate projects but dole them out piecemeal as chores and errands. II-D's rarely assign work to an employee who gets to complete the project from beginning to end in a continuum flow process. Consequently, assignments feel like odd jobs.

Two-dimensional leaders delegate tasks but not responsibilities. II-D's assign a task and never tell you what responsibility or function it is related to or what or who it is for. II-D's try to carve up jobs into piecemeal tasks to assign them in a way so they can jump into the process at any time they think is most beneficial for them to take credit for the outcomes. The way the work is assigned makes it more difficult for those doing it because if you knew what it was for and why, you could research, compile, and construct work more efficiently. What happens is that after you provide the assignment, the leader keeps coming back to request that you provide additional information on specific parts of the assignment, which you could have done had you known what the purpose of the assignment was.

Three-dimensional leaders delegate roles and responsibilities. III-D's master the art of delegation with accountability absent of micromanagement. It is how they oversee organizations that are amazingly robust and healthy and which have a deep bench of those who competently can continue to move the operations forward. Delegating responsibilities means people are assigned to fulfill roles and take charge of entire functions and processes. They get the opportunity to become the "face" associated with the project.

Training, Timing, and Trusting Delegation

Great leaders relish delegating when employees are ready for it, because guiding others through the process of handling responsibility is what builds their leadership acumen to create a deep bench of competence that makes the organization more robust. If I am a smart manager with foresight, I will want my organization to function in what I call the "Delegation Performance Pyramid." I will look to develop other managers so that as the organization grows and I get the opportunity to move up, the organization below me, down to the base of the pyramid, also stays healthy because I've trained others to manage well the resources necessary to coordinate our common mission. The health of the organization below me creates a level of safety for the higher position I desire to move into and remain in. If those below me fail, the organization collapses and downsizes, and I may find myself back in my old job or out of work. Appropriate delegation creates a robust organizational synergy that can be nurtured with training accompanied by appropriately timed assignments of responsibilities. This builds trust as progressively successful outcomes are achieved.

For organizations to function within a "Delegation Performance Pyramid," they must understand how to train team leaders, supervisors, managers, department and divisional heads. The training needs to be not only theory taught in formal classroom environments but also must be accompanied by structured time on the job that delegates experiences to trainees that progressively increase their responsibilities. Appropriate feedback takes place between the trainees and management, so they both grow to trust that learning is taking place. This process is documented and is designed to achieve a series of successful outcomes that verify and reinforce that both the trainee and the mentor agree on issues of mission, resources, and context that are imbedded in the parent company's culture. This is the foundation for the on-the-job trust that allows for widespread delegation to a cadre of leaders throughout an organization.

In contrast to the above process, one- and two-dimensional leaders create and operate in an environment that can be visualized as an "Inverted Pyramid" that bottlenecks too many activities and decisions through the leader. One- and two-dimensional leaders may appear to be workaholics; they give the impression that they are consumed with so many responsibilities that all is resting upon their shoulders. In reality, their egos dictate that they try to get credit for all activity that goes on around them, so they fail to delegate appropriately. II-D's take in the contributions and ideas of others and then disseminate them in such a way as to make them look like their own.

Two-dimensionals compartmentalize work, which frustrates the workers who now can't make the many daily routine decisions they are accustomed to making. Instead, all those decisions must be routed through and approved by the II-D leader, whose main motive is to ensure that everyone above and below in the organization understands that it is the leader's activity and decisions that are going forward and no one else's.

When employees are not empowered to handle responsibilities, delays are created, as they have to compile information and write memos that detail enough of the background material for the II-D to understand and make a decision. The challenge is, when information comes across the desks of I-D and II-D leaders, rather than pass it on to the appropriate people in the process, they often sit on it for inordinate periods of time, wondering,

How can I get name recognition out of this? How can I make myself look more important or powerful? How can I go after so-and-so over this? I-D's manage information to further their personal agendas and vendettas. II-D's manage information in a way that seems a bit more mission focused but still is overshadowed by personality quirks born of the leader's likes and dislikes. The organization, however, would benefit so much more if it obtained synergy from appropriate delegation that shares, rather than stifles, responsibility and recognition.

One- and two-dimensional leaders think they are safeguarding their jobs by only providing partial information, yet they often set up the process for failure. Many organizations are crippled by leaders who do not really know the mission, so they routinely want to keep secret many things about which there is no need for secrecy. The mission-focused people within the organization will try to tell them why the mission requires that certain information be shared with employees, partners, and others. It often falls upon ears that have been shut by hubris born from how these people feel powerful acting upon the mistaken belief that the knowledge they possess is only important if someone else does not have it. Often the things that I-D's are secretive about involve information that others either already have or care little about but which can fuel powerful initiative when shared appropriately.

Three-dimensional leaders inspire empowered employees to give all to the mission. Loyalty to the mission is of chief importance. Many people try to ingratiate themselves to leaders by saying, "Leader, I will be loyal to you!" When followers say that to me, I advise them, "What is more important is that together we are loyal to the organization's mission. If I stray from the mission, I want people who can get us back on track quickly. If people are loyal only to me, we quickly can become the blind leading the blind." The mission is the beacon that should guide our sense of purpose and gauge the success of our achievements, not how many people "suck up" and are loyal to us.

Many of us have had dysfunctional leaders who demanded

loyalty. These types of I- and II-dimensional leaders get elected to an office or appointed to a job, and then they appoint other I-D's and II-D's, who then hire and promote others who also are like themselves. Many I-D and II-D leaders demand loyalty. But all my leaders who were mission focused never had to demand it, because we all were focused on a common mission and giving our devotion and loyalty to it.

Leaders should work with people resources in such a way that they reach their potential for mission achievement. To accomplish this, leaders must invest in their human resources, so they will be the most useful and productive for the organization. To negotiate the process in a mission-focused way that is good for the organization means we are competent leaders who recognize that *how we go about our leadership activity is equally as important as what we set out to accomplish.* Good process leads to good outcomes. If we go about our missions the right way, we should get the right results. Three-dimensional leaders are committed to converting within the context in a way that honors the organization's mission and encourages and supports others to be the best representatives of it they can be.

Chapter Eight

Getting Synergy from Diversity: *A Football Analogy*

Great teams obtain synergy from their diversity to effectively negotiate the context.

To win at the game of football requires working effectively with human capital to obtain synergy from the diverse types of players so they work together to achieve "collective competence" as a team. A football team has some people whose bodies are very large and wide and are good at squatting low and driving forward to push other people aside, and they make excellent offensive linemen. A football team also has some people whose bodies are very powerful and agile and are good at outmaneuvering or overpowering offensive linemen and, having done so, are good at dragging ballcarriers to the ground. These make excellent defensive linemen. Some body types are good at throwing and make excellent quarterbacks. The running backs are people whose bodies are very powerful and agile and are good at running swiftly, squeezing through tight spots, and outmaneuvering others. Other types of bodies have longer limbs and arms that are great for running swiftly and catching things coming at them from various angles, so they make good tight ends and wide receivers. There are other smaller, skinny people on football teams who are good at kicking. Without this diversity, a football team cannot be successful.

The challenge to a team getting synergy from its diversity is that each of the different body types is wired differently psychologically to approach the game from varying viewpoints. An offensive lineman is wired to protect and to push opposing players aside aggressively or to hold them back from advancing to tackle whoever has the ball. The psychology of a running back is to avoid others and run over anyone who cannot be avoided. The mind-set of a defensive lineman is to catch and tackle others aggressively. The mental focus of a quarterback is to hang tough and do whatever it takes to deliver the ball to another player. A kicker is focused on accurately placing the ball onto various sections of the field or through the goal posts.

Each type of football player is focused on the mission of winning the game, even though they approach the game's mission from different psychological viewpoints. Great leadership coaches to get these diverse viewpoints to mesh together as a team to win games. While it is challenging to relate to the diverse perspectives to negotiate them to cooperate collectively, each one absolutely is necessary for team success.

Effective leadership works training plans to get diverse individuals to reach their full potential for team success. People feel fully empowered as they channel the full potential of who they are wired to be in to a great team effort. Great leadership empowers individual gifts and gets them to work cooperatively so they achieve more together than any of them can achieve individually.

A Football Analogy for Understanding Mission, Resources, and Context

The *mission* of a football game is to win by scoring more points than the opposing team. This mission can be broken down into accomplishing two strategies. The offensive mission is to score, and the defensive mission is to prevent the other team from scor-

THE THREE-DIMENSIONAL LEADER

ing. The offensive mission is accomplished by receiving a kickoff, running until tackled, and then proceeding to negotiate a series of four downs. The short-term mission of the four downs is to advance ten yards, which earns you a new first down and gives you the opportunity for four more downs. If you are successful at accomplishing the short-term mission often enough, you should get close enough to advance the ball across the goal line to score.

The offensive mission to score is accomplished by three strategies: a) running or catching the ball across the goal line to score touchdowns for six points; b) kicking field goals to score three points; and c) adding one point after a touchdown by kicking an extra-point field goal.

The defensive mission to stop the other team from scoring is achieved by accomplishing several strategies: a) tackling the opposing players when the quarterback hands him the ball; b) create a fumble by knocking the ball out of an offensive player's hands; c) intercepting a pass that was intended to be caught by one of the other team's players; d) blocking the field goal by knocking the ball to the ground when the other team attempts to kick it. The defensive mission suddenly can become a scoring mission if one of its players can pick up a fumbled ball, one that is knocked to the ground by a blocked kick, or intercept a ball thrown by the quarterback. If one of those things happens, the defensive player can try to run the ball back for a touchdown. The defense can score by getting a "touchback," which is pushing back the offense far enough to tackle one of its players in the end zone that it should be running out of and away from.

The basic or main *resources* both teams deploy for accomplishing their mission is each places eleven players on the field. Both teams have ancillary resources called coaches, trainers, physicians, water boys, cheerleaders, and stat people. Players have equipment resources such as cleats and helmets and pads for their knees, thighs, and shins. Since both teams basically have equal resources, the game, presumably, will be decided by which one more effectively deploys its resources to execute each play to achieve its mission.

The *context* in which a football game takes place is the field, the boundaries of which are one hundred yards long and fifty yards wide, with ten yards for each end zone, in front of which are goal posts, through which the ball must travel to score field goals from kicks. The context includes the arena or stadium. In open-air stadiums, the context includes weather conditions. Windy conditions can affect the travel of the ball when it is kicked or thrown. The conditions of the field or ground could be slippery, muddy, or icy. Conditions could be snowy or extremely hot and humid. Negotiating the context also means that you must be conscious if there will be sun in your players' eyes if they look up to see a pass coming down to them from a certain sector of the field.

Effective mission strategy means negotiating the context of the following challenges: If you are a team that is from a warm southern climate, and you are going to play a team in a frigid northern climate, you must get your team to the environment early enough in the week to get them acclimated to the temperature they will play in on the weekend. The same is true when visiting a stadium that is very high in altitude or in a very hot section of the country. If in a domed stadium and yours is the visiting team, you may have to negotiate the context of the noise fans make to distract your players from hearing well enough to understand various plays called in the huddle and by audible signals at the line of scrimmage. By contrast, the home-team fans will be quiet when their team calls its plays.

Each team deploys its eleven people resources into various offensive and defensive configurations called formations in an effort to achieve their short-term missions of counteracting and overcoming the other team's various strategies. Here is a play-by-play analogy of how mission, resources, and context are negotiated during a football game. My team receives the kickoff and runs the ball, getting tackled at the twenty-yard line. We now have four downs, or chances, to fulfill our short-term mission, which is to advance the ball ten yards to the thirty-yard line to earn the right to get another four downs. During our first play, or down, we attempt to run the ball and are stopped at the line of scrimmage, making no gain on the play. During our second down, we attempted a pass, and when the quarterback dropped back to throw, two defensive players tackled him five yards behind the line of scrimmage. Has the mission changed? No. This loss means we have to advance fifteen yards (instead of the original ten) to get to the thirty-yard line to achieve a first down.

Now it's third down, and "long yardage" is needed to achieve the short-term mission of getting a first down. Our offensive coach calls another pass play, the object of which is to throw the ball deep down the field to one of five people who will run out at least fifteen yards with the hope and intention that one of them will catch a pass at or beyond the thirty-yard line. The offensive plan is to organize its eleven resources so that five players will be blockers whose mission is to stop the defense from getting to the quarterback, who is player number six and will drop back and throw the ball. The remaining five players, two backs, who line up in the backfield, and three receivers—the tight end, the split end, and the wide receiver—will run out to get away from the defensive players so they can catch the ball.

As the offense lines up, the defense moves into a blitz formation and positions seven players to rush through the offensive line that consists of the center and four other blockers. Note that the defensive strategy does not change the offensive mission to get a new first down by advancing the ball fifteen yards. The offense now has to make an adjustment to how it has organized its resources on the field to convert within the context of what the defense is doing. The quarterback makes the adjustment of his players by calling an "audible" signal that gets two of his players, who were supposed to run a pass pattern, to reposition themselves to block the extra people the defense hopes will run around the line of blockers and sack the quarterback before he can throw the ball.

If the offensive conversion is successful, the offensive blockers will hold off their opposing defensive players, so the quarterback is protected long enough to throw the ball to one of the three remaining players running down the field, looking to catch the pass. If the ball is caught and moved down the field far enough to get a first down, the short-term mission is accomplished. If the ball is moved across the goal line, then a touchdown is achieved, so the mid-range mission to score is accomplished. If these short-term and mid-range missions are completed often enough, the team should fulfill the ultimate mission, of winning the game by scoring more points than the other team.

An important thing to note is that the changing circumstances on the field and the various offensive and defensive strategies do not change the mission to achieve enough first downs and touchdowns and field goals to outscore the other team. Converting within the context requires constant resource adjustment while remaining committed to and focused upon the mission! The winning team generally is the one that achieves synergy by getting its players to work well together to collaborate as a team rather than act as independent agents on the field.

One-dimensional leaders and players pursue self-interest at the expense of the organization's and the team's mission. Two-dimensional leaders may pursue the mission, but they fail to negotiate the context by deploying resources as strategically as possible. Three-dimensional leaders coach and cheer others to achieve collective success. Team synergy is achieved when the output of the combined parts is greater than their mathematical sum. Synergy is achieved when $1 + 3 = 6$, which means that one leader and three followers who work well together, focused on a common mission, will accomplish the work of six people who work individually in an uncoordinated way.

A Lawn-Mowing Analogy Shows the Effectiveness of Collaborative Synergy

If two people living side by side in track houses, with lots of the same size, individually mow their lawns and then rake and bag their leaves, they will accomplish two lawns in two man hours. If they take down the fence between the yards and work together, they will accomplish two lawns in 1.5 or less man hours.

How this synergy is accomplished is that the two people work together to mow the first and then the second lawns. Near completion of the second lawn, one person begins to rake while the other finishes mowing. At that point one mower is more efficient because, as the space to mow grows smaller, the two mowers have to make too many maneuvers to keep from bumping into each other. Soon the lawn is mowed, and now both people are raking. Near the end of the raking cycle, one person begins to bag the grass clippings while the other finishes raking. Soon both are bagging together and removing them from the lawns. Thus the two people working in a coordinated manner achieve synergy.

Great leaders scan the ranks of their volunteers and their paid work forces and determine who can be plugged in where to maximize synergy. Three-dimensional leaders build strong teams by (i) understanding the mission and the context; (ii) understanding how the organization's people and their individual gifts and talents contribute to collaborative success; (iii) empowering those people resources to use their gifts and talents to negotiate the context to fulfill the mission.

Great leaders build deep benches of pinch hitters who can step in and keep the franchise operating smoothly in the event that the first-string player no longer is able to perform. Great leaders produce other leaders who also develop teams with deep benches of pinch hitters and runners. Thus the operation can grow and be perpetuated in a healthy way with a consistent culture upon which the success rests.

Three-dimensional leaders work from an "enterprise perspective" in a way that benefits the entire organization—not just his or her personal department or section. Working with your own department in mind only makes you a II-D, because you are not conscious of the bigger picture and the context the larger organization must negotiate. This II-D focus is generally what perpetuates silos that may achieve individual or local program results in a way that forfeits enterprise synergy.

Corporations struggle because too few of the managers within their acquisitions take on an enterprise perspective to do business the "tried and true corporation way." Departing from those procedures often results in a loss of the core-mission synergy that made the parent venture profitable and successful.

The Ten-Thousand-Foot View of the Context and the Tunnel-Vision Focus on the Mission

Great leaders project visions based upon a ten-thousand-foot objective view of the context while they are able to tunnel in to focus on the mission. Leaders must see the big-picture overview of the context in which the organization operates, while divorcing themselves of emotional attachments that color or tint what is viewed, so they negotiate objective facts rather than react to their feelings. To be irrational means to act emotionally out of context of the facts.

By focusing on the mission details, leaders can set operational timetable checkpoints and milestones necessary to achieve the detailed process steps that fulfill it. Thus they can set an appropriate pace that ensures the team members arrive at objectives on time.

One-dimensional leaders make decisions based upon who they know, and if they know you, they are going to listen to you whether you have the mission in focus or not. Because I-D leadership is all about "me" and not the mission, I-D's gravitate toward and listen to whomever strokes their egos or supports their presuppositions. Two-dimensional leaders tend to make decisions based upon someone's job title, whether that person is contributing to accomplishing the mission or not. The II-D's may at least make sincere attempts to rely upon those whom they think should know what the mission is. A II-D leader does not have a clear understanding of how the mission unfolds within the context and, therefore, is at a disadvantage when trying to discern who and what will or will not accomplish the mission. Three-dimensional leaders, by contrast, grasp the context and thus understand which information is significant and how it relates to achieving mission-oriented results, and they empower the appropriate subordinates who can accomplish what is required.

III-D's ensure each person knows his/her part within the organization and how their roles and responsibilities within their respective departments contribute to the overall finished product, process, and mission. When people stray, III-D's sense it and nudge them back into appropriate channels. Followers must cooperate with the mission or vacate the team. Employees thus see how doing their specific parts help the organization to convert within its context.

Great leaders provide followers with clear direction, well-defined processes, appropriate materials, and timely information. III-D's delegate responsibilities, and they appropriately nurture people to handle them. III-D's franchise their operations, initiatives, and programs so they don't become a one-dimensional "cult of me" that is centered around the leader but easily are moved forward by others who work the parent organization's (PO's) way.

Three-dimensional leaders have the courage to interact with team members and followers with an honest heart that is frank about the aspects of their jobs where they most likely are to fail or fall short, either because they find those tasks distasteful, uninteresting, or rather challenging because of the way they are wired.

Leaders should be honest not as an attempt to manipulate team members to cover their shortcomings but to achieve better accountability and mutual support to increase collective achievement. Different team members excel at different activities. It makes sense to draw upon the team resources to achieve synergy.

Three-dimensional leadership successfully handles an organization's mission by deploying its resources within the context of its social, political, and competitive environment to achieve outstanding results. III-D leadership is an organization's best opportunity to successfully negotiate the three elements of mission, resources, and context. III-D's are focused upon accomplishing the mission by effectively utilizing people resources for the good of the organization.

Two-dimensional leadership tends to fail to help the organization to reach its full potential, either because it lacks the people skills to effectively work with human capital, or it lacks insight into the context in which the organization's mission is unfolding. The second failure is related to the first shortcoming. The "context" in which a mission must unfold consists of the institutional historical background, the organizational and cultural framework, the partner perspectives, and the various local circumstances that include the social, political, and economic environments in which the resources must be deployed.

Only managers and people at the local levels, in the various branches, and their surrounding areas have an understanding of the specific components of the local conditions or the contextual setting that impacts how operations must be conducted to fulfill the mission effectively. Like Sun Tzu's *Art of War,* Thomas Sowell, in his book *Basic Economics,* has articulated the importance that local knowledge plays in organizational success. If a leader does not know how to get the people relationships throughout the organization to collaborate effectively, there will be communication breakdowns and mishandling of resources needed to effectively convert within the context.

One-dimensional leadership is about "me." Two-dimensional leadership is about "us"—in the sense that "us" is about "me and the people in my immediate area of responsibility." Three-dimensional leadership is about "we," which includes the organization's mission and what is good for every branch, department, and division and its constituents throughout the greater context. III-D leadership is focused on organizing and facilitating a set of circumstances that are favorable for those throughout the organization to excel at their job roles and responsibilities.

Part Two

Mission

Chapter Nine
Mission Matters Most

Mission is the reason and purpose the organization exists. Mission fulfillment is the reason why we exist within the organization. The company, institution, organization, church, or team recruits a leader to fulfill a specific mission. Mission fulfillment means doing what we are paid or tasked to do as efficiently and effectively as possible. For leaders to achieve success, they must understand that *mission matters most!*

The mission is the main thing, or objective, to accomplish. The first step to success is to keep the main thing the main thing. Leaders must keep the mission in focus. What is good for mission achievement must guide every decision. A leadership mantra should be that "mission matters most." Without a mission there is no reason for the organization to exist. People will attach themselves to a cause that seems worthy and is greater than themselves. Leaders should hold up the mission as that worthy cause to which people should rally.

Leaders should be able to articulate the mission clearly in a sentence or two. Remember, Martin Luther King, Jr.'s mission was equality. His vision was "I Have a Dream," and his values were nonviolence. To achieve a vision, leaders must work as consistently as possible toward their mission within the framework of the organization's stated values. Vision provides inspiration, and values are the heart that beats after it, while mission is the soul where the other two meet and are infused into action. Wise leaders, like Martin Luther King, Jr. elevate their mission to rallying status. Great leaders elevate the mission by infusing it with the inspiration of vision and the passion imbedded in the organization's values.

Mission is the soul and nitty-gritty fundamentals that the organization accomplishes day in and day out. Mission statements should be something like this: "Manufacture product x; manufacture x number of product x every hour, day, week, et cetera. If the organization wants quality, it needs to manufacture with .xxx errors or defects. Service an average of x number of vehicles during an x period of time. Provide x number of services to x number of clients during an x period of time." Overriding mission statements can be "connect customers to cars"; "connect clients to jobs"; "connect clients to benefits"; "make accurate determinations."

Mission is more significant than the mere pursuit of an individual humanistic horizon of self-fulfillment. A mission is not merely "customer service," but "service that focuses on connecting customer loyalty to specific products or outcomes." A leader who holds up an appropriate mission will give people a reason to come to work each day and pull together for a cause that is meaningful and significant. Most people are working for the organization because they signed up to help fulfill the mission. Even common products and services—like household soap and cleansers—improve life by cutting down on germs and diseases and by making things sparkle. The world would be a far worse place without them. These product attributes are reasons why people will join a company and work hard to ensure that almost everyone obtains the benefits of using them. The same can be said about many government organizations and those companies that provide services. Employees signed up to work there because they believe the service adds value to and enhances people's lives. The mission to provide those services and products matter. Great leadership connects people to the mission and keeps the focus there. Mission fulfillment to manufacture or provide services or make deliveries is what matters most to employees and drives the economy, making the world of trade and industry go around.

Because customers will pay an equitable sum for the opportunity to obtain the quality of life the products and services provide, the company makes money, which it shares with its employees in terms of salaries and benefits. When the company and the employees dedicate themselves to a common mission, there is a triple win. The customers win, the company wins, and the employees win.

One-dimensional and two-dimensional leaders make lots of decisions that leave people scratching their heads because they do not make sense within the overriding mission context. Decisions that I-D and II-D leaders make are not rooted in a mission focus, so they tend to frustrate those who are mission oriented. II-D leaders make decisions that tend to be good for their friends or their department or section of an organization but, in actuality, are out of sync with the context of the organization. Three-dimensional leaders serve the people who work the mission.

The competitive process in the marketplace is an arena where continual testing takes place. Every day the competition has the potential to do that which makes sense to the customers and influence their purchasing decisions. The organization that fulfills its mission and appeals to the most people wins the sales territory, gets the most walk-ins, provides the most services, and earns the most income. Effective leaders must conceptualize the organization's vision into a step-by-step mission-implementation process, commonly known as a strategic plan. A strategic plan explains how we will use what we have to accomplish the mission that gets us to the vision, while working within the stated values and not straying from them. Strategic plans can be broken down into mission-accomplishment milestones, such as a sixth-month benchmark, the one-year benchmark, eighteen months, two years, et cetera, as components of a five-year plan.

To accomplish the short-term benchmark missions, each department, unit, or ministry branch must have a goal-champion or a goal-getter. A key role of the goal champion is to develop workers and/or volunteers who subscribe wholeheartedly to the vision, mission, and values, as well as being equally committed to the strategic plan process that gets the organization to that future destination. The absence of a strategic plan and people who are committed to it is a vacuum through which an organization can easily evolve into what Bill Hybels calls "a loosely connected federation of sub-ministries"[11]: or units to which people are more loyal than they are to the parent organization. Consequently, says Hybels, people will identify more strongly with the department's sub-unit than the overriding concerns of the larger organization.

Chapter Ten

Fulfilling the Mission through the Art of Leadership

Leadership Profile:
Robert A. Cocroft, Brigadier General (U.S. Army retired)

President/CEO, Center for Veterans Issues, Ltd.,
Milwaukee, Wisconsin
President, National Association for Black Veterans (NABVets)

A strategic plan can be useless without appropriate leadership to implement it. Below is a discussion with Brigadier General (Retired) Robert A. Cocroft, who is leading a national veterans' organization and a not-for-profit agency to implement their strategic plans. General Cocroft states, "The art of leadership is *not* getting people to do what you want them to do. *It is getting people to* want *to do what you want them to do.*" There is a difference between having a job title and being a leader. Strategic plans are fulfilled by people who are led by those who understand the art of leadership.

Brigadier General Cocroft is the President/CEO of the Center for Veterans Issues, Ltd., in Milwaukee, Wisconsin. He also is president of the National Association for Black Veterans (NABVets). The general reminds us that though the words "for black" are in the organization's title, people of other races are not excluded from participating, and membership is open to all races. The emphasis of the organization is to improve the plight of all veterans. In addition to the headquarters in Wisconsin, the organization maintains an office in Washington, D.C., where Larry Stokes handles appeals of veterans' claims.

General Cocroft wrote the strategic plan for NABVets and obtained the funding to operate the organization that originated as the Interested Veterans of Central City (IVOCC), founded in 1969 by several returning Vietnam veterans. General Cocroft got involved in 1971, when he exited active duty, and in 1973 the organization evolved into the NABVets. From 1973 to 1974, General Cocroft became the first board chair as the NABVets began incorporating other black veterans' organizations.

"The NABVets has had it ups and downs," says Cocroft, "but currently is on a fairly strong footing." The organization gained national recognition, but its chapters have come and gone. In the last couple of years the focus is to keep local chapters together, and this greater emphasis has paid off. The general notes, "We have had some phenomenal growth the past couple of years where we are now in twenty states and about thirty-five cities."

Leadership for "Creating a Positive Lifestyle"

General Cocroft believes the future of his organization lies in those who become members of NABVets, knowing what the mission is, and concentrating on improving the community. He says,

> The motto we've had for many years, "Creating a positive lifestyle," is to be applied to the community. The National Association for Black Veterans (NABVets) is focused on community service, maintaining the historical record of African-American

veterans, including building monuments to memorialize their military achievements and service, and empowering and assisting youth. NABVets' local chapters are expected to commit to the mission and dedicate themselves to fulfilling it. They also provide quality claims services to all veterans, and they are accredited with the Federal Department of Veterans Affairs (VA).

Cocroft's vision for the National Association for Black Veterans (NABVets) is to recruit active members in sufficient numbers to provide enough clout to confront issues that impact the lives of black veterans and black Americans. Cocroft provides the following historical background that makes his organization's mission a necessity.

The life of a black vet is different from those of a member of the majority race in America. Coming out of the Vietnam War, there were vets who received less-than-honorable discharges, many of which in the early years of the war were issued administratively without benefit of the due process of a formal court martial. Blacks served disproportionately in combat front lines. Vets returned to America raw from Vietnam combat while they still had four to six months of service and found it difficult after combat to put up with the military functions they now perceived as petty activities. The disproportionate number of administrative bad discharges provided to black vets is not a concern that other vets' organizations have.

General Cocroft also notes that the Federal Department of Veterans Affairs (VA) denials of Post-Traumatic Stress Disorder claims and the claims backlog problem also disproportionately impacts African-Americans.

Another thing that is key to us is the award of Post-Traumatic Stress Disorder (PTSD) claims by the U.S. Department of Veterans Affairs (VA). We have anecdotal evidence, but not data, that indicates blacks receive fewer awards for PTSD than the majority of the population. Similarly, when you take into account that many of us come from an urban setting, most of the problems that you hear about disability compensation awards, etc., are related to the larger city VA regional claims offices as opposed to those that are in less-populated areas. So that is another issue of concern for us right now.

We also are sensitive to veterans who were discharged and subsequently were diagnosed with AIDS and how HIV impacts the black community. AIDS impacts the black community more disproportionately than it does the white community. That is more of an issue for us than it may be for the American Legion, Veterans of Foreign War (VFW), and the Disabled American Veterans (DAV). So those are the kinds of issues that we confront that more traditional organizations do not, and therefore there has to be a voice speaking for those particular issues. These are reasons the NABVets exists.

The organization leverages technology to represent veterans in negotiating the VA claims process throughout the nation. NABVets operate an 800 number advertised through its *Eclipse* magazine and the NABVets Web site. Local chapters have local Veterans Service Officer Liaisons (VSOL). They are not accredited claims representatives, but they facilitate veterans to sign a power of attorney for NABVets to represent them, and then they forward the claim to a certified NABVets service officer who ensures timely and accurate claims are mailed to the VA Regional Office (VARO) nearest the claimant's resident. All claims officers are on the payroll. General Cocroft advises on some important issues related to using volunteers versus employees.

Volunteers are not allowed to process claims. All of our claims officers are on payroll; I won't allow volunteers to process claims, even though some may be qualified. The NABVets has more control over employees than it does volunteers. Volunteers are good in some things. The VSOLs are volunteers, but they are not allowed to process claims either. They can assist with gathering the information, but accredited Veterans Service officers process all claims.

While you can bond both employee and volunteers, employees can be hired and fired, so you can demand a certain quality of product from them, and you can evaluate them on that basis. With a volunteer, if you start demanding stuff they may walk on you and mess with cases or take cases with them. You've got all kinds of potential problems with volunteers. Volunteers may try to take ownership over cases, feeling they own them rather than the organization. But an employee works a case that is owned by the NABVets that has the power of attorney to represent the veteran.

We have claims officers located in Milwaukee, Wisconsin, and Tacoma, Washington, and we have accredited a couple more in Denver and some others are coming on line. Technology makes it possible for veterans seeking claims services to call in and use our automated data information process. Additional information is captured on the case through our local chapters' VSOLs, who ensure the materials get sent in to one of our accredited claims reps, who will develop the case. Naturally, any case that is appealed is sent to Washington, D.C., and Larry Stokes handles the appeal.

Constituents, Communications, Conventions: The Keys to Keeping Local Chapters Viable

Cocroft knows the essentials of holding an organization together include communication and holding conventions to keep your issues and mission before your constituents. The general sees that only a small portion of veterans actually participate.

After Vietnam, a lot of vets, black, Hispanic, and minorities did not join vets' organizations mostly because of the way they were treated. Only about thirty percent of America's vets belong to an organization. The VA operates the largest medical system in the world yet only serves about twenty-five percent of the nation's veterans.

In order to keep an organization together you've got to have communication tools and training and hold conferences and conventions, and individuals have to have the wherewithal to attend those. Historically we attracted a lot of veterans to the organization who had need as opposed to those who were sufficient in their own personal resources. The focus is to still help veterans who are in need and who make up a large percentage of our organization, but at the same time, we need individuals who have the wherewithal to assist and help other veterans. So using computer communication technology and telephones and as the older veterans become [less financially encumbered] and are more able to travel, they are more able to attend conferences and conventions in various parts of the United States. This will help us.

General Cocroft explains how and why he made the journey from a military general to a social advocate.

I've always had a concern for people. People are the most important thing in life. We're only guaranteed so much time on this earth, and I think of how Warren Buffett donated money to the Bill Gates Foundation. Warren Buffett first took care of his family and provided for his kids. He then donated to the Gates Foundation ... rather than trying to duplicate and replicate and parcel it out himself. I admire Buffet, who made all this money in his life but knows he can't take it with him, so he left it where he thought it would do great good. What I'm saying is that if you love people, you don't want to see them miserable. You want to try to ease their misery and do something positive. That is pretty much it. In going through the military, one thing I was taught is to be technically and tactically proficient and to take care of your people. An extension of caring for me is to deal with veterans.

I asked the general about his views on leadership and its essential elements the military teaches. He says ...

The military teaches leaders to be technically and tactically proficient and to take care of your people. Leadership begins with values and your proficiency, and then you will be able to exercise the art of leadership, which is to get them to want to do what you want them to do. If military leadership training did not work, you would not have so many companies trying to hire former members of the military; you wouldn't have so many employers seeking ex-military people.

Underlying leadership principles are values. It's hard to quantify leadership traits on a résumé, but they show up in the workplace. The values that most of us were taught as children are hardened and heightened through military leadership. Integrity, honesty, honor, dedication, loyalty, are all virtues that underlie military leadership. To be technically or tactically proficient means something to others who are looking to you for what to do, especially in crisis situations. You don't want to go into combat with people who don't know what they are doing and are unsure of themselves. You can get people to do what you want them to do out of fear, and there's also a whole bunch of other ways that are not the best way. The art of leadership is to get people to "want" to do what you want them to do.

"Protection" is the value that fuels military leadership. In his book *Wild at Heart*, John Eldredge indicates that protection is in the male DNA. He says this is why little boys play games of battle and war in which they pretend to get wounded time and again and yet continue to struggle to get up to fight on and prevail. Eldredge says that little boys play these games because they are programmed to understand that, when mature, they may be required to protect their families. What is in their minds as they play, says Eldredge, is Mom, apple pie, and the American way of life. Perhaps men and women are attracted to the American Military for these reasons. Cocroft's response to this is ...

I remember playing cowboys and Indians, I remember playing a lot of war too when I was a kid, and it was always to be the good guys. When I was growing up in the fifties, it wasn't that long after WWII. The military is the indoctrination of a lifestyle and a culture. It is more than just an orientation. It breaks you down as an individual, and the training builds you back up into an image of who they want you to be.

Everyone doesn't comply. You have your mavericks, etc., but that author is right. Somewhere in the American Culture we've always had this notion that we are citizen-soldiers who go off to defend America when we have times of crisis. But it is the military orientation and indoctrination that creates a bonding of the people who are there together. The bonding takes place through the indoctrination of the notion of patriotism and we're doing this for the defense of the country and to protect our families. That is why it is so necessary that every time America goes to war, we have an underlying moral authority to wage it. When you don't have that clear moral authority to go off to war, we get caught up in situations such as today in Iraq and thirty years ago in Vietnam.

When military units come out of war with titles like "Band of Brothers," it's an indication of the bonding that takes place. It's the bonding that takes place on the night right before the D-Day invasion, when you had all these men in all these boats waiting silently in the dark, not knowing what they're fighting for. When soldiers don't know what they are fighting for, they know they are fighting to protect each other. The patriotic notion of moral authority, however, remains essential.

General Cocroft acknowledges that one can exercise leadership technology and values to get people to want to do the wrong thing "if you all are of that mind-set. Hitler was a leader, but he was a bad leader. He exercised leadership for an evil purpose." General Cocroft wanted his junior leaders to focus on working with people in such a way that they willingly bought in to the organization's mission and desired to achieve it. He says ...

When I was interviewing officers for assignments in my command or to be on my staff, I would ask them, "What is leadership?" Sometimes the candidates had not thought about the issue that much. So I would rephrase the question and give a clue: "What do you believe is the 'art of leadership'?" Many people would say, 'Leadership is getting people to do what you want them to do.' I believe and would explain that "the art of leadership is getting people to want to do what you want them to do."

In addition to NABVets, General Cocroft is leading an initiative to address homelessness through "The Center for Veterans' Issues" (CVI), a not-for-profit organization in Milwaukee, Wisconsin, whose mission is to provide advocacy and services to veterans, including mental health, youth issues, and housing. Because numerous instances of homeless are rooted in choices people make, he says, "Ending homelessness is unrealistic, but as a nation we have the resources to impact it to a great extent!" Some people become homeless because of unfortunate circumstances or because someone else makes choices over which they have no control. Some children are homeless because one of their parents takes drugs or drinks excessively. Regardless of how people end up in that situation, each day people come to realize that if they reach for help and can obtain some assistance, their situation can improve. As a society we need to have services available to assist them.

Cocroft is committed to address these issues because, for him, "ending homelessness among black veterans is a priority when thirty percent of the homeless male population are veterans, and of that number, approximately sixty percent are black." Cocroft continues, "Lyndon Johnson's plan to end poverty was a good one. The challenge was the implementation. Bussing to solve educational problems became an implementation problem. CVI meets the challenge through a continuum of care. Clients are required to engage in volunteerism as part of their therapy that provides a heavy dose of a sense of responsibility." Cocroft explains the initiative and the strategy to help veterans overcome their homelessness:

> CVI is the largest homeless veterans' transitional site in the state. It owns permanent housing, so once veterans pass through our transitional program they can obtain a permanent

residence. CVI also works with the community in its "Veterans United for the Community Services" initiative, through which volunteers gain experience in all kinds of service fields, such as handling lawn care and snow removal for the elderly. What we find is that veterans who help others and volunteer become less focused on their own problems and issues. We run various programs, such as a mental health program, and are just embarking on an economic development program.

Cocroft is relying upon lessons learned from more than a decade and a half of experiences to lead new initiatives to assist the changing demographics of his clients. He says, "We have an employment and training model to identify individuals who are homeless, get them some training, get them in a work track, and assist them to save money so they have the resources for a security deposit on an apartment they will rent someday soon. Through employment they are able to afford their own housing." He continues,

> What we are finding now are more individuals with dual diagnoses, mental illness, and chemically addicted (MICA). It takes a much greater effort to transition them into the general population of society. We are getting about thirty percent of these individuals into an employment track so they get a job. About thirty percent we end up helping to obtain VA disability compensation and pension or Social Security Disability or retirement. The remaining thirty percent is our greatest challenge. With continuing supportive services, we are able to assist these veterans to enter the world of work and sustain themselves in the general population. However, to remain successful, they must continue to receive supportive services.

General Cocroft is taking implementation a step further to set up a business that will be the actual employer for some of the Center for Veterans Issues' (CVI) homeless veterans. The CVI Business Development initiative plans to operate a call center that will employ clients and other people. Cocroft says, "Call center services are a growing industry that because of computer and telephone technology can be handled from any location regardless of where the client and end user are." He explains his business model.

> We put together a business plan for a call center to focus on providing services for the manufacturing sector, health care services sector, and construction and more. We want opportunities to assist our employable clients and individuals to go into any occupation they qualify and can train for. Our economic development model concentrates initially on providing services to businesses through a call center. I'm working on obtaining our first contract now. For those clients with lower verbal skills, we have put together a business plan and are in the process of implementing a lawn care service.

Obviously, General Cocroft is not singlehandedly accomplishing his work with NABVets and CVI. He is leading these organizations by working with their employees, volunteers, members, constituents, and clients by exercising the art of leadership. He is caring for them by getting them to do what is best for themselves and what is best for the fulfillment of the organizational mission.

Chapter Eleven

Mission Fulfillment Is Defined by the Context

The context in which your mission unfolds contains the variables that must be negotiated to achieve success. "Human capital development" is what I consider to be the mission of many churches, religious, and not-for-profit organizations that provide services designed to assist people to improve their lives. That mission is so challenging because people are complicated and sophisticated and require complex approaches to helping them negotiate the contexts of their lives to resolve their issues and overcome their challenges. When dealing with MICA patients, as does General Cocroft, a thirty to fifty percent employment rate, therefore, is a great success.

Success can be defined by determining where you are starting. For an organization emerging from bankruptcy or near bankruptcy, success can be defined within the early phases of reconstruction as meeting expenses and not increasing debt. Peter Drucker advised General Electric Company (GE) CEO Jack Welsh that unless you are number one or two in any business, get out of it. For the General Electric Company at that time and place, Drucker provided great advice. By following it, Welsh led that company to become perhaps the greatest company on the

THE THREE-DIMENSIONAL LEADER

planet. Because GE had the potential to achieve as the number-one or number-two business in any of its chosen industries, its starting point was quite high. What will a successful GE look like in the future? Perhaps it no longer needs to be number one or two in energy, let's say, because it needs to get at the front of the learning curve of energy sources, such as wind-power generation and other "green" sources of energy.

For a pension fund, the determiner of success is "moderately increasing stable gains." Peter Drucker's 1976 book, *The Pension Fund Revolution,* described how they emerged to shape the investment industry because cumulatively they contribute greater amounts of monies than does any other segment of society. The pension fund "institutional investors" need secure investments in blue chips and mutual funds that will grow at a moderate rate over a long period of time. The influence of pension funds on the market has been quite significant.

Regardless of your context, success is achieved by attaining win-wins.

One-dimensional leaders operate from
a win-lose frame of reference.

Two-dimensional leaders operate from a
win-breakeven frame of reference.

Three-dimensional leaders operate from
a win-win frame of reference.

One-dimensionals operate from an "I win and I don't care what happens to you" frame of reference. Two-dimensional leaders operate from an "I win and I hope you will be okay" frame of reference. Three-dimensional leaders operate from an "I win and I want to make sure you also win" frame of reference.

Both one- and two-dimensional leaders make decisions as if they are in isolation, and no one else within the team or larger organization will be affected by it. Two-dimensional leaders make decisions as if their team is all that matters within an organization. Three-dimensional leaders make decisions with a view of the big-picture context of what the larger organization is trying to achieve in relation to its customers, suppliers, and partners.

One-dimensional leaders may not intentionally demolish other people, but because they have such a narrow-minded focus, their decisions often make sense only to them and their devotees. Other team members and departments lose when I-D's win or get what they want. When II-D leaders make decisions that only benefit their team or a member on it, the outcomes can be very harmful and take an initiative in a direction that undermines the other departments involved with the process. III-D leaders make decisions with a perspective of how the entire organization must function, including the procedures its various departments must follow for a process to be undertaken. Thus they go about their business providing a win for their team while ensuring other departments also win in the process.

A surprise or unforeseen change in circumstances generally requires a change in strategy but does not change an organization's long-term mission. Don Giek, of Don Giek Consulting, says a key leadership responsibility is keeping your eye on the ball. "The ball" is the mission—the main thing—the reason the organization exists. Organizations do not fail in their missions; people do. Fixing organizations that have either strayed from their missions or failed to handle resources appropriately requires regrouping to overcome what caused or allowed the situation.

Organizational challenges result from two causes: people and circumstances. If they first are caused by circumstances (which often are the result of decisions made by people outside the organization), they are perpetuated by the failure of people within the organization to address them appropriately. A leader first must raise the hood of the organizational vehicle to see what, and who, are causing the challenges and dysfunction. Let me tell you a story about a leader who had to negotiate surprises that were overcome while never losing sight of the mission.

Leadership Profile:
Joseph P. Sluszka, Executive Director
Albany Housing Coalition, Inc.

Joseph P. Sluszka is the executive director of the Albany Housing Coalition, Inc. (AHC), located in Albany, New York. The Albany Housing Coalition (AHC) provides housing services to veterans who have fallen on hard times. The Coalition has existed since 1980 and has had four executive directors, whose tenures endured long enough to acknowledge. It is a respected organization and is considered a cornerstone of veteran support in the community. It is not uncommon for politicians, from the mayor to state assembly and senate and federal congress and senate-elected officials, to show up at events sponsored by the AHC. These officials interact with Executive Director Sluszka on veterans' issues, programs, projects, and to seek assistance for individual veterans.

Sluszka is a three-dimensional leader who negotiated his mission through many unpleasant surprises. Three weeks after he took over his current position, he received foreclosure notices on two major properties. In addition to those challenges, notice also arrived that the City of Albany was suing the organization to close one of the properties. Sluszka had suspected that some of the executive board members felt that the past director may have deceived them about the organization's financial status, and when the foreclosure notices and lawsuit arrived in the mail, these suspicions were confirmed in a stunning way.

Remember, all this occurred within three scant weeks of him taking the job. He and the board had barely gotten a chance to know or trust one another. Sluszka assured them that he could get them through this as he dug in to face the challenges and to enable the organization to continue to fulfill its mission. All that Joe had learned about the supportive housing industry, real estate management, community relations, and leadership was about to be tested.

Joseph Sluszka learned from board members that it was their

opinion that the former director constantly engaged in a game of blame shifting. Every problem the board got wind of, the past director explained away as being a mistake either the City of Albany made or because someone else had dropped the ball in some way. He reportedly assured the board not to worry, because he was taking care of things. During the end of the former executive's tenure, he protested to the board that the City of Albany was persecuting him and the Coalition. Since the City had previously provided exemplary support for the Coalition, someone should have looked deeper into the former director's insinuations.

The AHC attorney advised the organization's dire financial state required filing bankruptcy. Sluszka was opposed to this because he believed that once the Coalition was on record in bankruptcy, its donors and supporters would pull away, making the financial situation worse, crippling the organization's ability to maintain daily staff and operations. When Sluszka asked the attorney what his fee would be to file the response, he was more convinced that bankruptcy was not the way to go. The lawyers' fees would double what the Coalition already owed to local vendors. Sluszka approached a local real estate attorney he had worked with in the past and convinced him to take on the matter pro bono. Sluszka then boldly asked the board to give him time to make a full assessment of all the organization's assets and liabilities and then give him a chance to turn things around. He also met with the mayor and got an agreement that gave him six months to reverse the situation. Sluszka was negotiating the context to build the community support necessary to overcome the challenges the organization faced.

While Joseph Sluszka was preparing to work on the Coalition's financial challenges, a public relations nightmare unfolded. Two veterans who were client-tenants thought they would help the organization by contacting the media and holding a protest with other tenants, advertising that as disabled, indigent veterans, they were about to be evicted by the foreclosure. This greatly complicated matters for Sluszka, because negative publicity could cause the withdrawal of community support. He also knew that no potential new owner would want to be known as the landlord that evicted disabled, indigent veterans. Sluszka would have to attack the challenge on two fronts: He would have to work to get the organization solvent while developing new housing arrangements for the current tenants of the properties in default.

Sluszka convinced the bank holding the mortgage to give him time to turn around the organization's finances and to try to find a buyer. He sensed the negative local publicity made it more unlikely that he would find a local buyer of the properties in default, so he was going to have to court out-of-town interest in the Upstate New York, large, inner-city multi-unit property. His more than thirty years of knowledge and experience in the supportive housing industry provided him with the understanding that New York City investors would find these Upstate urban properties attractive. He listed both defaulted properties in New York City newspapers, and within several weeks he found a buyer for one of them. This sale provided the Coalition with enough money to pay off the mortgage and put $120,000 in the organization's bank accounts. No viable buyer was found for the second property, so Sluszka negotiated a deed in lieu of foreclosure. Eventually he was able to relocate the tenants into other properties owned by the Albany Housing Coalition.

Josepeh Sluszka's leadership and integrity proved that the board's decision to hire him was a good one. His philosophy of leadership involved the following: build support, keep close tabs on progress, train and trust your managers, and, most importantly, instill team spirit and dedication to the organization's goals. In this case, the rallying point was maintaining a valuable resource for homeless veterans.

After four years under Sluszka's leadership, the organization is fiscally strong. The company has purchased, rehabilitated, and opened a new twelve-room permanent home for homeless, disabled veterans. The Albany Housing Coalition's case-management staff has grown from three to eight and includes a new employment program. The organization's veterans' services program is recognized on the state and national level as one to be emulated, and Joe is a frequent workshop presenter at conferences within NYS on veterans' housing issues.

Sluszka successfully negotiated the challenges his organization faced, in part because he was not "functionally fixed" and emotionally tied to his resources, but shrewdly used them to negotiate the changing context. To be "functionally fixed" means that you view your resources solely in terms of their traditional use. Your narrow or restricted focus prevents you from seeing their alternative uses. For instance, properties are the most important thing for an organization that provides supportive housing, because they are the reason the organization exists, which is to provide clients with a place to live. If Sluszka placed himself under a mandate that the AHC had x number of properties and could never part with one of them, he would have set up himself and the organization for failure. When leaders are functionally fixed, they view the world through self-imposed restrictions that prevent them from seeing alternative uses of available resources. Sluszka's decades of housing experience gave him the insight to leverage the organization's critical asset. Housing is real estate that provides equity that can be sold and leveraged. Had Sluszka's predecessor thought that way, the situation might not have plunged into a crisis.

Joseph Sluszka's plans for the future of the Albany Housing Coalition includes additional housing services and possibly leveraging resources to provide options for veterans to enter in to affordable homeownership. As we have seen, if anyone can accomplish this, it probably will be him.

Chapter Twelve

Three Strategic Missions Styles: Operations, Products, and Customer Service

Strategic styles can be categorized by three basic focuses: operations, products, and customer service.

Operations: An organization with an operations mission has a culture focused on efficiency, order, speed, and processes that are accurate and error free, like distribution, logistics, and production.

The work environment tends to be managed by measurement, control, hierarchy, cost-consciousness, teamwork, and adherence to rules. Change must be implemented in these organizations incrementally, because effective execution requires the precise coordination of numerous elements within the context.

Products: An organization with a mission to provide products may emphasize operational autonomy and employee independence to support research and development experimentation, invention, learning, and technical know-how. Work environments are intentionally competitive, constantly changing, and, usually, resource-rich. Because products evolve, these companies should adapt the easiest to change.

Customers: Organizations with a mission to serve customers stress responsiveness to them. They should extend the same to employees who are empowered to serve customers. The company culture needs to be collaborative, service oriented, qualitative, upbeat, and should have a more "bottoms-up" approach— meaning the focus should be on supporting the service providers. Change should be part of these companies' cultures, because they should be focused upon innovation that meets customers' changing needs.

History, nonetheless, is littered with companies that failed to adjust to customer desires. Customer-oriented companies are most successful when they listen to customer complaints and praises as a source of information about what customers want and are willing to pay for.

Operations management focuses on achieving efficiency in arranging and monitoring recurring activities and processes to control, distribute, manufacture, and/or purchase products and services. While all organizations rely upon some form of operations management, it comprises the core competency of certain types of organizations, such as delivery services and product manufacturers. If you have an operations mission, you need a strategy to obtain meaningful measurements and analysis of your organization's internal processes to ensure they are operating in a way that efficiently delivers, manufactures, and/or provides what customers value. Place emphasis on getting complete, accurate, and timely data from customer feedback. While you can get external data from customers by surveys, it is challenging to obtain feedback that accurately represents a good cross-section of customers. The goal is to translate soft information from surveys into internal hard data that provides quantitative measurements of what employees do that impact customer perceptions of quality products and services, timely deliveries, and other elements in the customer value proposition. Of course, you must strike a balance between the cost of obtaining the data and the value it provides.

If your organization's style is centered on providing products, then your systems should focus on processes and procedures that enhance employee performance, especially in product research and development, product evaluation, and market analysis. The data comes from external sources that feed you information about customer preferences; its scope is wide to include broad cross-sections of potential clients, and it tends to be soft, meaning it tends to be based on client opinions and feelings—although sometimes it could involve hard facts, such as if products arrived at particular times. The challenge is obtaining data that provides information that can be acted upon and transferred to product outcomes that deliver competitive advantage.

When considering strategic objectives and critical success factors that meet external customers' expectations, leaders should ask the following:

- What does the public think about our services, products, and offerings?
- What challenges do potential clients encounter when they interact with our offices, stores, or branches?
- Why are the operations of competitive service providers, which are nearby and similar, chosen by customers over ours?
- Why is the opposite true in other places?
- How do we adapt to changing customer demands and industry developments?
- Are there emerging service areas that we should enter?

Information technology (IT) makes it possible for companies to design customer-centered applications that focus on real-time responses to consumer-choice patterns while also capturing data for marketing, tracking sales, and customer-acquisition information. IT captures the customers' viewpoints so leaders can base actions not on the priorities of functional fiefdoms, but on the overall corporate objective of providing what satisfies customers.

A project I did for a service organization included determining the number of "personal service encounters" (PSEs) the organization could expect to have with categories of clients throughout their lifetimes. The services offered determine the circumstances under which a potential client is likely to seek a PSE. Organizations can position themselves to meet clients' needs at those strategic service opportunities.

Customers will only return for additional PSEs if their first one is positive. For organizations to win clients and maintain them throughout their life-paths, they must manage the customer relationship at each encounter. Customer-relationship management (CRM) is personal-service encounter (PSE) management. There are three phases in the relationship an organization has with its customers: *acquisition, fulfillment, and retention.* During the acquisition phase, clients will be attracted not only because your advertising is persuasive but also because offices, stores, or outlets are located conveniently.

Customer expectations for obtaining a superior product or service delivery must be fulfilled during the next phase. Fulfillment means the customer obtains satisfaction and will return. Excellent sales or service support is achieved when employees cross-sell and up-sell, making customers aware of other products that may benefit them.

The mission to retain customers requires organizations to be able to tailor product offerings to customer wants. Organizations that are proactive in response to clients' needs earn a long-term relationship with them.

The answers to two mission-focused questions help leaders avoid making missteps with service organizations. The questions are:

1. "How will our customers respond to this decision, course of action, direction, initiative, and/or strategy?"

2. "How will our employees who provide services to our customers respond?"

Asking question one and ignoring question two can lead an organization to strike a good path to the customer's door but fail to deliver what is expected once the door is opened. Asking question two and ignoring question one can lead an organization to design a great service-delivery strategy with exquisite operations that employees everywhere would envy, only to discover that the end product or result does not resonate with and is not desired by potential customers.

Leaders must understand their resources in relation to the mission that is to be fulfilled, and there is an opportunity cost associated with each deployment of resources. Since resources tend to be limited, the opportunity to deploy them to do one thing is generally at the cost of not being able to deploy them to do another. Thus one-dimensional leaders make critical mistakes by assigning their resources in a willy-nilly fashion, often in pursuit of some seeming crisis, which, when analyzed within the greater context, often is realized to be a momentary phenomenon or distraction that is blown out of proportion by the leader's emotional response to it.

The assignments that result from these perceived crises pull the organization away from focusing on its core mission. These assignments frustrate workers within the organization who quite often instinctively know what is going to help fulfill their core mission and what is going to detract from it. Companies that experience high employee turnover would do well to analyze the cause, which likely is misguided leadership that frustrates and repels employees from the mission. Because any one of us can suffer momentary lapses of focus, it is good for leaders to empower their team members to call them back to the main task when they stray from a three-dimensional mission focus.

Chapter Thirteen

Leadership and Mission Challenges in Government

The challenges with leadership in government are rooted in the fact that government reserves its most influential decision-making positions for the family members, friends, paramours, the significant others, and the chief donors of politicians and their key supporters. The challenge with this leadership-procurement system is that most of those appointments involve people who do not have any actual experience in what they are tasked to manage or oversee. While they may say they have an appreciation for a government agency's core missions, they may lack the leadership abilities to get large numbers of people across multiple departments to work effectively to accomplish them. Often those appointed to high-level government positions worked their way up through the party ranks and may have first obtained a job in city, county, or state government. They may have been involved in a union or some other organization that coordinates with government or worked for a state legislature, where they may have assisted in analyzing and crafting legislation. Later they are appointed to positions of authority within those actual agencies, yet they have no management ability, no leadership skills, no people skills, and no track record showing they have the ability to coordinate and steer large numbers of people and departments to fulfill their missions.

It should be readily apparent to even casual observers that government departments often are headed up by people who can quote chapter and verse of the law but have no operations management ability to translate that information into effective processes that coordinate large numbers of people to work together effectively to provide the services at the local level where citizens access them.

I have spoken with many government employees who worked their way up into mid-level and then senior management, where instead of being able to put to work their vast knowledge of the system and the processes for it to operate well, they experienced endless frustration under the unrealistic visions of political appointees. Alexander Pope (1688–1744) said "a little learning is dangerous,"[12] and I-D and II-D leaders often learn just enough about an industry to identify a problem, while they fail to learn enough about the context and the processes that negotiate it to understand how to solve the problem. With great confidence and fanfare they charge forward, blissfully ignorant in their half knowledge, seeking to build their careers around a slogan-like initiative, such as "Homeless Veterans." The leader, however, does not even know enough about his or her self-proclaimed mission, agency resources, and the processes that negotiate the context to even add verbs to the slogan, so there is some actionable or directive information associated with it.

Many gifted public servants appointed to higher-level positions actually do have a three-dimensional focus and know their jobs are to work toward providing efficient operations and services. As a result of their efforts, we see efficiencies in reduced lines at many Department of Motor Vehicle offices and at many local Department of Veterans Affairs (VA) medical centers and clinics. But government services are legendary for unenthusiastic employees, long waits in lines, and for giving customers grief as they try to unravel red tape. Just Google "long lines at DMV" and see how widespread the problems continue to persist. Nation-wide, the VA continues to struggle with its claims backlog. Every four years Americans experience the recurring trauma of long lines at the voting polls.

Many gifted civil servants and upper-level leaders in government programs often achieve productivity, functional alignment, and coordination of services despite executive management. Typically, politically appointed managers are classic one-dimensional leaders whose agenda is to wield power and achieve name recognition. Thus they feel very satisfied touting slogans while they undervalue the processes that support the employees who actually serve clients and help them overcome their issues that underlie the problem. I-D and II-D leaders know very little about how to organize the actual services and the duties of the people providing them. Because they often are too arrogant to learn, they consequently make one poor decision after the next—often ordering managers to interfere inappropriately with processes upon which clients and partner organizations rely. The leader's impetuous behavior thus has a negative impact on the way employees work.

People within government will tell you that "politically appointing executives is the way people in power employ the people they know and trust to get jobs done for them." The challenge is finding someone they know who has expertise or at least a background in the processes they are supposed to manage. I have asked many political appointees, "What did they tell you about the job and what you are to do here?" and most have replied, "They said I don't have to know what the employees do to be able to manage them." Then, with an air of superiority, they state, "My job is not to embarrass the governor." I try to advise them that this is accomplished by making decisions that assist employees to do their jobs well. When I try to explain that employees are the organization's greatest asset and are delivering what the public relies on, many of the politically appointed I-D upper managers see that as some sort of threat to their power and prestige, and they begin to name-drop the various politicians who have assisted them to get their jobs. This indicates to me that rather than have a focus on employee and organizational mission and productivity, they are focused on those whose influence got them the jobs.

Because one-dimensional leaders do things based upon *who they know* rather than what you and your employees know, they usually do not allow knowledgeable people to do what they are capable of accomplishing. One-dimensional leaders are identified by how little they focus on the front-end mission, which are the real reasons the agencies exist. One-dimensionals spend little time negotiating the actual context in which employees must operate to do their jobs well. They fight with and throw their power against people in the context. They don't understand the perils to operational synergy from ignoring other departments, functionaries, partners, and operatives within the context. They wrongly think it advantageous to withhold information from or go over the heads of those within the context. Two-dimensional leaders may care about the mission, but they fail to learn how to accomplish it by authorizing work processes that are effective throughout the given context. So their decisions only resonate with a few of their closest associates in the context.

If you do not know or learn what your employees do, you never will be able to judge the quality of their performance or the quality of the products and services they provide. This is one reason why government management information and control systems often fail to count the individual employee productivity that translates to customer and client satisfaction, which is the foundation for organizational success. The leaders who oversee management-information systems setup often override the views of long-term civil servants in favor of their own rudimentary knowledge.

It is very challenging to achieve organizational health in environments that are heavily influenced by political appointees for at least three reasons. If politicians are elected presumably to carry out agendas, it makes sense for them to hire leaders who are focused on and willing to implement them. Unfortunately, appointed leaders tend to emulate the politicians who gave them their jobs. Politicians have a legitimate need for name recognition because they must run for office, but the appointed leaders of agencies do not. Nonetheless, many appointees are focused on seeking the same name recognition needed by the politicians who appointed them, so they spend their time dreaming up costly but not necessarily effective initiatives in hopes of making a headline that includes their name. Instead, they should be focused on the thoughtful and steady management of the day-to-day operations of their organization's front end, where the public actually obtains services that are meaningful to them. This focus requires valuing and placing emphasis on the employees with whom the public interfaces to obtain services. Valuing and esteeming employees is not what the typical political appointee has in mind when he or she gets a job.

The second challenge is that politicians and their appointees often promise initiatives and focus on programs and projects that cannot be implemented within the reality of the organization's actual operations that have been set up to achieve its primary mission. The organization may not be positioned to implement the newly mandated initiatives. Politicians and their politically appointed managers may lack operational knowledge of the agencies they oversee so that in whatever initiatives they undertake, you effectively have the blind leading the blind. The politically appointed leaders often have the least institutional knowledge of agency operations and lack the historical perspective on the relationships within the context that coordinate to fulfill the essential missions of the organizations they now head. This does not stop them, however, from charging headlong into initiatives that actually undermine operational and employee synergy and effectiveness. When midlevel managers try to challenge these directives or steer them into channels that are compatible with existing operations, the politically appointed leaders cite that they are working on behalf of the chief executive of the city, the county, the state or federal government, or they are implementing the will of the city council, county or state legislature, or the congress or senate. What often happens is appointed leaders leverage political will in a heavy-handed way that fails to negotiate the context and undermines effective organizational operations. This is not to say that government chief executives, councils, or legislatures actually know what the politically appointed managers are doing on a daily basis.

The third reason why government often fails to achieve what it has set out to do is that politicians and their politically appointed leaders fail to consider how consumers actually respond to program and service offerings. Many government service initiatives are viewed as "underutilized" because they are set up and administered in a way that is counterintuitive to how private businesses and citizens operate and function. Many government leaders design program offerings for the public and never interview or consult any of the private citizens, businesses, or not-for-profit organizations they say their programs are designed to assist. You only can help people in the ways they want to be helped. If you never ask people how they want to be helped and in what ways your services will be meaningful to them, what can you really accomplish? You may design programs that seem like great initiatives from an "ivory tower" perspective, but they will resonate with few others in the context. Sadly, the actual outcomes of many government initiatives amount to little more than the press releases touting them.

Too many appointees believe they have their jobs because, in some intrinsic way, they are brighter, better, and smarter than the employees they now manage (or, in their minds, "rule over"). Or they may believe they are of better political pedigree than the people around them, who may be of the same political party but just didn't land a "big job." Because one-dimensional leaders arrogantly view employees lower in the organizational hierarchy as "beneath" them, it is not surprising that they are unable to learn mission-oriented operations from them.

Because upper managers of government organizations tend to come and go every three to four years, there is considerable inconsistency in their ability to fulfill their missions. Because midlevel managers who have worked their way up through the civil service system generally possess the organization's institutional memory, executive leadership would be wise to tap into and make effective use of those resources. Far too often, however, this is not the case.

The dedicated employees and midlevel managers within various government organizations have a long history of interfacing with the community and other agencies to coordinate and fulfill their respective missions. Because people can only do what they know, if the appointees do not learn what the employees know or have actual work experience in what they are tasked to manage, they impose what they know (and what they don't know) upon the process.

Many midlevel government civil servants have worked nights and weekends, documenting and recording processes trying to educate appointed leaders to get them to understand how the system works, so they can implement appropriate initiatives. Employees hope their supervisors can talk sense to the appointees. It takes years for them to go around a learning curve, however, and realize that what the civil servants proposed (based upon their years of successful experience) was indeed the correct thing to do. The behavior of many politically appointed leaders infuses inefficiency throughout the organization and needlessly delays productive activities. It deflates employee motivation by implying that their opinions, bred of years of dedicated, selfless service, mean nothing. It is a great way to lead an uninspired and de-stimulated work force.

Numerous government employees relate experiences of how appointed leaders often disrupt and undermine well-established, fruitful working relationships with partners that have provided successful outcomes for the public for more than a decade. Sometimes the appointees forbid employees to discuss program issues with those in other agencies, even though those other employees are well aware of them. The appointee feels they have to defend information that long-time employees and community partners know from their years of working together that there is no issue to defend. Government civil servants and their community part-ners often share the same perspective and history of the data and, therefore, have the same conclusions. But because the appointees do not understand this, they feel insecure, as if they have to hide the information and the decisions to be made in relation to it. Failing to inform long-term partners about the process, however, makes the other parties feel betrayed, as though they are being treated in an underhanded way. Institutional working relation-ships break down and are replaced by fragmented coordination that results in inefficient processes—all born out of a lack of trust and cooperation.

Many government managers try to work around appointees to maintain good working relationships necessary to coordinate services, despite how appointees come along and undermine them. These managers are not always successful, because they can be threatened with insubordination and ultimately compelled to go along with the boss's decisions. By the time appointed gov-ernment executives get around a learning curve (and some never do) and have exhausted all their efforts at imposing what they think they know upon the mission, they have lost all credibility with the middle managers, employees, and partners, who are so frustrated that they want nothing to do with them.

The leaders should be embarrassed that so many things they have tried to do are outside the parameters of the context. The groundswell of employee frustration that boils over and the nega-tive public opinions and complaints about the misdirected top appointees seems to fall on deaf ears, because few appointed leaders ever are disciplined or removed from their jobs. Some will be in the third and fourth years of their tenures before they have learned enough about the civil service and union rules, federal and state laws that govern how operations and programs are set up and administered, and other work processes and procedures to approach anything near the level of managerial competency, and even then many never reach it. History is littered with political, military, and business leaders who failed to come around a learning curve but instead tried again and again to impose what was mission fatal considering the context.

In government, as soon as you think you have the current crew of appointees around a learning curve, there is an election, and a new politician is appointing the next crew of agency leaders, beginning the painfully frustrating learning curve all over again.

There are two major skill sets required for leaders of government organizations. One is program knowledge. This can be taught and is easily learned—if the appointee has a learning mind-set. The other is people-management skills that guide how one leads, oversees, and manages large groups of people that make up the organizations that provide the work the public relies on. I have been advised that the only way politicians can reward those who help them get in to power is by giving or creating jobs for them. There is pressure upon any political system to employ people who, for whatever reason, want or need a job. Some people just want to be "the leader" of something, so they seek a government-appointed management position that is accompanied by a nice job title, office, automobile, and travel expenses, and an entourage of people to travel around with them and do their bidding. These perks feed their egos, and the more the ego is fed, the more it grows. The more the ego grows, the less focus there is on the mission.

One-Dimensional and Two-Dimensional Burgeoning Bureaucracies

One-dimensional and two-dimensional leaders increase bureaucracies in unproductive ways. A challenge for the economy is that when government leaders say they want to help us by creating a program, they mean they want to create a bureaucracy that will require managers, administrative staff to handle the payroll, benefits, and other employee-assistance programs that go along with it. To oversee and monitor these government programs, additional bureaucracies are created.

Legislative bodies respond to crisis or perceived crisis by creating committees to study issues and make recommendations for an official response to them. Legislatures often receive additional pay for each committee they chair. While there are legitimate public concerns that need to be addressed, the number of active committees can become a self-aggrandizing exercise that provides lawmakers within income in exchange for very little outcomes that affect change. It actually may be worse for the taxpayer when these committees succeed in creating a program that gets passed into law and is funded because of the bureaucracies necessary to support them.

New programs may require offices or buildings. Every new employee will need a desk, a computer, and office supplies. There will be mileage expenses and per diem travel expenses, and on and on the expenses will go. A new government program requires tremendous expenditures that must come from other productive sectors of the economy to support it; otherwise, deficit spending increases, which is often the case.

There is a vast difference between creating a bureaucracy and fulfilling a mission. Politicians may like bureaucracies because the large groups of people, buildings, and institutions associated with them are easy to hold up as an example of what is being accomplished for the public. One-dimensional and two-dimensional political leaders also like institutions and buildings because they add to their "officialdom" by placing their names upon them. Shortly after the attacks of the World Trade Center in New York City on September 11, 2001, a politician repeatedly tried to add something meaningful to the process by saying we need a national 800 number so parents can phone in to find out information about anthrax, as they are terrified for their children's lives and want to know more about the deadly poison.

I heard the politician say this no less than six times on different occasions. I thought, *There already are county health agencies, state health agencies, and other public health forums where people can obtain information. Any information about anthrax and other toxins can be provided through those organizations. We don't need another bureaucracy for this.*

For this politician to get her way, it would have required the public to endure the expense of phone banks, people to answer them, desks at which they would sit, managers to oversee those people, secretaries for the managers, and office rental. The cost of government would increase by paying for the health insurance expenses and retirement benefits of all those employees.

Max Weber on Bureaucracy

The man known as the Father of Modern Sociology, Max Weber (1864–1920), provided the structures for which contemporary bureaucracy is known. Weber said that bureaucracies "are founded on legal or rational authority which is based on law, procedures, rules, and so on." Characteristics include positional authority of a superior over a subordinate, readily viewed in the traditional organizational chart, where hierarchical power stems from the legal authority invested in certain positions. Weber said that efficiency in bureaucracies is achieved by clearly defined and specialized functions, hierarchical structures of decision making, and well-documented rules and procedures. Successful leadership is accomplished by technically trained bureaucrats and a workforce appointed to positions based on technical expertise as well as promotions based on competence.

Contrast that with what takes place very often in political bureaucracies today that have devolved into monolithic, cumbersome organizations that tend to be unresponsive to the public, stifling of the individual employee, and highly resistant to meaningful change. Is it any wonder when the people leading them know little about the technical aspects of the organization's mission?

While the 2008 financial crisis, brought on by subprime lending, was unfolding, I wondered how many Securities and Exchange Commission (SEC) civil servants saw the dangers but were overridden by their politically appointed layers of management. Those civil servants are the institutional memory that, in my opinion, if listened to, could have prevented the crisis. I wonder what they perceived about the government's easing of credit restrictions that provided loans to people whose incomes could not support them. While the loans were made more palatable to the lenders by assigning higher and fluctuating interest rates, those same strategies meant that consumers would be less likely to sustain payments, due to changes in their income-to-mortgage payment ratios. If those payments are not made, the lending institutions holding the mortgage notes will have less cash flow to pay their expenses, including the salaries of their employees.

The subprime lenders made commissions from these loans that were passed through and approved by investment banks and the credit rating and approving agencies, which also made money from their efforts in the process. Insurers and others involved in the securitization process may have culpability because, while mortgages are attached to a physical piece of property, having too many of them in developments and neighborhoods populated by subprime borrowers is an undue risk. Brokers and dealers passed on this gratuitous risk to the public by selling mortgage-backed securities and debt with housing values propped up by subprime loans as collateral. The SEC is supposed to regulate the securities market to protect investors. It failed at being proactive at this mission.

The Senate and House of Representatives banking committees also failed in their duties to oversee America's banks, financial markets, and insurance companies to help the nation avoid financial crises. The government leaders who sit on these committees historically are the largest recipients of campaign donations from the sectors and institutions they are tasked to oversee. One can see how such a system lends itself to being taken advantage of by one-dimensional and two-dimensional leaders who do what is expedient for them and their friends but which is disastrous for "we the people" throughout the national context. Perhaps these leaders will make three-dimensional responses in the aftermath.

The litany of publicly displayed foibles played out by various branches of government during the aftermath of Hurricane Katrina that hit New Orleans, Louisiana, on August 29, 2005, is evidence of the ongoing challenges of leadership competence in government. The mayor allowed a one thousand-seat train to leave the city empty rather than heed warnings to evacuate his citizens. He also allowed scores of school buses to be ruined by floodwaters along with other mobile pieces of city taxpayer property. During a time when people around the nation were praying for the citizens of his city, he presented even further disturbing behavior when he took the Lord's name in vain over the radio airwaves.

The governor failed to allow the federal government to exercise its authority to send in its troops. Much of the gubernatorial indecision apparently stemmed from that politician's overriding desire to protect her "image" based upon statements and communications of an aide. If getting credit for initiatives is one's primary focus, then there may be reluctance to bring in the assistance of others, because it means sharing credit. If politicians or leaders are most concerned about name recognition and image, then assuredly they have surrounded themselves with people who will make that boss's focus a number-one priority. Only one-dimensional followers would take on a job whose focus is centered on fawning over the leader's so-called image. Three-dimensional performers will seek positions that provide a focus on the mission, because they want to accomplish something beyond the name recognition and perks they garner for themselves. Unfortunately, there are too many I-D's to go around.

Chapter Fourteen

Mission-Focused Mentoring

While I-D leaders fawn over something as superfluous as their image, which actually is determined by the opinion of others whose viewpoints are not within our control, competent leaders are focused on strengthening their organizations so they can accomplish a mission. One activity that I believe distinguishes III-D leaders is they understand that the ongoing health of their organizations depends upon developing a deep bench of future leaders. While all leaders are busy and must set priorities, none is more important to an organization's future than leadership development through mentoring.

Mentoring can be formal and informal. Conducted properly, it can shorten the learning curve for up-and-coming leaders. What a lot of potentially great leaders need are mentors to help them achieve their full potential, so they function as robustly as possible in as short a time as possible. There are several challenges to mentoring. One is that if you never were mentored, you may not have an appreciation of how valuable it can be. You also may not know what it looks and feels like to mentor someone else. Unless one is accustomed to the dynamics of being a schoolteacher or a college professor, mentoring may seem awkward and uncomfortable.

Mentoring versus Micromanaging

Mentoring is not micromanaging. You feel micromanaged when someone who lacks expertise exercises undue control over your expertise. By contrast, if someone has expertise and comes alongside you to support you and assist you to do your job better, you would feel mentored. You would feel that the mentor is enhancing your experience and adding value to you as an individual, and that quality is added to the outcomes of processes in which you are being mentored.

Mentoring Requires Investment

Mentoring can be an expensive proposition. For example, some professional football teams hire aging, outstanding quarterbacks to mentor a younger quarterback who is being groomed for the starting quarterback position in the near future. Part of the seasoned quarterback's job is to sit on the sidelines beside the younger player, who at the moment may be the third-string quarterback, and explain what is taking place on the field during each play made by the current starting quarterback and why things unfold, develop, and turn out the way they do, and what possible adjustments the quarterback could have made.

In literature the Greeks introduced the concept of mentoring in the epic *Odysseus,* where "Mentor," the son of Alcimus, is friend and advisor to Odysseus. Athene takes his form and becomes the guardian and teacher of Telemachus.[13] Mentoring generally involves an older, more skilled, and experienced person taking an apprentice under his or her wing to reduce the learning curve of the novice who needs guidance to be able to reach his or her full potential. In the medical field, surgeons and other doctors enter into mentoring relationships with their interns. Many union apprenticeship programs are founded upon the concept of mentoring. Mentoring is why rookie police officers rarely are allowed to patrol alone.

Mentoring, however, is something that only the most forward-looking III-D leaders really understand and intentionally make part of their leadership development and succession-planning initiatives. Mentors have to be people who can still perform well enough for others to learn from them but are willing to allow the sometimes fumbling and awkward apprentice to get in to the game to do his or her best.

The mentor has to have the patience and grace to tolerate the apprentice's efforts, which may not be up to the same level of performance of the mentor, but which accomplishes the job adequately enough so that the organization's mission is not compromised. While mentors know the ins and outs of each situation and how to advise the trainee to negotiate them, they must have the ability to pass on wisdom in a selfless manner that builds the future not for themselves but for the good of the organization that will be relying upon the apprentice for its future survival and vitality.

One-dimensional leaders believe their leadership prowess is displayed by how things fall apart when they are not present. The success of a mentoring relationship, by contrast, is proven by how tremendous activity continues when the mentor is not present. Only the healthiest of leaders can make themselves suitably expendable because they have appropriately mentored. Professional football teams have challenges in succession planning when they try to create a mentoring relationship between an aging quarterback and a younger one. The aging players do not want to play second or third fiddle and sit on the bench with the prospect of being there primarily to assist the less-experienced athletes. Since many seasoned quarterbacks still have incredible game life in them and can play at an amazing level, what would work better for them is for teams to develop a player-coach role that allows the number-one player to feel comfortable as the starter while also helping their team organizations to prepare the next crop of superstars who will succeed them someday.

It Takes Three to Mentor

Many would-be mentors blow the opportunity for their teams and, in my opinion, for their own legacies when they fail to mentor. While it is commendable to have a competitive spirit that scraps to obtain the lead role or the equivalent of the starting quarterback job, one also should see the bigger picture. Teams should work to achieve a win-win-win role between the seasoned players and the potential up-and-coming stars. A player-coach role could reduce the rivalry between the experienced players and the understudies to create a more comfortable and intuitive process that allows the latter to carry on the former great player's legacy. I would be honored for a younger up-and-coming player to attribute his or her success to how I provided essential guidance that pushed his or her career forward at a critical time of development. These accolades will be possible if we discern the mentoring opportunities that are before us and make the best of them. Our organizations may be counting on us to do so.

It takes three to mentor: the organization to set up and support the initiative, a willing employee mentor, and a cooperative apprentice who is eager to learn. An organization must be willing to pay two people who often will be doing the same job, or nearly the same job, or will be crossing assignments enough that others will think they are doing the same job. One of the employees must be performing the task, while the other employee is mentoring and overseeing the same process. The shortsighted will call this "a waste." I view mentoring as an essential part of a healthy organization's leadership training and succession program.

In addition to sending employees off to conferences, which have the ancillary expenses of travel, meals, and lodging, an organization also can invest in on-the-job mentoring programs, whereby less-experienced employees periodically are brought alongside more experienced employees who assist the apprentices in undertaking assigned projects and duties. The mentoring process incorporates time (money) for the more experienced employees to provide feedback that provides the novice employees with the opportunity to benefit from the critiquing. Many successful companies have these types of processes in place as a key part of their strategy to develop continuous generations of employees who are learning to understand what has made those companies successful and what will be necessary to lead their organizations to future accomplishments.

For organizations that have learned how to learn, mentoring programs are an institutionalized process. The best way to learn and grow is to teach or mentor, because it compels us to analyze how we do what we do and break it down into process steps that easily are explained for others to grasp.

Chapter Fifteen

Strategies to Negotiate Leaders Who Care Little for the Mission

Making Mission-Focused Decisions

Leaders make three-dimensional decisions through a process that asks these questions:

- Does the proposed action or initiative align with our mission?

- Can the proposed action or initiative be accomplished with our resources?

- Does the proposed action or initiative make sense to and resonate with those in our context, especially customers and the partners and others with whom we must coordinate to reach them?

The resource question and the context question are intertwined. The people in your internal and external context are your most important resources. You answer these questions by asking others and consulting with them—especially representatives of the employees who are the chief resource and must successfully accomplish the work the initiative requires.

Proverbs 15:22 says, "Plans fail for lack of counsel, but with many advisers they succeed." Your analysis and consultation must be broad based because successful implementation requires people throughout the context to be on board to do their part. Too many initiatives fail because a headstrong leader charges into them only after getting consensus from a small number of hand-picked clones who suffer from "groupthink."

Yale University's Irving Janis (1918–1990) coined the term "groupthink" as "a collective in-group's unwillingness to realistically view alternatives."[14] No one in the group is encouraged to critically evaluate the opinions and directives of the leader, and the opinions of industry experts either are ignored or not even consulted. A phenomenon I have observed in dictatorial I-D leaders whose organizations suffer from groupthink is that they isolate their teams from alternative opinions, strategies, and viewpoints. They often accomplish this by ordering their subordinates to not discuss information with outsiders. The leader's incessant demands for "loyalty" sends clear messages to those around them that "if you want to keep your jobs, you will articulate only what I think, and you will shun anyone or anything that is contrary to my opinions."

Groupthink prevails because of the "Asch Effect," which is how social pressure produces "the distortion of individual judgment by a unanimous but incorrect opposition." Solomon Asch (1907–1996) conducted research to see whether or not people would "conform to a majority opinion that obviously is wrong." "Only twenty percent of Asch's subjects remained entirely independent; eighty percent yielded to the pressures of group opinions at least once! Fifty-eight percent knuckled under to the 'immoral majority' at least twice."[15]

Three-dimensional leaders resist giving in to group pressure to turn their backs on their mission, resources, and context (MRC) perspective and values. Organizations are at risk of groupthink because they tend to take on the personality of the leader. If the leader is one-dimensional, he or she will tend to attract and hire others who know less about the MRC than he or she does and who will make the leader's wants and whims their priority. If the I-D leader is a bully, he or she will attract others who enjoy bullying and forcing their narrow opinions onto others. They will attract people who use the power of their positions to force their style preferences upon others, regardless of how superfluous they are to the mission or regardless of how ineffective they are at accomplishing it. I-D's also are compatible with people who really have no strong opinions, motives, or desires and so are comfortable to passively go along with whatever the leader wants.

Groupthink can have disastrous outcomes. There have been many articles written about its contribution to the 1986 Space Shuttle *Challenger* disaster, aboard which teacher Christa McAuliffe died. Two engineers of the Morton Thiokol Corporation, the contractor responsible for building the solid rocket booster, stood their ground in warning that O-rings in booster joints could fail, resulting in serious consequences if the shuttle was launched in cold weather. The Shuttle *Challenger* was launched in thirty-six-degree weather. After numerous delays that pushed the launch back several days, leadership overrode the concerns of the experts who had built the rocket booster and its O-rings. Some reports cited that senior leaders felt pressure to perform the launch for the public, which had been built up to expect a launch and then let down during the several delays. II-D leaders, who, by definition, fail to negotiate the complete context, created their own sense of pressure to "perform" for the admiring public that anticipated seeing the first schoolteacher launched into space. In the process science and engineering concerns were forced to take a backseat.

While it is very challenging to resist a boss's directives regardless of how off base they are, there are several strategies for dealing with leaders who are not mission focused. None of them, however, make for an ideal work situation. Three-dimensional employees would rather spend time at work pursuing missions rather than negotiating the prerogatives of I-D and II-D leaders.

One-dimensional leaders do not care about the mission. I-D leadership is all about "me" the leader and not the mission. As I stated earlier, when you are dealing with I-D leaders, you do not negotiate your mission. You only can negotiate your I-D leader's wants and whims, regardless of how far removed from the mission they are. When you are dealing with I-D's, you do not whistle off to work to accomplish job responsibilities that are stated on your employee-evaluation form. At work you only can do what the I-D wants when he or she wants. This obviously can be very frustrating for employees who are focused on and in tune with MRC dynamics.

Filtering Information Does Not Always Work

One manager, who obviously wants to remain anonymous, strongly urged me to include what follows: He advises that he deals with I-D leaders by filtering the information he passes along to them, so he has some impact on their output. With a I-D it is not "garbage in and garbage out"; it is "good information in and garbage out." Even when I-Ds are given appropriate information, they try to turn it to their personal advantage and are not focused on organizational processes and so tend not to make appropriate mission-focused responses to it. You will have more opportunities to filter information coming from those below you on the organizational chart than you will for those above you on the organizational chart.

People above you and your boss more often than not will communicate first with your boss, who then filters the information to you. Sometimes leaders who either are on the same stratum with or above your boss may come directly to you to get around your boss. This may happen because they may feel your boss tries to manipulate assignments in a way to further his or her personal agendas. I have been in the unfortunate situation of having leaders above me contact me for assignments, requesting that I do not advise my I-D boss. In such instances, I notify my I-D boss if the leader above me is asking me to compromise my integrity or my organization's mission, violate company policy, or to backstab my boss. Generally in those instances, my estimation is that I am going to need the protection of my boss. Because if someone is willing to compromise the organization's mission, my integrity, and be vindictive to my boss, they are not worthy of my trust, and under no circumstances do they obtain my collusion. I usually advise the person making the request that "I do not think what is being asked of me is appropriate, and I cannot participate in it." If the other leader is persistent, I ask, "Do you have any idea how my boss is going to feel or treat me if he/she finds out that you are asking me to do this?" If they persist, I advise "that as soon as I get off the phone, I am calling my boss to advise him or her of this conversation." I nip it in the bud!

If, however, I do not think my boss will believe that the other leader would pull such a stunt, I advise the other leader that I will not participate, and I do not tell my boss about the conversation. There are times when other organizations come to me directly because they do not want any other interactions with my I-D boss. Sometimes they invite me to participate in initiatives or functions and ask me to make sure that I do not bring my boss or even let him know about the event, so he does not crash the party and try to muscle his way to the front of the room and make a speech to give the impression that he has initiated and been integral to the process. Sometimes I am able to participate in those events and sometimes I am not.

Since in certain environments, like government, bosses can come and go every three to four years, I may be able to participate in such an event to keep intact long-term working relationships and to support the employees who must continue to negotiate them after my boss and I are gone. When I get such requests, however, I advise that "there is no guarantee I can attend, because I cannot always control my schedule. If my boss schedules something for me during the same time as the event, I obviously will have to do what my boss prefers, since, per the request, I cannot notify him or her of a conflict."

Once, a boss's secretary and I tried to manage a disciplinary matter by filtering information to him, as he had a history of inappropriately insinuating himself between employees and their supervisors. We suspected an employee had a history of getting her supervisors to compromise themselves, so she had leverage to swear them to an unholy alliance, in which she would have the upper hand. She had used up all her vacation, sick, and personal time allotted for the year, and her supervisor had requested my assistance, as I was his supervisor, to work toward getting her to come to the office on time and to be there more often. I caught the employee arriving at the office more than an hour late on two occasions, and she tried to compel me to "let her slide." I did not let her "slide" and arranged with my boss's secretary to accompany me and the tardy employee's supervisor to deliver her termination notice.

We had worked with our legal and personnel departments to ensure we had an airtight case, and then we advised our boss of the pending action, which legal and personnel had advised us to take. He insisted on being part of the team that went to deliver the message and paperwork. He knew of the many previous challenges we had had with the employee and the numerous violations she had committed. On the day of the action, however, our I-D boss did not show up to the office, as pre-arranged, so we all could carpool to the meeting. He also did not answer calls to his cell phone. Instead he called us an hour before the scheduled meeting and said that he had taken the employee to lunch and had broken the news to her gently. She claimed he had sexually harassed her, and a compromise eventually was reached that included her staying on the job.

It does not always work to try to filter information to I-D bosses. The boss can do what he wants, when he wants, within reason. Even when you filter to protect them from themselves, you may not be successful.

Reporting As High As Possible
Above the Challenge

Another strategy for dealing with I-D's and II-D's includes try-ing to report a level or two above them whenever possible. Report their behavior to higher levels than that if you get the opportu-nity. I-D's and II-D's, however, are good at covering their tracks and often establish work procedures that make it difficult to go around them. Going over or around them is risky because your actions can be interpreted as being disloyal to your supervising leader. You also may find that your evaluations reflect that you are not doing what your leader wants you to do. But when leaders undermine the mission and make resources ineffective, so they can't accomplish it, and when they compromise organizational processes throughout the context, you may feel you have no other choice than to try to stop it in any way that is appropriate that does not break the law or commit insubordination. Only you can determine when you have had enough and upon which hill you will fight on to the point of being fired.

Whenever possible, document in e-mails and memorandums what your leader wants you to do and what you believe your job is supposed to be, including what the organization is relying upon you to achieve and what course of actions you recommend pursu-ing that are consistent with what the organization is expecting from your role. Try restating your leader's directives and then your position while not being rude, coming across as arrogant or insubordinate. Keep in mind that you most likely will have to do what the leader wants—at least for a while. A signal that you are not involved in a fair exchange of information and a healthy give-and-take discussion about strategy in pursuing an initiative is that your leader will not write back to you but will pick up the phone and conduct business "off the record" in a verbal "hearsay" manner. Without written proof of the directives, you have little defense.

A corrections officer once told me how a prison superin-tendent tried to make it look to his bosses that he had reduced assaults at a facility by internally changing the definition of a "reportable incident." If inmates attacked one another or an officer, he would not allow it to be reported as an incident. There were far-reaching consequences to this one-dimensional leadership directive. Consequently, no arrests were made of the inmate perpetrators, and no negative information was added to their files. This endangered guards because the inmates figured out that they were not experiencing negative legal consequences for their violent behavior. The lack of reporting made the inmates more eligible for parole. This meant that felons who continued to be violent were more likely to get out of jail and back onto the streets.

The corrections officers and many other personnel tried as often as possible to report to others higher up throughout the greater context. In about a year the superintendent lost his job. His I-D behaviors tarnished his reputation, violated his oath of office, and endangered the employees he was supposed to oversee and protect. Employees should find ways to get out from under a leader who does such things. Loyalty to honorable processes is a higher calling than loyalty to a misguided leader.

I once had a boss who would verbally state to me, "Just let this stay between us. There is no need to have any communication with people upstairs. Let's not involve them in our business." After a while I realized my boss used this tactic when he was giving the leaders above us different information than he was giving me. Sometimes his agenda was at my expense, and sometimes it was at their expense or at the expense of others. I let my mission, resources, and context (MRC) values determine my response to this particular boss, who floated between being a I-D and a II-D leader. Whenever the initiatives included the directives and input of the leaders above us, and they included me in their e-mails, I would include them in my e-mails, so they could see what was supposed to transpire from my end, and they would have something to compare against what my boss may have been telling them.

On a couple of occasions, a II-D leader on my boss's level contacted me and sent emissaries with a request that I interpreted would undermine my organization's mission and definitely would do something that I knew my boss would not want. On the other side of this equation, my boss would order me not to engage in normal work processes that caused appropriate interaction with the other II-D leader. I grew tired very quickly of being pushed and pulled by the two leaders, and after about a month of it, I called the chief executive and asked if she could assist me to negotiate a situation between two of her leaders. I explained that their actions made me feel like I was back in junior high school with two immature people trying to involve me in their game of one against the other. She agreed that I should not have to put up with such behavior, and I then asked her to advise the two of them that if they want to fight with each other, they should not use me and my program as their pawns. The other II-D leader stopped trying to pit me against my boss, and he let me know that there are times I must interact with the other leader and program and that I should be free to do so.

The Inconsistencies of Two-Dimensional Leadership

Two-dimensional leadership is a broad category that encompasses leaders who wander in and out of mission focus. Two-dimensional leaders are inconsistent in pursuing initiatives that are in line with their organization's long-term vision and values that should guide their efforts in negotiating their mission, resources, and context (MRC). II-Ds have personality quirks that make it difficult for them to maintain an MRC focus and identify what relates to it and what does not. II-D's are unpredictable regarding when, where, and under what circumstances they will be mission focused. Their idiosyncrasies keep them from being consistently objective.

When dealing with a II-D leader, you actually will find many instances where the leader's mission focus allows you to implement ideas that are consistent with long-range MRC strategies. What you will find most challenging, however, is that because II-D leaders fail to perceive and appreciate the context, you will have disagreements about how to go about implementing the initiatives. If you try reporting above you, your challenge is to get those above you to understand the context enough so they realize that the way your II-D leader is forcing you to go about implementation is going to frustrate others throughout it.

When I-D's and II-D's are on a leadership ego trip, they make decisions that they believe will draw the most attention to themselves as the leaders. They use decision-making opportunities to do whatever they think gives them prestige as the leader. Their discussion reveals that they are consumed with being "in charge" and being "the leader." At times, their speaking becomes exercises in meandering around topics, trying to make sure they make enough references to their position and the role they have in steering things, and how they are leading their people and managers. These behaviors communicate that the leader's focus is not really on the mission, nor is it on the resources that they have available to fulfill it.

Part Three

Rallying Resources

Chapter Sixteen

People Provide Potential

Resources consist of people (managers, employees, volunteers), time, real estate, machinery, information technology, computers, equipment, suppliers, partners, networks, money for investments, inventory, salaries and benefits, travel budgets, operations budgets, and research and development budgets. Human capital, however, is the most promising resource available to achieve an organization's success. People provide potential. People are also the most sophisticated and challenging resources for an organization to manage. People provide the most potential for both failure and success. Three-dimensional leadership is especially adept at working with people, for when the human resources are handled properly they are incredible assets for an organization.

Even in highly mechanized operations, people make the most critical decisions. People push the buttons that turn on and shut off the machines. People set the tolerances, the performance thresholds, the run-times, et cetera. Leaders never should underestimate the amazing potential people have to achieve outstanding results to support mission fulfillment.

Popular movies create drama around how people are the ultimate heroes. The setup is that the hero must achieve the mission and save the day by overcoming great odds. This is achieved by exercising extraordinary ingenuity in the middle of bad circumstances as things are not going as planned, and all the hero's supports are removed. The person has to overcome by the sheer whit of improvisation.

The story lines involve a common person who is like "every man" or "every woman." The common person suddenly is caught up in the middle of extraordinary circumstances, whereby fulfillment of a mission provides an outcome that has significant consequences for others or the entire planet Earth. We find it compelling for the protagonist to fight against the odds to accomplish a noble thing that requires triumph over "the system."

The system typically is a bureaucracy or a group of individuals who all see things the same way in contrast to how the hero sees them. The tension contrasts the hero as the odd man out. The drama intensifies when he is stripped of all the supports that one would expect a hero to have. If the protagonist is a police officer or detective, he is stripped of his badge. If the hero is a combatant engaged in armed battle, he runs out of ammo or loses his primary weapon. Often the hero is stripped of the machinery that normally would carry him to victory. He loses his horse, his car, his plane, his boat and has to improvise to overcome seemingly insurmountable odds.

We can draw many parallels between the dramatic hero and the organizational leader, both of whom deal with all kinds of challenges that threaten to impede the fulfillment of the mission. They both have to overcome every obstacle and setback to skillfully and artfully negotiate fulfilling the mission for the greater good of the organization. Thus the factory stays open and the employees keep their jobs, and the investors' futures remain bright as the company makes a profit against all odds.

When all the machinery fails and the best organizational planning falls short, it is people who will successfully negotiate the context to make success happen. Get the "who" right and you will get the "do" right. It is people with great hearts who persevere through unpredictable circumstances to achieve success. People in dramatic settings are like the quintessential organism that will slip through every entanglement, negotiate every obstacle, and rebound from every setback to reach the goal and achieve the mission.

Regardless of the investment that corporations make, their success ultimately depends upon people. A retail chain's investment in capital improvements to make store and façade beautification can increase visitor foot traffic, but how those visitors become shoppers and the profitability from their transactions depend upon how well people provide customer service. Return on equity ultimately depends upon how your people handle and sell assets to increase their value over your liabilities. Before a capital investment can meet the needs of customers, it must be effectively implemented by managers and undertaken by construction workers. Upon these people depends the quality of your investment. People determine the outcomes of investments in equity. It is people who negotiate and time purchases and sales to take advantage of market fluctuations to make a profit for your organization.

For people to be effective, however, they too need attention and care. Machines tend to perform in prescribed ways. There are rather predictable mechanical or other physiological reasons why equipment fails or performs well. Thus one can establish preventative maintenance schedules to keep machines operating. Machines, moreover, tend to be functionally fixed to perform the tasks for which they originally were created and are not easily cross-trainable. Sometimes some can be reprogrammed and retrofitted to do things other than what they originally were intended to do, but they do not provide the potential for flexibility and adaptability that humans do.

While people can be flexible to adapt to different circumstances, they are complex in how they respond to them. There can be numerous and varying reasons why they fail to perform to their potential. When determining why people perform poorly, we need to analyze whether or not it is the individual who has the challenge, or is it related to the way the system is designed in which he works, or does the challenge lie within the circumstances or context that may be out of his control? Does the underperformance lie with the supervisor, manager, or leader? Or are both the employee and the leader experiencing challenges in the situation? Helping people to make appropriate adjustments to improve their performance requires discreet and circumspect troubleshooting and analysis, as much or more so than one would do with very sophisticated machinery.

Three-dimensional leaders inspire and show people how to be heroes to fulfill the mission in the face of an evolving context and changing circumstances. It values and empowers individual ingenuity so it can be applied to the mission at hand. III-D leaders facilitate circumstances that are favorable for their people resources to succeed at their jobs. Thus the mission is converted within the context, much like how a football quarterback must adjust to the tactics the defense has deployed by spontaneously calling an audible play, which varies from the original play received from the coach on the sidelines. While the mission does not change, the individuals must be empowered to adjust their methods to accomplish it.

Empowering People

Without being empowered to have the ability to call such audible plays to make spontaneous adjustments to the defense's tactics, the quarterback and the offense he leads is at a distinct disadvantage. I-D leaders hamper fulfillment of the franchise's mission when they micromanage by tight control that does not allow workers to exercise their individual ingenuity to adjust to the situations that unfold on the playing fields of their classrooms, offices, shop floors, and other environments.

A typical I-D leader mistake is to fail to treat workers in the same manner they want them to treat customers. If a customer comes to a store or an outlet and asks, "Can I have this product or service delivered or provided to me this way?" an employer would hope an employee would say, "Certainly!" Or if the service or product cannot be delivered that way, the employer hopes that the employee will explain to the customer how it can be provided another way to achieve nearly the same outcome the customer originally desired. Yet when employees are trying to convert within a particular context—especially one that is unfolding in a rather different way than the boss planned—I-D's abruptly shut down employee initiative by saying, "No, you can't do it that way." Remember, there often is more than one way to do something well.

In unfolding and developing situations, customers can get frustrated when employees have to take the time to explain all the background details to a leader before they are allowed to make certain adjustments to convert a certain way within the context. The most satisfactory customer outcomes are achieved by employees who are properly trained and empowered to make adjustments on the fly.

Values Are the Engine that Powers Employee Behavior

The values with which employees are treated are the determining factor as to whether or not they reach their potential for organizational success. By working with managers and supervisors to ensure that the organizational values are consistently reflected in the employee evaluation and discipline process, the organization ensures that only those with the right values remain within and get promoted up through the culture.

Values are essential to implementing an employee-evaluation process. This is because to interpret whether or not human behavior is consistently compatible with the company's goals, we must have a clear understanding of the actions, activities, and behaviors that go into performing the job duties and assignments. Understanding and articulating values are the foundation for determining not only the "what" of a job but also the "how" of the job. Values tell how one should behave when not only performing specific job duties but also when interacting and interfacing with others both inside and outside of the company.

Values articulate the desired attitude with which all employees are expected to perform their jobs. Values determine team synergy and customer satisfaction. These values should be articulated not merely in the strategic plan, but they should be drilled down into the employee-evaluation forms that supervisors and managers use when assessing performance. To achieve a cohesive organization, leaders must instill evaluators with a sense of mission fairness so that each employee is evaluated by the same values standards. Fair and impartial evaluations and assessments encourage subordinates and team members to believe that the values and the mission they support really do matter most. Employees with the right values should be empowered and trusted.

Leadership Empowers—Management Controls

Colin Powell says, "Leadership is the art of accomplishing more than management ever thought was possible." III-D leadership gets the results beyond what the leader personally can achieve. Management denotes a more limited span of control. Leadership provides inspiration, direction, and an impetus that permeates every stratum of the organization to impact the behaviors of management and line employees to have a positive outcome on performance. One of my definitions of leadership is, "Leadership is the capacity to encourage and empower others to use their abilities, gifts, and talents to the fullest potential to achieve the objective." Leadership encompasses and exceeds the boundaries of management.

On Sunday night, October 19, 2003, I saw Peter Drucker on the "Charlie Rose Show" on PBS, WMHT television. Drucker said that he had thorough, tough bosses who did not believe there were limits to what people could achieve when given the right tools and circumstances. Following his first and second books, *The End of Economic Man*, published in 1939, and *The Future of Economic Man*, published in 1942, General Motors invited him to come and take a look at its operations in the mid-1940s. At GM, Drucker said he realized there was a role called management that was tasked with taking resources, including people and things, and making sure they all work together to achieve the business process. He described business as "organized activity," not merely as buying cheap and selling high.

In 1954 Drucker published his most successful book, *The Practice of Management*. This book laid the foundations for understanding how people are a chief resource and play a prominent role in achieving within the context. Drucker's work illuminated the following:

- There is no business without a customer. This was the foundation for the marketing mind-set, as business became focused upon what the customer desires.

- Management is a practical art, like medicine. It's getting the best out of people.

- Leaders need to answer, "What is my product?" "Who is my customer?" and, "What is my value?"

Three-dimensional leadership adds value to the company's people resources and gets employees focused on determining what the customer values and what they are adding to the customer's experience or value proposition. Employees within effective organizations answer the question, "What am I doing that the customer considers valuable or value added?"

Drucker views the ideal manager as a symphony conductor who has the tools of his financial office, the production score, and understands the audience. He or she loves the musicians, the music, and the process of engaging them and motivating them to provide a performance that the audiences love. The company that supports the musicians (employees) has organized them to produce a product (performance) that the audience (customers), the conductor (leader), and the musicians all enjoy. There is no "us versus them" mentality in this view. People are working cooperatively to put out a product that both they and the customer love.

Drucker viewed workers as a resource, not merely a disembodied cost. American managers were slow to embrace his concepts. The Japanese did so first and by the 1970s had achieved business processes to generate product quality and captured dominant market shares on the world economy.

Kenichi Ohmae, in his book, *The Mind of the Strategist: The Art of Japanese Business*,[16] explains it was intuitive for the Japanese to understand Drucker's view of companies as the center of the communities in which they are located. Here is why: After World War II, Japan had to rebuild its economy from that devastation. Entrepreneurs, scientists, and engineers came together to form companies to produce products to sell, but during the early years of these ventures, markets were not yet developed, so the company employees had no income. People lived on the factory grounds and shared a communal type of existence, where everything essential for living, including shelter, clothing, and food, was at first provided from what the company could scrape together. People became very loyal to the company, and the company became very supportive of them. As products were sold and the employees were paid, they purchased homes in the community. The communal spirit of the nurturing company, however, continued, and the close relational ties between it and what was good for the greater community extended to where the employees moved. What is good for the people is good for their collective productivity within the company, and what is good for business is good for the employees who are the people in the community. The Japanese business mind-set encompassed leadership that extended beyond the concept of managing the company's inanimate production processes into investing in people to obtain the best services from them.

Drucker studied demographics as the basis for social analysis. During the 1960s, he saw that 90 percent of all the scientists the world had ever known up to that time were alive and at work at the same time. Many managers within companies and institutions came from the ranks of these scientists. Drucker noted that the largest body of employees was educated managers. He called these people "knowledge workers" and said that future success would be based upon how well the knowledge workers worked with the actual worker. How leaders deal with their people resources make or break organizations.

Drucker says that leaders must ensure that what they are working on is a "shared vision." Make sure the vision is rooted in where you are in relation to the operational context and in what makes sense to the students, constituents, clients, employees, and volunteers. One might say that Drucker understands that "mission matters most," and what matters most in management is to get your people resources to keep their focus on what matters most. When managers are not focused on the company's mission, which is why most employees signed up to work there, they lose credibility with those employees. Drucker says, "Don't confuse motion with progress." Don't be busy, yet non-productive. Don't be busy, yet unfocused. Drucker's most famous question is, "What is your business?" Another way of saying this is, "What is your mission?" or, "What is the mission the company has given you to accomplish?" One-dimensional leaders, who make the focus of their work "me" and not the main (or core) mission, do a disservice to their workers and organizations. Drucker says, "Management betrays workers by being self-serving."

Followers Must Respect You before They Will Share Your Vision

I once was asked to participate on a leadership communications team that consisted of department heads and managers from every segment of the organization. Our mission was to be the spokespersons for the organization's new mission, vision, and values initiative that the executive leaders had done a pretty clumsy job of handling. They dragged out the process for so long and had acted and continued to act contrary to the stated mission and values that they proved to almost everyone they were the only ones in the organization who did not understand them in the first place.

When this set of leaders got into power a few years earlier, they failed to go around their learning curve gracefully. When they wanted to impose what they thought they knew upon the process and would ask the most competent and experienced employees why certain situations existed, they failed to listen to how to go about our business. When the leaders could not get the answers they wanted, they would act condescendingly, speak sarcastically, and preface comments with "As you know ... " or with "Of course you know ... " Later they would call their subordinates on the phone and belittle and insult them for their views.

Word spread of this treatment of their subordinates, which spoke volumes to us under-managers that our senior leaders could not be trusted and would turn on any of us in a moment. It also proved that they cared far more about themselves and their agenda than they did our mission, and they were too arrogant to know the difference.

Because the leaders had been so arrogant, rude, and cruel to the department heads and under-managers, no one wanted to be associated with them. Many of the managers believed that the senior leaders had done so many wrong things and had lost so much credibility with the workforce that to be perceived as speaking for them and carrying out their "grand idea" of our mission, vision, and values would make us guilty by association. Many of us organizational leaders knew what our mission was and had been disseminating information consistent with it all along. Rolling out this so-called grand new vision was not going to add any value to the branding of the organization, relative to the effort required, and was not going to inspire employees to perform differently. The mission, vision, and values were new to only the senior leaders. Everyone else had grasped them long ago and had grown very frustrated trying to get the senior leaders to understand them. Having the senior leaders give what everyone perceived as lip service to them now was futile.

Senior management hired consultants who advised that to implement their new initiative, it had to be communicated through all the department heads and their key managers. Thus our senior executives pulled us together to be briefed by the consultants and empowered as spokespersons for the mission, vision, and values initiative. At the first meeting, a team of the senior executives briefed us and then left us with the team of consultants.

The team of five consultants began laying out the process for ensuring that employees at all stratums of the organization would understand and function consistently within the parameters of the stated mission, vision, and values initiative. A participant raised her hand and said, "Now wait a minute. What exactly are you asking me to sell here? I do not want to go out and look foolish in front of my people by speaking for what has gone on around here lately."

Several other participants joined her in this sentiment. What the consultants did not know was how badly the senior managers had treated many people in the room and, thus, had lost credibility with them. I had been cursed at by a senior leader over petty issues on more than one occasion and had experienced a leader who nitpicked over vacation time during summers and around the holidays. A hallmark of I-D leadership is that it often degenerates to control issues over time and attendance. Since a I-D does not have a vision to manage subordinates to achieve the mission, they manage their time. This leader was a joke among field employees for the nonsensical things she would place on the agency intranet with the intention of inspiring employees to share best practices. The problem was that her idea of best practices had no relationship to our mission. While I did not want to be perceived as being joined at the hip with the person who was perceived by many seasoned and gifted employees as "ridiculous," I could see the value of the initiative—especially for fertilizing the new crop of employees who were coming into the organization.

To lighten the mood in the room and get the consultants out of the line of fire, I joked, "It appears that we have to resolve some ambiguity about what should be communicated." Another participant interjected, "I know what they want me to say. I am just not going to be perceived as speaking for the group that just left the room!" Most of the participants expressed anger and frustration about how they had been trying for so long to get the senior leaders to understand what our organization was all about, and now they wanted us to go out and speak for them. It was not going to happen. I think it was readily apparent to even a casual observer that some of the designated spokespersons genuinely did not trust the mission, vision, and values initiative because they did not trust those from whom it was coming.

The meeting ended, and the consultants were tasked to go back to senior management and clarify with them what exactly they expected the group to accomplish. Later that day I saw some of the consultants, and one said, "It is so frustrating being a consultant. You just never know what you are walking in to." Senior management made one more attempt at pulling together a communication team. Senior executives gathered with division and department heads to review how the mission, vision, and values initiative needed to be disseminated to every employee and permeated through every level of the organization. There was always tension in the room when certain members of the senior executive team were present. Some of these people had been so consistently rude to so many people in that room, regardless of how well they did their jobs, that none of us trusted their integrity. Someone asked, "Is this message going to change?" The answer was, "No. These are our stated mission, vision, and values." Since in many people's minds our executive leaders had failed to lead in a productive direction consistent with the stated mission, vision, and values, there was a long, pregnant silence. We were dismissed to disseminate the information. We never had another meeting.

Mutual respect between leaders and followers is necessary to achieve a shared vision. When leaders come in to an organization and fail to be gracious and graceful, they immediately lose credibility with the workers with whom they must partner to be successful. To gracefully round the learning curve, leaders must conduct themselves in ways that facilitate productive collaboration with employees. Failure to do so during the earliest moments and days of a leader's tenure sets the tone for the future success or failure of any initiatives the leader undertakes.

Poor process on behalf of the leader forfeits opportunities for him and followers to learn from each other. Learning is so important to an organization that the workplace should be viewed as a classroom, where self-esteem and sense of trust and safety play key roles in how one is postured to achieve. Needlessly dumping on subordinates just because you have the power to do so dissipates the emotional and social capital one needs to get organizations united to focus on a common mission and vision.

Learning Is a Resource

The ability or capacity for people to learn is a key resource for organizations to leverage. People can only do what they know. The more they know, the more they can do. People can grow when they are willing to learn and have the capacity to assimilate more information and apply it to their jobs. Operational synergy is achieved first by hiring people who have natural curiosity and are genuine lifelong learners.

Since people only can do what they know, it is important to determine what people really know and whether or not they are willing to learn more before you hire or promote them. Temperament, tendency toward arrogance, and educability determine how well people will fit in with your organization and team. Leaders need to be especially careful to obtain synergy from diversity when selecting a "knowledge team," that is an inner circle of managers and employees that act as a think tank and incubator for new ideas to assist the organization in keeping up with emerging industry developments.

Peter Drucker saw management as the input of the mind brought to bear upon the work. General Electric, IBM, Citibank, and General Motors all sought out Drucker, who became the first management consultant. He was one of the first people to determine and espouse that future success is based upon lifelong learning. Understanding the relationship between knowing and doing, Drucker says, "You can't deliver a service without trained and quality people. Most companies fail to realize that they are in the people-training and development business."

For people to be effective on the job, they need a perspective on these four things:

1. the mission: the main thing to be accomplished.

2. the vision: the frame of reference required to see the future state of how the world will be when the mission is fulfilled.

3. the values: the attitudes and behaviors that characterize the actions that fulfill the mission.

4. the culture: the framework of values and customs that characterize how operations are conducted.

When making daily decisions, leaders must do so with a long-range vision that is consistent with these four perspectives. Do not undermine them just to get something done today.

Those selected as a knowledge team of advisors should be chosen not by job titles, but because they have demonstrated the ability to actually achieve something on their jobs. Review their résumés to see not merely what committees they have been on—as if being on committees are an end in itself. Rather, select those who have demonstrable contributions to decisions, polices, and procedures that actually have made a difference for the service-delivery front end of the organization and its management work-facilitation middle and back ends.

The Who-Do Principle: Get the "Who" Right to Get the "Do" Right

Because people are the most important resource, you have to get the right people on your organizational bus. The "Who-Do" principle is "get the 'Who' right and you'll get the 'Do' right." Jim Collins's *Good to Great* study concluded that company leadership is the key determinant of whether or not an organization succeeds or fails at its mission. He compared companies that were in the same industries and competed within the same economic environment. He concluded that those that succeeded did so because of leadership, and those that failed did so because their leaders either led them astray or were "asleep at the switch" and failed to make appropriate decisions at critical junctures. The book *Good to Great* bears reading because it has dozens of concise case studies that detail exactly how leaders make or break organizational performance.

Collins says that the first thing organizations must do to effectively drive their corporate vehicles down the road to mission success is get the right people on their busses. I attended a training program with other senior managers where the facilitator asked how we know we are leaders and how do we evaluate our effectiveness as leaders. One of the attendees' responses bears noting here. Rather than cite some performance that the individual was able to steer the organization into achieving, one attendee said, "I know I am a leader because I end up on the board of almost everything I get involved with. I am in demand as a leader." Because of our job titles, many of us were asked to sit on numerous committees and boards. I later discovered that employees referred to the leader as "the kid," because he had never held a management position prior to getting a political appointment to the government job currently held and never initiated a definitive decision. The individual managed by default.

In all my dealings with this person, I observed that the style was to be receptive of suggestions and to agree to our plans to implement initiatives. But rather than participate, the manager would defer or deflect every tough decision on to me and my people, which we readily and competently could handle once we had the "go ahead." Whenever there was the slightest hint that something might go wrong, however, the individual would copy our bosses in e-mails to us, pointing out what problems existed— but did it with language that was accusatory toward us, while making sure he or she appeared to have little or nothing to do with the process. I would respond by forwarding to this person and our bosses an earlier e-mail that had laid out the process, showing everyone's involvement, while I detailed what my side of the organization would do to overcome the challenges.

This manager's behavior, in my opinion, was divisive and cowardly. There was no attitude that "we are all in this together." At the slightest hint of a challenge, this individual was going to be the first person off the Titanic, and no one else was getting into the lifeboat! Some managers, like this one, perceive them-selves as great leaders—most probably because they have a job title. A job title, however, does not a leader make.

Three-dimensional leaders conduct their day-to-day opera-tions in ways that communicate to their human resources, "We are in this together, and you are vitally important to mission ful-fillment. When the going gets rough, I will not abandon you." I am reminded of Ben Franklin saying in the Continental Congress just before signing the Declaration of Independence in 1776 that "we must, indeed, all hang together, or most assuredly we shall all hang separately." Leaders who operate in all three dimensions understand that sticking together provides the organizational integrity that is necessary for their human resources to negotiate the context.

Chapter Seventeen

Rallying, Readying, and Rustling People Resources

Rallying Resources

Human resources must be rallied to the mission by leaders who are conscientious to do what encourages them to commit their minds, hearts, and souls to the effort. People choose to work in an industry or company because they understand and believe in its mission and will rally around those who uphold and support it. The leader's action either rallies or repels followers from the mission. The leader's job is not only to rally the right resources but also get them ready to serve by training and equipping them. Rustle means to move or work quickly and energetically. When resources are properly trained, motivated, and empowered, they are energized to achieve the mission with vigor and energy.

Rally the Resources and Release Them to Achieve

Effective leadership involves people management. People will join, rally around, and be devoted to causes they feel are worthy. The most effective leadership rallies people resources to the mission, orients them to the appropriate processes, and then releases them to achieve within that context. Because people are the most sophisticated and complicated resources, they should not be neglected in favor of focusing on technical operations or equipment maintenance. It is always a mistake to ignore how people respond to processes and to each other. Leadership must continually devote concentrated attention to ensuring that the people who do the work remain focused on achieving their missions as they negotiate their daily interactive challenges with each other. How we train people to appropriately negotiate relationships will make or break our team dynamics and the ability to achieve mission focus. Three-dimensional leaders are careful, however, not to allow relationships to undermine the mission.

Once the people are brought together, the leader must form them into an effective team and inspire and direct them to focus on the mission that drew them to the job in the first place. Effective leadership realizes that people who are well focused on a common mission will figure out a way to fulfill it, even if the machines and other processes are not operating optimally. Leaders need people skills to effectively rally and direct people to achieve the mission.

Four Types of People Resources (Employees)

There are four types of people resources or employees.

There are those who:

1. can and do.

2. can't but will.

3. can but won't.

4. can't and can't.

"Can and do" employees perform their jobs successfully. They possess the functional capacity to follow through with the actions, activities, and behaviors that accomplish their jobs effectively. Bosses, coworkers, and clients all appreciate "can and do" employees.

"Can't but will" employees at first lack knowledge and/ or ability, but once you equip, train, and give them adequate time to round the learning curve, they will perform their jobs successfully.

"Can but won't" employees possess the functional capacity to do the job but fail to do so either because of attitudinal, emotional, personal, or personality problems.

"Can't and can't" employees are not capable of doing the job regardless of what you do for them or provide them. They lack aptitude and functional capacity for job fit.

"Can but won't" employees, however, are the most challenging to deal with. Because when they are held accountable, they suddenly are able to fulfill their job duties. As soon as the boss's back is turned, however, these employees fail to perform adequately.

I once saw Jack Welch, former CEO of the General Electric Company, on the *Charlie Rose Show* on WMHT Public Access TV express the four types of employees in terms of performance and values. He said:

1. There are employees who make their numbers, and they have our values. We make a place for them to grow and get promoted throughout the organization.

2. There are employees who don't make their numbers, but they have our values. They get additional training and chances.

3. There are employees who make their numbers, but they don't have our values. These are very challenging to deal with, because they get the job done but often are making themselves a pain to deal with for people throughout our system.

4. There are employees who don't make their numbers, and they don't have our values. This is an easy one for us. They get moved out of the system.

Peter Drucker says, "Don't do business with people whose ethics and values do not match your own." Organizations do themselves and employees a favor when they assist those who can't perform to realize there is other work for which they are better suited. The quicker these decisions are made, the happier the organization and the employees will be. You must choose the right people resources to get the right jobs done. Three-dimensional leaders will make appropriate adjustments regarding employee hiring and retention. When one is mission focused and intent on supporting a team to negotiate its context, one sees the necessity for suitable and timely personnel adjustments. It takes honesty and humility to acknowledge hiring mistakes. Courage and compassion are required to correct them.

Recognizing Talent

One-dimensional leaders hire people they know. Hiring decisions are not based upon job requirements and whether or not the person actually has the skill sets to do it or is capable of learning them. If the potential employee has something in common with the boss, he or she gets hired. As this process gets replicated, one can see how one-dimensional and homogenous an entire organization can become.

Two-dimensional leaders will tend to make better hiring choices because they at least have some perception of what the real mission is. Because they do not understand the context, however, they often choose people who are as shortsighted as they are. Two-dimensional leaders tend to hire to II-D followers. Three-dimensional leaders demonstrate that they are aware of the context by analyzing the duties and skill sets required to do a job and how it must be done within particular circumstances. They then associate those with a job title, and they select an individual for that job who has the abilities required to do it or who has demonstrated the capacity to learn the skill sets required.

I believe there are three main reasons why poor hiring choices occur:

1. The job design and posting process fails to clearly define the duties and requirements of the job in relation to the organizational cultural context in which the job unfolds and thus encourages the wrong applicants to apply for it.

2. Those involved in the screening and interview process fail to completely understand the complexity of the actual job to clearly explain the duties and requirements of it, and, therefore, they cannot screen appropriate applicants.

3. The applicant really does not care what the duties and job requirements are and does not care what the context of the organization is and how to work within it but wants the position in order to get a paycheck or the "esteem" he or she thinks the job will provide.

People who are anxious to get a job (or a paycheck) may say anything they think interviewers want to hear. Once they are on the job, however, they do what they want to do rather than what the job requires. Part of the remedy in avoiding unsuitable hires is to delegate applicant screening to people who are actually doing the job (or nearly the same job) and empowering them to be on the interview team.

Effective job-candidate screening is done by those who understand what actual actions, activities, and behaviors will be required of employees to negotiate the context of the jobs they are being hired to accomplish. When you do not understand the mission or the context in which it must unfold, you do not have a clear idea of how to recognize the talent that can achieve it.

I once had to spend several days negotiating with a boss to get him to understand that we should not hire a person who had been fired by another branch of our organization due to multiple offenses. If my boss had a better understanding of our internal and external contexts, he would have known that once our personnel office went through a formal process of firing someone "for cause," that person would be inappropriate for providing services to the population of clients my boss said he wanted to help. So stubborn was my I-D leader that not only was my time taken up with the issue, but I had to consume valuable organizational time coordinating with employees in our personnel office to repeatedly explain to him why this person ought not to be rehired. Here is how the process unfolded:

My boss called me and mentioned the name of the individual who got fired and said that he wanted to do what he could for this person. I asked my boss why the person was fired. My boss said, "Oh, he did a few things that showed poor judgment, but the real reason is that he does not get along with his supervisor." I advised my boss that if someone shows poor judgment and can't get along with supervisors and others within the team environment and community context, he or she is definitely not a headache we need to take on. Since this person had shown no indication that his attitude or behavior had changed in any way since he was fired a few days ago, we would be setting ourselves up for him to have problems with our clients and coworkers, and we would consume a lot of our administrative time managing and putting out fires.

After another twenty minutes of not being able to talk my boss out of this extremely poor decision, I thought if I could just get him to actually see why this person was fired, he would be more reasonable.

I advised my boss that we were going to have to justify rehiring this person to our personnel office, so I was going to have to review the paperwork given to the employee that detailed the exact reasons why the personnel department had fired him. My boss said he already had copies of the material and would bring it to me. I was discouraged to discover that the fired individual had committed four major offenses, in addition to a host of minor offenses. First, he had physically roughed up a teenager whom a local school had brought into the office as part of a field trip exercise. Apparently, the teenager and some of his buddies viewed the field trip as an opportunity to get out of school and clown around—as teenagers are prone to do. Physically tussling with and choking the teenager, however, was an inappropriate way to try to get the young man to pay attention. The second offense involved a sexual harassment confession that was supported by numerous e-mails to the victim, who worked for a partner organization.

The third offense involved him responding inappropriately to a complaint and verbally dressing down and making accusations to the leader of a client organization in violation of department policy, rather than completing paperwork so that another branch of our organization formally could investigate the matter. The fourth offense involved how the individual showed extremely poor judgment and was insubordinate by trying to accompany a female client to the home of another client when the issue the female client had stated clearly was the responsibility of a partner agency within the office. The fired individual argued vehemently with his supervisor, who took him aside to prevent him from leaving the building alone with the female client, when a short while earlier he had confessed to overstepping professional boundaries with members of the opposite sex. My boss did not feel that this series of offenses were grounds for firing the individual.

The next day I had another forty-minute debate with my boss, during which he ordered me to hire the terminated individual because he had promised him that he would help him. I advised that the fired individual would have to be rehired into the regional supervisory structure that had just gone through great pains to fire him, and we were going to have to negotiate the context of that structure to get him rehired. Later that day I arranged a conference call between us and the regional manager who had participated in all the disciplinary actions and the firing.

During the next phase of this exercise in I-D stupidity, the regional manager spent about fifty minutes explaining to my boss how the fired individual was a friend of hers whom she had advocated to have hired. She again reviewed the list of offenses and said there were more, but she did not want to violate the fired individual's confidentiality by reciting what he had not chosen to reveal to my boss. My boss said that if we rehired the individual, we could overcome his first offense by sending him to anger management. The regional administrator advised that he had already had that training but failed to be rehabilitated and adjust his behavior. The tussle with the student was only the latest of his offenses of that type. My boss said we could overcome the sexual harassment offense by sending him to sensitivity training. The regional administrator advised that he had already been to that training too, yet continued to show extremely poor judgment in the area of his dealings with members of the opposite sex.

When my boss still would not be deterred, the regional manager advised that the former employee could not work in any of the offices within commuting distance of his home because there were restraining orders against him due to threats he had made against personnel working in them, which, given his past violent behavior, was being taken very seriously. My boss's final argument was that the man was well seasoned, and since the organization had invested so much money in training him, it would be a shame to let him go. The regional manager and I advised my boss that the fired individual apparently had not taken his training to heart, because his behavior so often was contrary to what he was taught, and although he had longevity of employment, one could not say that he was a valuable, well-seasoned employee.

Besides all of the reasons related to inappropriate behavior and extremely poor job performance, I felt that we would be exposing the organization to a lawsuit and the possibility of liability, because if we hired the person whose employment had been terminated, he may have grounds to argue the firing was improper. The individual may have been able to find an attorney to make the case that, previously, he could not have been as poor an employee as his first managers claimed because he was rehired by a different branch of the organization. Though the numerous offenses were well documented by the previous set of managers, an attorney could have argued that the documentation could not be an accurate representation of his client, because our branch of the organization felt he was not that bad and had rehired him.

When the regional manager finally talked my boss into coming off the suicidal "let's hire the loser" ledge he had climbed out on and stubbornly was clinging to, he sighed and said, "Well, I guess there is no way we can help this man." My boss then told me to contact the fired individual and advise him that we could not rehire him, and explain to him all we did to advocate for him. I advised my boss that I felt no obligation to explain anything to the individual because I had had no dealings with him and had not promised him anything.

"Besides, even if he were to receive a negative answer from me, he is still going to call you for an explanation, because he knows you—not me." I called the fired individual, as ordered, and he said he wanted to discuss the information with my boss, just as I had predicted.

One-dimensional leaders and one-dimensional followers gravitate to each other. When an I-D becomes a leader, he or she tends to attract I-D followers—people who are like-minded in their "it's all about me/us" focus. Left unchecked, I-D's will draw upon each other's misguided ideas and tendencies, and the gravitational pull will weigh down and draw energy from any and all in the larger organization who have dealings with them.

Hire People Resources Who Demonstrate Triple-C Synergy and Imagination

Desirable employees are those who have demonstrated the ability and capacity for communication, cooperation, and coordination, as well as the competence to learn and do what the job requires. Potential employees should be able to demonstrate, and their references ought to confirm, that they have done their previous jobs with a high degree of triple-c synergy. Organizations obtain synergy between its divisions, units, business teams, and personnel when they communicate, cooperate, and coordinate.

Desirable candidates should have imagination and a natural interest or curiosity that gives them the capacity to perceive the context and which motivates them to search for answers and solutions within it. When answers can't be found, imagination leads us to ask the right questions that lead to the correct answers. Imagination is a foundation for people being able to take in information and deploy it in some useful job-accomplishing ways—especially when the connections are not readily apparent. No one thinks out of the box apart from having an imagination. Imagination helps us to envision how to move from the theoretical to the practical. It helps us take what others don't see and organize it as a resource to accomplish desired ends. Imagination is the cornerstone of building structure out of ambiguity. For an individual to exercise useful and productive imagination, he or she must have the mental aptitude and perception abilities necessary to figure out how to do a job within a particular context. If these are present, there is the likelihood that competence and great job performance will follow.

Résumés may indicate the core technical skill sets one has to perform a job. While you definitely need to hire people who have the correct technical competencies, you also must find someone who will be a good citizen within your organization. More often than not in today's small-world, globally integrated environment, you need people who have the intangible relational skills that facilitate cooperation, communication, and coordination with people from multiple cultures and customs. You want to ensure that you are attracting, interviewing, and hiring someone who has the capacity to perform with a III-D organizational perspective.

To recognize talent, hear loudly what is not being communicated on a résumé. Beware of people who merely list the boards and committees they've been on. We should not be impressed with people's job titles, because within each one there are people who are performing commendably and others who are not. The people who tout being on boards and committees also should tell you what the mission of those organizations were; what resources they were utilizing; and how those resources were deployed to fulfill the mission. They also should be able to tell you how they assisted the organization to negotiate its circumstances to further the mission and overcome or work through challenges to fulfill it. They should be able to tell you how they assisted the organization with fundraising, acquiring the talent needed, and the general and specific contextual environment in which the organization operated, along with how he or she specifically contributed to the successful negotiation of the operation. Regardless of job titles, if people can't articulate these issues, you have not found someone who has the actual competent job experience you are seeking.

Beware of empty suits who have sat on boardroom chairs wiping up dust with the seat of their pants and who continue to try to increase their nonperforming influence by touting what committees they've been on. What you do not read in their curriculum vitae are the accomplishments they achieved while on committees or how they helped the organizations in any way while they held their positions. If the potential hire cannot relate to you specific details that answer those questions, then most likely the organization realized little or no benefits from that person's involvement. Many people like to get themselves appointed to various committees and boards because they think it gives them "name recognition" and cachet that will look good on their résumés. "Name recognition" is not an organizational mission for most outfits.

Organizations need their missions fulfilled. They do not exist for people to join them for the purpose of "name recognition." In cases where this does happen—which is all too often—individuals are allowed to increase the "status" of their résumés at the expense of the organizations they are failing to serve. Hiring these "name seekers" because you are impressed by their résumés allows them not to achieve anything once again—while they "keep their name out there"—as they call it.

We should be impressed with people who have used their job titles and memberships to assist organizations to actually achieve the purposes for which their charters say they exist. Those interviewing and conducting reviews and assessments of applicants should conduct 360-degree evaluations to see what the candidate did or did not achieve while holding job titles and sitting on boards and committees. A 360-degree evaluation means that the evaluators analyze the prospective hire in terms of what people in the same job title report about them, as well as getting input from those at every other level of the organization. If you want an employee, board, or committee member to have an enterprise perspective, I strongly suggest you get their former or current enterprise's viewpoint of his or her performance.

In the 360-degree evaluation process, the more removed one is from the core environment in which the job candidate operated, the less weight an opinion or input should have. If people in the more distant 360-degree environment, however, did not enjoy working with the candidate, this may be a strong indication that the candidate talks about fulfilling the mission in the home office but cannot carry it out in the larger context in which the organization must operate and coordinate to be successful.

One- and two-dimensional leaders who may have some good motor skills in a particular area, but who lack contextual insight to understand "mission resources and context," are in no position to guide others effectively, as they do not possess the intellectual clarity of the overall purpose to plot strategy for their organizations.

When interviewing, first determine what the candidate's current or last organization's mission was in relation to the roles and responsibilities required for the job you seek to fill. Know what the critical skill sets and operational success factors are for the job. For instance, does the job require analytical ability to obtain various pieces of information to determine how to categorize it for clients and construct appropriate responses? If so, you must screen for two skill sets during your interview: 1) the ability to analyze and 2) the ability to make the proper written response based upon it. Interpersonal skills are needed for any position involving direct contact with other people, including supervising and managing. If a person you are interviewing has difficulty making a decision and choosing a course of action following analysis, you do not have the right person for the role, or additional specific training in decision making is needed for the individual to be successful.

Beyond mechanical or motor job skills, the most crucial ability necessary for success within a team or organizational environment is the ability to get along with other people. Relational intelligence is required for individuals to interact and make positive contributions within organizations that are healthy because workers must successfully negotiate the internal context by getting along with each other. One must be able to work within the organization "the organization's way." One who has a history of establishing and maintaining mission-focused relationships to coordinate cooperative business and work activities are the most desirable employees. These are the people who are getting their jobs done in ways that are not painful to the people and organizations with which they interact.

Chapter Eighteen

The Quality of Leadership Determines the Quality of Followership

The quality of leadership determines the quality of followership. For the members of an organization to attain the collective achievement for which they have been gathered together in the workplace requires them to be led at all strata by leaders and managers who understand the corporate mission, appreciate the complexity of their human resources, and know how to negotiate the context so the resources effectively are positioned to achieve their goals. Because people only can do what they know, it is essential that leaders be learners engaged in two fields of study: information pertaining to their industry's services, product lines, applications and maintenance programs, and managerial leadership. My goal with this book is to improve your learnership, which will improve your leadership, which should help you improve your followers' ability and capacity to perform.

Three-dimensional leaders learn to mold people into teams that are focused on a common mission and thus can accomplish far more than a loosely associated collection of even super-gifted individuals. The puzzle below illustrates how great leadership is achieved. III-D's empower others to function as robustly as possible within the operational framework that best fulfills the mission. Giving credit to others, who also work hard to achieve success, is essential to the team process, as it encourages people. Valuing and appreciating employees is an admirable quality that characterizes those whose followers appreciate serving with them.

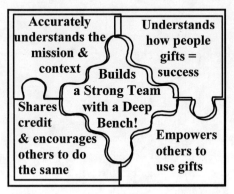

III-D leaders understand why people are attracted to the organization. They rally workers and volunteers around those attractive mission dynamics and bring them together as a team to work within a cohesive framework of organizational values to fulfill the common mission.

The ServiceMaster Corporation lists these mission objectives:

- Honor God in all we do
- Excel with Customers
- Help People Develop
- Grow Profitably[17]

The leaders at ServiceMaster believe that God has given each employee dignity, worth, potential, and freedom to choose. The firm begins by looking to God for help and accepting and developing the different people He created. Former ServiceMaster Chairman and CEO Bill Pollard says, "Profit is a standard for determining the effectiveness of our combined efforts." Leadership must recognize and develop the inherent dignity and worth of employees and volunteers who perform mundane tasks, such as mopping the floors. Leadership at ServiceMaster is focused on how the principles of dignity and worth translate into employees finding meaning and purpose.

Leadership Is Service

ServiceMaster's leadership objective is to serve employees by inspiring and supporting them to develop as professionals. Here is a statement from its Web site:

> A career with ServiceMaster means continuous learning, the chance to move up based on merit and the opportunity to enhance your business and leadership skills. Our goal is the continuing development of each worker—to prepare them for their present job responsibilities while setting the stage for continuous career growth.[18]

Investing in employees should return their long-term commitment. In John 13 of the Bible, Jesus washes the feet of his disciples. In doing so, he taught them that no leader is greater than the people he leads, and even the humblest of tasks is worthy of a leader to perform. Thus our role and obligations as leaders involve more than what a person does on the job. We are involved in what that person is becoming and how the work environment is contributing to that process.

ServiceMaster wants its leaders to establish a work culture that communicates a sense of mission that transcends the tasks to provide a sense that employee efforts and activities are adding up to something more significant than what physically is accomplished. "How well its employees serve depends on how they're motivated, respected and trained. Servant leadership helps employees find meaning and purpose at work."[19]

Three-dimensional leaders organize people well and treat every member of the team with dignity as they mobilize them with a tremendous sense of mission purpose. III-D's do not play favorites and thus greatly limit the politics that become the distractions that cause organizations to be driven by the personalities within them rather than by a common focus on their missions. III-D's encourage others to use their personal styles as long as they are focused on getting the job done in a way that benefits the entire organization.

Highly effective leaders ensure that each person knows how his or her efforts, roles, and responsibilities contribute to the organization's overall finished products, services, and mission fulfillment. Great team leaders manage team members who are thoroughly familiar with the organization's vision, mission, and values, and who also understand how the department, unit, or ministry function in which they've chosen to serve contributes to achieving the organization's overall objectives. The workers see and understand the big picture and fully know and do their specific, individual parts to contribute to it. Because they see the context, they cooperate fully with other parts of the organization, because they know what it takes for them to negotiate it.

Stewart's Corporation: Successful Resource Alignment

Leadership Profile:
Bill Dake
CEO, Chairman of the Board, Stewart's Corporation

"All men can see the tactics whereby I conquer, but what none can see is the strategy out of which victory is evolved."
Sun Tzu[20]

The Stewart's Corporation is a thriving upstate New York convenience store business that offers limited restaurant-style seating. The corporation cites its competitive advantages include that it is two-thirds family owned and one-third employee owned, which provides employees with an excellent incentive to achieve sales of its signature dairy products, coffee, and other food items. In 2006 the organization grossed one billion dollars in revenue, with $30 million in net income. The company is debt free and owns the real estate whereon its 325 stores are located, and it continues to grow. In 2007, the corporation donated approximately $2 million, mostly to local charities. The company motto is "We are closer to you," and with its stores permeating eastern and central Upstate New York and Vermont and stepping into Massachusetts, its proximity to the customer is getting better all the time.

The year 2005 marked Stewart's sixtieth anniversary. Highlights that year included Cornell University naming it the producer of the highest quality milk in New York State, and its chocolate ice cream finished second place at the World Dairy Expo Championship in Wisconsin. All business starts with a product and/or service, and Stewart's certainly has quality products. The company knows, however, that it is its people who manufacture, account for, market, distribute, and sell those products that make the difference in the service delivery that achieves business success.

Because the Stewart's Corporation recognizes that its employees are its chief competitive resource, I am including an interview with its leader, Bill Dake. He says that because Stewart's is a growing business with a stable operations model that has placed it in a strong financial position, it can afford to make good decisions that contribute to long-term growth as opposed to quick decisions that might only achieve short-term profits. The chain has enjoyed double-digit growth for decades.

Bill Dake is the mostly retired chief architect of the Stewart's business system that has achieved the success stated above. To many in the Upstate New York region, Bill is a business legend whose reputation started when he graduated college as an engineer and put that training to use by making adjustments to his family's dairy equipment and the operation began turning profits. He tends to be easygoing and does not seem to take himself too seriously. It is obvious from his passion and success, however, that he takes his work seriously while he also believes it should be upbeat and enjoyable.

The Dake family negotiated the context well from its inception as it transitioned from an ice-cream delivery business in the 1920s, to become the Saratoga Dairy in 1935, and then the Stewart's business in 1945, when they purchased the Stewart's dairy plant and started store operations by selling ice cream from a couple of shops. Dake explains how their store operations evolved with much controversy that made the Dake family local folk heroes.

> In the 1950s we went to put milk and other items in our stores, but the State of New York had milk laws that said you couldn't do that, much like they have beer licensing today regulating who can sell it and where. It's not to protect the public but to maintain the status quo in the industry. We wanted to sell milk in our own stores, delivered from our own plant, because the little old truck driving around was a totally inefficient way to deliver milk to customers. The state said no, so we took them to court and won. We got so much publicity that overnight we had 15 percent market share. We had much bigger trucks going to our own stores, delivering in volume, and passing on the savings to the customer. This was 1958, '59, and '60.

Dake said that the local industry was not happy about Stewart's early success.

"Everybody else thought we were terrible because we had a different paradigm for delivering the product, and when we took 15 percent of the market, we had to take it from somebody. The other guys were furious with us."

Bill explains how his industry peers failed to catch on to the strategies that would have made them competitive. They tenaciously clung to the home-delivery model, and even when they finally got around to delivering to larger grocery stores, they were still using little trucks, and the inefficiency, plus the extra cost the bigger stores had to charge, left no savings to pass on to the customer as the Stewart's model did. Bill says the other business owners made excuses as to why they could not employ the Stewart's product-delivery model. They said their businesses were different. But Dake says they really were not. They just found it easier to say, "My business is different," rather than adapt and change.

Bill said the experience was an early payoff in their business model.

> It taught us to be vertically integrated ... Much of our success comes from the integration of our manufacturing and distribution systems, retail, and development operations. That same coordination between departments gives our shops the support they need to provide service and value to our customers.

Dake knows that the customer's experience at Stewart's lies in how his managers deal with store employees to get the job done, and he instructs his managers, saying, "We can afford for you to make a long-term fair deal [with employees] that is good for both sides." But mission definitely matters most with Dake, because he admonishes mangers to "look at ROI on decisions. Does it really make 'cents' (pun intended)? Sales need to be the result of decisions, because there is 'opportunity for rewards if you hustle.'"

Stewart's Vertical and Horizontal Relational Context

Bill Dake speaks most about relationships. He understands that his business is highly relational. He knows that the overwhelming majority of business problems involve human-relationship issues. The opening pages of Bill Dake's Stewart's managerial manual advise managers that "our success comes from relationships."

The cultural context that Stewart's has achieved is "vertical and horizontal win-win relationships." People relationships make stores run well. Numerical relationships make accounting meaningful. Dake says, "'Vertical integration' is accomplished as product flows from manufacturing to warehouse to shops. 'Hori-

THE THREE-DIMENSIONAL LEADER

zontal integration' is between functions like accounting, personnel, marketing, operations, and facility." To avoid the "silo effect," Dake wants these corporate functions interrelated and cross-pollinated, so "everybody knows" how they all come together to support the main mission.

A Stewart's store manager informed me that while his store is supported with vertical relationships the corporation provides from production to delivery and marketing, he drives sales by focusing on the horizontal relationships with the store's employees and their relationship with customers. The relational reach encompasses the physical store environment and extends to the immediate surrounding community. For him, the "vertical" relates to the internal corporate context, and the "horizontal" relates to the local store and community context.

The Dake relational philosophy assists Stewart's to negotiate its community context by facilitating reconciliation of its suppliers, business partners, and customers. During times of price or market volatility, such as when dairy prices increased a few years ago, Stewart's stores had signs that explained the market dynamics in a way that placed no blame and made no one the bad guy. Below is a segment of a New York Farm Bureau article entitled "Stewart's Tells It Right," written By Alan Knight, Contributing Editor, who recognized a job well done by the Stewart's leadership, "who took the initiative to place signs on the dairy cases of its stores to explain the [milk] price hike in terms both consumers and farmers could appreciate."

> Dairy prices have been low, causing some dairy farmers to go out of business. Because there have been fewer dairy producers, supply has been decreasing while demand has been increasing, causing butterfat prices to more than double. Higher dairy prices help dairy farmers stabilize and grow. While we're pleased dairy farms are doing better, we understand the impact of higher prices on consumers. It's an issue that we can't fix, but we can try to help by offering a promotional price on our 1 percent milk.

The New York Farm Bureau featured Stewart's positive action on its Web site[21] and in a May issue of *Grassroots.* Stewart's not only achieves good relationships with its community partners, but it also achieves it in its internal operations.

The vertical corporate relationship allows managers to have the advantage of "handheld ordering," the response to which is "frequent deliveries." Bill Dake says that the Stewart's Stores successful operational model

> ...is leveraged from the tremendous support and service relationship the corporation has and provides to its line managers. At Stewart's we are vertically integrated and horizontally integrated. The stores and managers are supported by unusual corporate support. We distribute about eighty percent of what we sell in a world where, from a retailer's standpoint, the service is going downhill rapidly. We spend an exorbitant amount of time and are in a position to provide a lot of support to the managers.

The Stewart's model treats managers as though they are franchise owners. One manager likened it to owning your own business that has larger corporate support and no debt on your part. The Dake manual notes that "customers are confronted with so much information that we must be remarkable to get their attention." The corporation has strong market penetration to reach customers from one-fourth of the households in the surrounding communities wherein the stores are located. The density of stores in its tri-state reach means that the Stewart's logo and branding is becoming familiar to more and more people. Its delivery vehicles are rolling company billboards. These corporate dynamics support store managers and employees who are called "partners."

Unlike many organizations, where "employee support" feels like a byword with no heart and soul behind it, the Stewart's Corporation provides its workforce with an employee stock ownership plan (ESOP), a profit-sharing program that gives those who run the stores the same sense of ownership and responsibility that the corporate founders have. Dake says,

One-third of the company is owned by the employees through the ESOP, and in our case we did the ESOP not to get money out of the company as usually is the process, but the family really feels that if the employees own one-third of the business, the value of the family's share will grow greater. The Stewart's ESOP profit sharing is over twenty-five percent of the net, and employees are fully vested after seven years. This is a different attitude from the guy who's trying to squeeze funds from an ESOP.

Because the manager gets one-third of the profit of the shop, he or she has an incentive to improve performance. Bill Dake says,

My biggest problem at times is that the manager gets so greedy to make money that he starts pressing his people more than he should, or he is trying to make profit and not grow the business. This incentive system has been functioning for thirty years. There are not very many that last that long, by any stretch of the imagination.

The incentive system directly effects a store manager's and his partners' compensation. Dake says they "fix what the manager can't control and provide variable compensation incentives for those things the manager can control." The corporate strategy includes that proceeds from various profit centers pay shop-level expenses, while marketing accounts pay the expenses the manager has no direct control over. The structure mitigates large fluctuations in income, such as from gasoline, to reduce volatility in the shop's profit and loss, which otherwise would more greatly impact the manager's income.

Several store managers said they appreciate how the corporation arranges the playing field, invests in them, and trusts them to make it possible for them to succeed. Managers know that shop activity must cover most costs, and because the system allows for their income to grow, they have the incentive to at least beat inflation by increasing sales profit by a percentage at least equal to that index. Thus the leader's pay can keep increasing equal to or ahead of the inflation rate.

The Stewart's Corporation partners with its managers to achieve reality-based objectives that are incorporated into its employee-evaluation process. There are many levels of control and loss prevention, including the registers, product-movement reports, inventory audits, and crosschecks in which the numbers don't lie. Bill Dake says,

> Our shop oversight is very, very good and very fair. It deals with what the manager can have control over. We have a facility account and a marketing account so that we can take the loss out of the system. The reason this incentive system has worked so well is that the numbers you're dealing with are very objective, so you are not dealing with subjective issues.

The objectivity that Stewart's has achieved in its operations-sales system lets managers know where they stand. The system extends to employees at all levels. After just four years, partners are vested, and if they hit certain targets during the year, they obtain a twenty-five percent stock bonus at year's end.

"The magnitude of our profit sharing," says Dake, is that "they work for four quarters and get paid for five." The corporate office continually encourages managers to invest in employees by ensuring they hit qualifying targets, such as working a minimum of one thousand hours annually. The corporation actually calls managers and advises that certain employees are close to achieving those hours and, with a little more attention to scheduling and a bit more additional effort on the part of the employee, he or she will meet the criteria for the annual period. These are retention incentives that provide a win for the employee and the corporation.

SHARE Management

Dake says that Stewart's engages employees in an ongoing process to give them the rationale to succeed at the relationships of store life.

It's not a static "how did you do? Sorry if you haven't figured out how it is rational to do it." We do not leave you to just fall on your face. "How" is much more critical than "what," which is the reason for the corporate support. Two things happen when people from the shops come in and go through the corporate headquarters and plant. The partners are dumbfounded at how much the people in the warehouse smile at me and them. And two, how much support everybody wants to give them. This is because we really know that if the profit-sharing partners don't sell it, we are not going to make it as a company.

I interjected that I have a seminar I teach on team relationships. One segment of it deals with how "Strength of Relationship Equates to Intensity of Change." People must trust you before they will commit to making an emotional investment to share risk and go the distance with you and do the hard work of overcoming challenges. Dake responded, "There are a lot of issues involving trust in making our operation work." He continues...

> You don't get people to change if they don't trust you. I think the bottom line to all of this is that you have to want to grow people in today's world. This means that for them to change, you must be a good enough teacher, and there must be enough trust so it's worth their while to change. You have to be a teacher. If you are a manager and you don't think you are a teacher, then you are lacking in a key element to your job. Whether you are telling someone something or selling someone something, you are teaching. I also make the distinction between communicating and selling. Selling is not merely telling; we use an acronym, "SHARE," when we do a review. Selling is a relational process. You can communicate, but that doesn't mean they reacted to your words; if you sold something, that means they got it; they bought what you offered.

SHARE stands for selling, honesty, activity, reasons, and externals. Each of these involves people. The Stewart's managerial training manual advises leaders to "use relationships" to run their stores, "because managing human nature is necessary to keep people in balance." The corporation instructs managers to "focus on people vs. things. It's not what you do, but how you do it" that will matter the most to the other partners within a store. Stewart's leaders are asked questions like, "Do you share enough so people don't doubt your intent or ability?"

Managerial responsibilities include following the Stewart's corporate guidelines for managing ideas, facts, and business details. Dake believes, "If managers can discern three-fourths of the facts and details while they are in the store, they can keep a handle on what is going on when they are not there." The contextual view includes grasping that the "where" and "when" of phenomenon is as important as "what" is taking place. Dake says, "This helps us find patterns to determine the causes of what is going on rather than merely observing the symptoms," or the end results. Dake admonishes his leaders, "Don't admire the problem," but look for the reasons behind what is going on and address those issues.

To have credibility with their subordinates, managers must "organize and follow up" to build respect and trust. Information is only as good as it is filed and can be retrieved when needed. Dake says that having a written log gives the "perception you are organized and in control," and inspires in others the "confidence that you haven't forgotten." He says, "Write it down and follow up," because it "shows you care" about what is going on. For Dake, keeping an accurate, well-organized little black book is like having a recent institutional memory that "makes managing share agreements easier." Share agreements are informal pacts between supervisor and employee. He advises that these agreements should and do change as employee home circumstances, or "externals," dictate. In other words, management must be flexible to realize that there are times when people have to take care of their family matters and maintain their jobs too.

GREAT Sales

Bill Dake emphasizes the relational aspects of selling through what he calls the "GREAT" sale. GREAT stands for greet, read, evaluate, associate, and try. He trains partners that to sell they must *G*reet the customer by acknowledging them with eye contact, a nod, and a smile. Greetings can be enhanced by speaking with the customer about the weather, a local, regional, or national event, or by making a general comment.

Partners also must *R*ead the customer to determine if he or she is a "rusher," a "shopper," or a "regular." You obviously do not want to detain a rusher, but you can engage a shopper and a regular.

Employees then must *E*valuate the ROI on sales, such as the gross profit (GP) from products. Store partners also must evaluate whether or not marketing and discounts are achieving multipliers (multiplying the sales of non-discounted items), and if there is a "tail," or residual increased sales of products once those items have gone off sale.

Up-selling is encouraged when employees *A*ssociate by selling products that go together, such as milk and eggs, a hard roll and chili, or dry gas to a gas buyer.

Anyone in sales may experience frequent rejections; Stewart's employees are encouraged to continue to *T*ry to sell by asking questions that may lead to additional sales. You try to sell when you offer free samples, for instance.

Frequent attempts and the deployment of multiple strategies will lead to "GREAT" sales.

Perceiving Patterns Means Seeing the Trends

Bill Dake emphasizes that good managers understand their context and see patterns of relationships between the components and phenomena therein. Patterns refer to trends. Seeing patterns means you are discriminating between more than the mere differences between elements in the context. Perception of the patterns involves understanding why those differences exist and what can be controlled, changed, or impacted to accomplish the mission or business success. The manager cannot be passive but must see the relationships and outcomes that contribute to profit and loss and must actively engage what he or she can control to increase the former and limit the latter. The last virtue of a failing organization is the tolerance of that which allows the business to decline.

Seeing the relational patterns between what is going on over the course of quarterly, yearly, or thirteen-month cycles, or five-quarter cycles, with breakdowns by product type, provides an opportunity to understand what took place in the store, so the manager can determine how to negotiate the local context to grow business. For instance, if there is a spike in activity, analysis that discriminates between the variables within the context can provide an understanding of why, so one can look for patterns that present opportunities for replication in the future. Once you know why something happened, you can develop the awareness to spot those elements within the context as they are emerging, so you can be proactive in responding to them.

Spikes in activity may have resulted from a nearby road being temporarily shut down that rerouted traffic, causing more customers to drive by and stop at your store. Seeing such a pattern gives a manager and store associates the opportunity to be on the lookout for other events or phenomena that temporarily can boost sales. In some communities there are continuous streams of events that provide such opportunities. These include parades, sports events, road repair, and construction projects. Awareness of the context is required to assist customers when such events take place.

One Stewart's manager says that he uses many human-relationship sources to obtain information to determine how to properly prepare to take advantage of opportunities within the local context. He says sometimes customers will come into the store and discuss that they are attending a local event that he had not heard about. If it is taking place that day, he does what he can with his available inventory to make visible those items that consumers who attending it could use but might not think of. This could be anything from sunscreen to bottled water or ice cubes if people are attending an outdoor fair or parade, concert or sports event. If it is raining or snowing, he will put a display of windshield solvent by the doors or by the counters. On days when it is sleeting or snowing, he will put snowbrushes on prominent display. Providing these items to customers is a service, because it reminds them of what they may need to better enjoy an activity or be safe on the road.

WISE Customer Service

Stewart's managers and partners are expected to be "WISE" when it comes to customer service. WISE means "What Is Someone Expecting." The goal is to be proactive in meeting customers' needs. I once wrote a song that had a line that says, "I searched the whole world over, looking for more things to want." The idea is that people don't know what they want until they see it or think about it. The partner's goal is to anticipate what the customer will want once he or she sees or is reminded of what is available.

Dake and a manager explain why growth is more essential than mere profit. Growth can come through increasing the number of customers coming into the store and the number of purchases each customer makes by up-selling them, which is as simple as asking them if they want to try or buy some particular item or asking them if there is anything else they might need. Many business leaders say that without growth, businesses die. You cannot sustain increases in employee salaries without increases in sales volume. You cannot expect to maintain the same business you did last year and increase profits by merely bumping up your prices by some percentage to try to meet the increasing costs of doing business. The main reason why this will not work is because you are not going to sell the exact same items in the exact same quantities as you did last year. There also are market variables that cause prices of items to rise and fall periodically, which then influence whether or not customers purchase them and in what quantities. These factors mean that you cannot rely upon merely tweaking your prices by cost of living indexes, for instance, to achieve monetary growth from sales. You have to be far more proactive and creative than that. You have to actively engage and negotiate your context.

Some entrepreneurs may decide that they do not want the hassles of handling a low-margin product, such as gasoline, which may only provide a five to six percent margin, but making gas available to customers increases their foot traffic into the stores that sell it, which can lead to growth in the sales of other products. In this sense, gas can almost be considered a minimal gain leader (MGL) that provides an opportunity to make greater profits on other items those customers might also choose to purchase.

CPR: The Confidence to Pursue Reality Managing Employees at Stewart's

Dake's manual advises that the corporation expects managers to "use reason to manage and teach others," as opposed to trying to come up with rules to arbitrarily pre-order responses to situations that could occur. You cannot operate a fast-paced convenience store and mini restaurant by establishing controls that synthetically superimpose artificial mandates to cover unusual circumstances. Thus Stewart's admonishes that managers use "reason vs. rules" to keep operations running smoothly. Overseeing employees in a fluid environment necessitates periodic adjustments to changing circumstances.

The corporation emphasizes employee-specific solutions to local store challenges. Dake's manual says that "deals need to be fair both ways for long-term success. Deals can and should be changed. You have to 'read' the other person to make a fair deal." Because Stewart's leaders value the corporation's employees, they advise managers to "see both sides." Ultimately, the corporation wants cooperative responsibility from both its supervisors and employees. "Fit, fix, fire" is a Dake mantra. Managers are to work with employees so they achieve job fit, and after reasonable attempts to fix what is not working, they are expected to fire the employee for the sake of mission fulfillment.

What do employees expect from their supervisors? The WISE

for employees is that they want good workplace arrangements or deals that facilitate their job success, while they balance school and family responsibilities. The Dake training manual instructs managers and supervisors to achieve a "balanced shop profile to serve customers." The challenge in dealing with groups of people is finding an appropriate mix of them that achieves team synergy. The profile not only means matching full-time and part-time employees to provide effective coverage but also should take into account which partners and associates work well together.

Dake asks managers to "invest in partners." One manager explained how he started out as a part-time employee and was gradually given more and more responsibilities, which included attending training meetings with the boss. The manager was being groomed for leadership before he even knew he was targeted for it. When opportunity opened for him to get into an assistant management position, he realized that he had already been trained to handle most of the new job responsibilities. I believe that employees want a leader who will invest in them so they have the tools to succeed and grow.

Dake compels his managers to have the confidence to pursue reality and "share good and bad [news or information] to make everyone successful." I have had many struggles throughout my career with my superiors who insisted that bad news never should be shared with employees. I believe employees like to know where they stand. Distrust is bred when the "reality" of the situation finally becomes known, and the employees realize that their supervisors or upper managers had access to information but did not tell them. It's better to get it out in the open and discuss it.

In a *USA Today* opinion research survey of 1,198 workers by Joe Young and Sam Ward, printed on February 26, 2008, Top Workplace Frustrations are poor communications by senior management about the business (17 percent), followed closely by general office politics (16 percent), and lack of teamwork (15 percent). All these workplace frustrations are directly related to how people communicate and follow through.

D. James Kennedy has said that "discrimination is knowing the difference between a garden and a jungle; the difference between music and noise; the difference between barbarism and civilization. Discrimination is the difference between bad and good. Without discerning these differences, our gardens will become like jungles; our civilization will degenerate to barbarism." When businesses fail to discriminate the differences and the patterns that contribute to profit and loss, they fail and do not know why.

At Stewart's "Smaller Is Nicer" A Big Network of Small Businesses

The Stewart's Corporation runs 325 neighborhood stores. Bill Dake says, "The characteristic of the operation is somewhat different in that we believe in SIN. 'Small Is Nicer.'" He explains ...

> We are really four hundred small businesses. We are a big small business, not a small big business, even though we achieve a billion dollars in sales. We are four hundred small groups working efficiently to support each other in a more candid and pleasant environment.

Bill Dake states that some of the advantages of his "big small business" paradigm include that the impact of employee personal responsibility is immediately known. "Everybody knows what is going on in the stores." Bill calls the environment "rational."

> There are several things that occur in that environment. One is that everybody knows each element of it. In other words, if you have one hundred people, and one of them goes over and sleeps in the corner, someone can say, "Hey, what do I care?" But if there are ten of us assigned in a store and three are on the job at any given time, and you go over and sleep in the corner, the impact of that immediately is felt. The others really will have a much, much harder time keeping up with things. We have a more rational environment with a smaller number of people. It's more stressful for some people because it's rational, but life is a lot easier this way, ultimately. The goal is to have a small enough group of people that reality reigns.

Three-Dimensional Leaders Thrive at Stewart's

To succeed at store level at Stewart's, leaders cannot be insecure or defensive. Bill Dake says that to enjoy Stewart's, a manager has to be a learner. "Listen and understand us before trying to impress us." A leader must be focused on the context. "Look outward versus inward to be aware and grow," says the Dake manual. Thus one-dimensional leaders, who want everyone to focus on them, cannot go far at Stewart's. Three-dimensional leaders, by contrast, are able to successively work up to larger and more profitable stores. The managers I have spoken with, who motivated me to interview the architect of this organization, have worked their way up to stores that are in the top 15 percent of the chain's producers.

> Success at Stewart's is achieved by working at what I call the "Level of Emotional Intelligence." Healthy relationships and how people support each other characterize Stewart's operations. Healthy relationships underlie its ownership philosophy, and how it achieves its strong market position.

I asked Bill Dake why he does not fear that the information he shared with me would be replicated by someone who would become his greatest competitor.

His closing remarks are …

> Because they don't have enough trust to execute it. The person who would steal it doesn't understand it. We are very open. We will tell anybody anything, because if they don't believe it, they can't get it done. There is a difference between you understanding what I say and you believing what I say. Unless you believe what I say, you won't act on it. Somebody said to me, "Bill, you should write a book." I said, "I have." It's this training manual, and several dozen backup pages beyond those.

Successful Integration of Resources

Dake is walking the walk. His managers are happy, fulfilled, and thriving. The Stewart's success comes from the integration of its manufacturing and distribution systems with its development and retail operations. The culture of coordination between departments is what gives Stewart's shop managers the support they need to provide service and value to customers. The Stewart's model of resource integration and coordination provides the synergy to win, win, win. The corporation is winning with suppliers and vendors. Its profit-sharing compensation system is winning with its employees, and the customer is winning by being able to shop conveniently while saving on numerous quality food and other store items. Bill Dake has successfully led Stewart's to its win-win-win position in the marketplace.

Chapter Nineteen

The Mechanics of Leadership Roles: Leaders, Managers, and Supervisors

Leadership can be found and is needed within every job title throughout an organization, even though some job titles have obvious leadership duties and expectations. For example, people expect CEOs to set the overall course and direction for the organization. People also expect that a supervisor will oversee the day-to-day activities of subordinates. Regardless of at what level of the organization a leader serves, his or her role is to facilitate a set of circumstances that are favorable for employees to succeed at their jobs.

The Role of the Manager

Managers maintain an organization's internal workings by planning, organizing, allocating, directing, and monitoring resources. Good managers negotiate challenges by redeploying and reallocating resources to fulfill their unit's day-to-day missions. Effective managers gather, organize, and arrange the appropriate resources and devise systematic processes that carry out work plans to achieve the goals of the organization.

People skills are the essential management competency, because work processes rely upon cooperating and coordinating relationships to accomplish the goals of the organization. People skills are needed to rally employees to the mission and oversee them in ways that inspire and motivate them to serve with their hearts to achieve organizational objectives, especially when corrective action is necessary because performance has fallen short of what was planned.

In terms of management hierarchy, a supervisor is the basic function of one who directs and oversees the work of others. Middle management provides directives to implement top-management goals. Supervisors direct the actual work of the organization at the service, manufacturing, operational, sales, and retail ends of the process. The healthiest organizations have three-dimensional leaders at all levels of supervision and management.

The Role of the Supervisor

Supervision involves appropriately interacting with employees so the organization obtains productive behaviors from them. The emphasis is on "appropriate" supervisory behavior because to be effective, supervision must be conducted according to the rules within the organization's context, including procedures established by the personnel department in coordination with union agreements, legal statutes, civil service policies, and state and federal laws. Keith Davis, author of *Human Relations at Work: The Dynamics of Organizational Behavior*, says the supervisor's importance in an organization is analogous to "the keystone" of an archway.[22] The keystone (supervisor) is the central, topmost stone of an arch (organization), without which the arch (organization) collapses. The keystone supervisor is essential because that role is designed to take the pressure of all the stones (parts of the organization) around it. By its strategic placement (or role), the keystone (supervisor) exerts its own pressure and, in

THE THREE-DIMENSIONAL LEADER

combination with the pressures that also are upon it, works to strengthen the overall arch.

The supervisor is the main support that joins the directives of managers to what the employees below them actually do. Supervision is a very challenging role that coordinates between upper management and the front-end employees to carry out the work. It is essential that supervisors be III-D leaders, because most of their days are spent representing management by interpreting policies, providing instruction and information, and routinely interacting with employees. Supervisors explain to employees not only what is expected of them but also how their work relates to the rest of the company's units and processes. An astute III-D supervisor greatly increases employee job satisfaction by providing them with intellectually satisfying rationale about how they fit in and why their productivity and efficiency are important to the company's success.

Three-dimensional supervisors are guided by a sense of mission and how the company's people resources entrusted to them can fulfill it daily. This mission and resource focus becomes the compass that guides responses to employees as situations arise. III-D supervisors lead their units to negotiate the elements within the context so the team coordinates to conquer work situations rather than losing mission focus and operating in chaos. Completing each task in ways that are consistent with the organization's values and objectives are the stepping-stones to long-term vision fulfillment.

Succession planning is accomplished by promoting into supervision and management layer upon layer of employees who have the capacity to achieve the company's mission. These leaders not only have the most institutional knowledge about the company but also have liked it and been loyal enough to its processes to deserve to be promoted. From the multiple ranks of such managers, a company should find it easy to select its top executives. The benefits of having such homegrown, dedicated, knowledgeable, and loyal layers of leadership within your own ranks is seen in the General Electric (GE) Company's CEO succession process when its former leader, Jack Welch, announced he would retire.

GE had an almost ten-year succession process. It developed a list of more than thirty possible successors to Welch. Of those, only three or four were from outside GE. Of the top ten, I believe at least nine were from GE. The three finalists were all internally developed GE managers. Of those other nine GE finalists who were not selected, most became CEOs of other companies. GE's corporate performance is a testament to what its succession of leaders continuously has accomplished for the organization for more than a hundred years. I previously discussed that mentoring, training, and delegating responsibility are how to grow leaders. GE and other top-performing companies do this exceedingly well.

Proctor & Gamble (P&G) CEO A.G. Lafely was placed in charge of that company in the year 2000. He began his career with the company in 1977, following a stint in the navy, where he oversaw retail and services businesses on a military base in Japan. He progressed through P&G's laundry, soaps, and beauty businesses, taking on successively greater responsibilities. When he assumed leadership of the corporate portfolio, Lafely knew the products and was bred of the company culture. He knew, therefore, how to successfully lead the corporation to acquire appropriate resources and develop, improve, and produce quality products that drive the company's business.

Contrast what P&G and GE accomplish through purposeful managerial development and succession planning with the long-term loss of synergy and trauma other organizations cause themselves by getting the wrong people in leadership. If someone is promoted around the age of thirty, he or she may be with the company another twenty to thirty years or more. If this person is not suitable to lead, the company either is faced with a long-term loss of synergy, or it has to go through the painstaking process of demoting or firing that person. In the meantime, however, that person is incapable of doing what the company really needs him or her to do. Organizations should avoid such self-inflicted wounds at all costs. But if the mistake is made, and a thorough diagnosis confirms the leadership lesion, do the surgery quickly. Whatever short-term pain is caused ultimately saves the company's life.

Chapter Twenty

The Employee Evaluation
and Mediation Process

A supervisor's job involves conducting periodic employee job evaluations. Job description and evaluation forms can be thought of as the organization's formal process of delegating roles and responsibilities to employees. The evaluation process should provide objective feedback regarding how the employee is handling the mission that is delegated to him or her.

It is all too easy, however, for an employee-evaluation program to degenerate into a personality contest. Human relationships often cloud objective judgment. If someone is nice to us some of the time, we all too often want to overlook their negative behaviors that continually undermine organizational productivity. Frequently, we hear people say in reference to a coworker that he or she is a nice person but fails to do this essential thing or that essential thing. The same people who avoid dealing with a non-performer because it is so difficult to communicate and coordinate with them say, "But he is such a nice guy." Even though these employees undermine nearly every work process they get involved in, coworkers repeatedly say they are nice people because they greet them warmly in the hallway or show up at office parties to wish them well.

When people have a pleasant personality and yet fail to do

the jobs for which they were hired, they are often not evaluated on the basis of their job performance. We allow our sentimental feelings to undermine our organization's mission and processes because those poorly performing employees greet us pleasantly each morning and give us cards on our birthday. We fail to evaluate their job performance objectively but instead evaluate them on the fact that they do nice things a few brief moments of the day and on special occasions throughout the year. Consequently, we do not deal in a consistent manner with their job-performance shortcomings.

There are people who routinely circumvent the execution of smooth workflow processes by their surliness, procrastination, passive-aggressive behavior, and tendency to withdraw their presence from essential activities. These people contribute to silo mentalities or single-handedly erect barriers and prevent cross-pollination of organizational principles, guidelines, procedures, and policies and thus hinder and undermine operational strategies, yet we say they are "nice people." They repeatedly fail to provide information on time and meet deadlines. They refuse to operate within established frameworks and decide not to participate fully in projects in which the rest of their teams and others throughout the organization are intensely engaged. They resist accountability and refuse to work within established channels. Yet we and others throughout the organizations say they are "nice people." Employees, however, should be evaluated upon the basis of their job performance, not how we feel about them as human beings. We can respect people as humans and still categorize their job performance for what it is.

The healthiest mission-focused organizations are those in which the culture, "a group's shared set of beliefs, values and assumptions about what is important,"[23] is consistent with the reality of two plus two equals four. "Nice people" do not undermine and circumvent their organizations' processes. Poorly performing employees do. The goal of an evaluation program is not to acknowledge that people are nice but rather to determine if they are contributing to their organization's mission fulfillment by engaging in their work in the ways that contribute to the entire organization working effectively. Employees should be evaluated upon two primary categories. To paraphrase Jack Welch, one is, "Are they getting our numbers?" and two, "Are they demonstrating our values?"

Earlier we discussed the four types of employees. Employees in category four are those who cannot do the job and so are subject to dismissal. If those in category three, however, who could do their jobs but won't, persist in the behaviors that fail to produce acceptable results, then over the course of a year, which should minimally provide evaluations every six months, they get categorized as category four and become subject to discipline and dismissal.

To be fair to the employee, the supervisor or employer must determine if the employee is trying to reach unrealistic goals given the circumstances in which he or she must work. Sometimes poor direction and management could contribute to underperformance. Remember my story about how the corporate management of a retail store chain did not realize that the dimensions of one store's stock room did not match the dimensions of a template that assumed all facilities were of the same size? Forcing the store into the mold actually made its local operations inefficient and contributed to lost sales. If the district manager of that situation fails to get corporate leaders above him to respond appropriately and allow for the local store variance, local management will be frustrated because they know they could perform better if they were empowered to do so.

When there are multiple stores or employees underperforming in a particular sector or unit, senior management should look at three potential causes: 1) centralized bureaucratic, corporate policies that hamper local achievement, 2) local management and supervision that fail to appropriately rally and deploy resources, including employees, to the cause, and 3) contextual environmental market factors, which will be discussed in detail later. Corporate salary-structure polices could make it difficult for local managers to hire qualified employees and retain them, so they become increasingly more experienced and valued employees. High employee turnover can be discouraging to local managers, who may feel like they can never make progress in building a team of seasoned and gifted individuals. High employee turnover also could indicate that local management is lacking people skills.

If an employee fails to improve, regardless of the different solutions and remedies applied, disciplinary action should be undertaken, and dismissal may result. Any dismissal should be administered with appropriate transitional assistance and severance benefits.

Resolving Workplace Conflict

Situations that merit dismissal tend to be rare. Situations where conflict must be resolved are more frequent. While I have used a variety of sources to mediate office and interagency conflicts to keep people mission focused, I most often refer to the "Thomas-Kilmann Conflict Mode Instrument" (CMI), which I obtained during a workshop I took. Handled appropriately, the CMI is a great tool to assist employees to overcome their interpersonal workplace challenges. I structure formal and informal mediation sessions by deploying techniques I learned from a Managerial Mediation course I took that provided materials from Daniel Dana, Ph.D. He defines Conflict as "a condition between two task-interdependent people in which at least one feels angry toward the other (though not necessarily overtly expressed) and finds fault with the other, and which disrupts work and morale in the organization."[24] If a leader does not teach his or her team members to mediate their disagreements and to overcome challenges related to their varying style preferences, a series of seemingly minor issues can build up into frustration and the loss of enthusiasm and morale that fuels employee job satisfaction and achievement. Left unchecked, these situations can digress into deep resentment and anger, which impedes unit effectiveness. These conflicts occur between coworkers, their supervisors, and people in every job title up and down the managerial and organizational hierarchy.

When it is my responsibility to intervene in a situation, either because it involves people I supervise, or if another manager has asked me to intervene in a conflict his or her peers and/or subordinates are experiencing, I arrange a training session I call "Negotiating Your Mission through Team-Based Problem-Solving Techniques." This sounds a lot more positive and less threatening than advising employees that they must attend a session to help them resolve their conflict. While I have conducted the training session in both large and small groups, I will focus here on a small group exercise that functions as an intervention to help employees to overcome challenges, so they can work harmoniously to focus on their mission. The exercise provides employees with a III-D focus on "how to get the most out of their working relationships."

Getting the Most Out of Working Relationships

For a "session" to be useful in resolving the challenge (conflict), the parties involved must be "psychologically minded" enough to have the functional capacity to understand how their feelings can result from perceptions. This functional capacity, in my opinion, is necessary for a session to have the opportunity to resolve misunderstandings that have led to the conflict. A person must be able to understand that if you think a thought, you get a feeling. Most people who feel a certain way long enough will act on their feelings. If a person is capable and willing to change his or her perceptions because new and relevant information makes it rational to do so, they will feel differently, and a behavioral change becomes possible.

Not all people are psychologically minded enough to analyze how their perceptions contribute to their feelings and how their actions and reactions result from them. For instance, if you think someone is going to hurt you, you feel uptight, anxious, and defensive, or you may feel a surge of aggression to defend yourself or strike out at that person before he or she strikes out at you. Another response is that you may feel that you want to get away from or avoid that person. You can experience these feelings even if the other person really intends no harm to you. We react to what we believe and feel what other people's intentions are. The unfortunate challenge that many organizations face is that people who are not psychologically minded have gotten promoted into supervision and management. Misunderstandings cannot be resolved if people have little or no capacity to realize that what they think others are thinking and feeling about them indeed may not be what other's are thinking and feeling about them.

People who are not psychologically minded tend only to see things in black and white. Such people have little capacity to make the appropriate adjustments in their perceptions that lead to behavioral changes that provide functional synergy within team environments where multiple personalities necessitate negotiating varying communication styles and viewpoints for people to understand each other and focus on their jobs. This perception and understanding is essential for relationships to move beyond the stormy interactions that often occur when groups form and which tend to occur when groups are faced with change that causes adjustments in their assignments and the individual members' roles and responsibilities. Harmonious relationships result when people grow to be emotionally intelligent with each other so their collaboration is not impeded by misinterpreting each others' intentions. This level of understanding is the platform from which teams launch to focus on their missions, rather than on how they are feeling about each other. It often takes work on each member's part, however, to get to where they are working in highly effective collaboration.

I have preliminary phone conversations to introduce myself, if necessary, and to advise the parties that I have been tasked to conduct a training session. I advise that the session will have the most value and relevance for employees if we use it to address issues related to some of the actual challenges they currently must over-come. Usually all the parties readily agree to participate in a small group-training session that focuses on their mission and how they can work more effectively together to overcome challenges and achieve it.

On "session day," I conduct a pre-meeting with management to discuss issues and determine what solutions might resolve the employees' conflict. I then conduct one-on-one meetings with each individual involved in the conflict. To avoid the perception that I am playing favorites, my agenda for the day's sessions indi-cate that the individual meetings will take place according to the alphabetical order of the employees' last names.

I start the day by addressing the parties in a group and state, "I want to meet with each of you individually to make sure I under-stand the challenges you each feel you are experiencing as you think about the mission the organization has tasked you to fulfill." I may put up a few slides that provide an overview of their mission and then one or two that address the issue or change initiative that has led to the challenges that bring us here today. In the group discus-sion, I try to build off what each team member states to get other team members to agree, build upon, and re-state the mission and perhaps the current challenge in their own words. This helps with team building, as the members accept one another's statements and validate one another's input. It also helps me to determine how much ownership and responsibility each party is taking to be part of the solution to overcoming the challenges. If a party is reluctant to state the mission, then he or she is reluctant to accept responsi-bility to help fulfill it. When there is positive energy and good eye contact among the parties as they discuss the overall mission, we are on the way to a successful training experience and constructive outcomes. If energy and eye contact is lacking, additional training may need to take place.

Individuals are Important

I advise that as part of today's training event, I next will con-duct individual meetings with each member to build upon what we discussed here and to ascertain your views on how we might address the challenges we face in fulfilling our mission. If one of the individuals is reluctant to continue to participate, I pull rank (or get a supervisor to pull rank) and make it a mandatory "job assignment" like any other required meeting. Because of the work done during the preliminary phone calls, I rarely have had anyone try to back out of the process.

I conduct a meeting with each individual that builds upon the trust I gained during the introductory phone call and group meeting. I show empathy so they will open up fully to tell me what is troubling them and express their perspective of the situation, but I do nothing that takes their side against their co-workers. If during the individual meeting someone asks me a question I'm reluctant to answer, I will ask, "Why is it important for you to ask that?" or, "Why is that an important issue to you?" My goal is to determine the perspective and presuppositions of each person and their predisposition to resolve the conflict. The individual meeting gives each person a chance to vent their feelings and frustrations, which can be a catharsis that produces a greater willingness to suggest or accept compromises during the group meeting that will take place later. Later, during a second group meeting, I will facilitate and mediate how the parties will address each other directly.

During the individual meetings, I show each person the Thomas-Kilmann Conflict Mode Instrument (CMI) and advise they should review it as a self-test. The purpose of the CMI is to get those who review it to focus on solution-directed thinking. The language of the questions provokes in most rational people conciliatory thinking, which will make the discussion that follows more productive. I state, "There are no right or wrong answers to the CMI questions. I am not here to grade you." I then allot ten to twelve minutes for the employee to review the CMI. I then instruct, "After this session, but before the larger meeting, please think over what your answers would be in relation to the CMI material on pages seven through nine to determine a self-assessment of how you tend to approach problem solving. Where

would you be on the Thomas-Kilmann Assertiveness-Coopera-
tiveness scale?"[25]

I then read Daniel Dana's description of workplace conflict,
and I ask, "Given that definition, would you say that you have
a conflict with at least one other individual involved in these
meetings today?" After hearing the employee's side of the story,
I explain: "I'll keep your statements confidential, but I intend to
help you and the other parties involved communicate constructively and deal with these challenges as fairly and positively as
possible. I hope that you recognize there are some personal benefits to you in resolving this conflict, and I am here today because
I am committed to seeing you folks work toward and hopefully
arrive at resolution."

The CMI helps employees enter into a solution-directed
frame of thinking, and during each of the individual sessions, I
advise the employee, "I am aware of some challenges taking place
within the office, and I am asking each of you your perspective of
what is going on." At times I may challenge a person's particular
perception or assumptions by interjecting questions, such as, "Are
you sure that a particular person or the other people really are
thinking what you think they are thinking?" Sometimes I will
ask a person if he or she would mind if I found a way to bring up
a particular issue in the joint meeting that will take place later.
I offer to do so without mentioning names or revealing who has
the challenge or concern. Care must be taken not to coach, chide,
criticize, or discipline during these individual meetings. Be careful not to take sides. If an individual pressures you to take sides
by saying something like, "How would you feel if this happened
to you?" or, "Don't you think that ... " respond with, "I know that
what you are experiencing is difficult, but expressing my opinions
will not help the two or three of you (or your group) find your
own solutions."

I ask each person, "Following this individual session, would
you take some time alone and visualize the ideal conditions that
would bring reconciliation with the other parties involved? In an

ideal or not-so-ideal case scenario, what would resolution look and feel like to you? What situation will allow you all to move on positively from here?"

The Mediation Session

Following a lunch break, I hold a group meeting with the employees, the goal of which is to conduct a "controlled engagement," whereby I raise the issues that are causing the conflict. I set up ground rules that we must own our feelings and not blame how we feel on others. This is done by using "I" statements to speak of situations. An example of an "I" statement is: "When this type of situation occurs, I feel like ... " This is very different from accusing others of intentionally making you feel a particular way.

I review what conflict is and restate what I read previously and continue.

> Anger, regardless of whether it is acknowledged or openly expressed, is the fuel that feeds the fire of conflict and always is present in any conflict that becomes an organizational challenge. Conflicts need not be loud, explosive, or violent to affect productivity or morale. In fact, superficially "polite" workplace relationships, that have an underlying tension, often have a greater negative effect on team-organizational performance and productivity. A goal of this session is to help us arrive at more harmonious and cooperative working relationships by reducing anger by increasing our understanding of each other to arrive at "the level of emotional intelligence" as we interact.[26]

I continue by stating, "Tension between you and your coworkers is distracting attention from productive work. Let's explore some ideas of how you are going to reduce the tension. Our purpose in meeting today is to provide an opportunity for you to work through your challenges, so we can reduce friction and work together more effectively. I ask that we all agree that the specifics of what we discuss here will remain confidential between us—although we may share actual solutions that involve our business process that may be evident to others. As a facilitator, I may not be very active in the discussion but will try to assist you to address each other as truthfully and constructively as possible, so that as a team you may find your own answers. My role as a facilitator is to prevent withdrawal and to support conciliatory gestures. I will act as a scribe to record any specific agreements reached. Who would like to go first in stating the issues that you think have brought us here today?"

The facilitator must risk the dialog growing tense, must interrupt statements that are accusatory, argumentative, inflammatory, and hostile, and ask that they be rephrased as an "I" statement. For instance, if one of the parties says, "Bob makes me feel like he thinks he is better than me or that he doesn't like me or respect my input," I interject, "Please give us a specific situation that made you feel this way. Please phrase your response in an I-statement, such as, 'When this happens, I feel like Bob doesn't respect my input.' Two people can experience the same circumstance and mentally process the information differently, and thus react to it with radically different feelings. It is essential, therefore, that we not assume the other person intentionally wants us to feel what we feel."

The mediator's role is not to limit confrontation but to channel it so the individuals begin making conciliatory gestures toward resolving every disputed issue. The parties involved must determine what issues they confront. The mediator interjects restatements to clarify what is being said to keep the focus on the issues and keep the parties from attacking each other verbally, which will cause constructive communication to break down. The mediator may say, "So, Peter, are you saying that when 'x' happens, you feel like 'z'?" or, "Peter, is that how you intended to make Jane feel?" If Jane or Peter starts speaking to you as the mediator, you ask them to address each other.

During the course of a session, people may say things like, "On Tuesday, Bob, you walked in and did not say 'good morning' to me, so I feel like you ignore me and do not like me, and you treat me like I don't exist and that my contributions do not matter to this office!" Bob then can explain how his intention is not to make the other person feel ignored or rejected. Bob may be one of the kinds of people who are a little grouchy first thing in the morning, or he may need to get some things straightened out on his desk before he feels he can interact with others. To keep channeling the discussion so it remains focused on the group's organizational mission, I try to get the parties to make references to as many specific work-related issues as possible. So, I might interject and ask, "Have you worked on any projects or assignments in which you had similar feelings that your contributions did not matter?" I then will let Bob and the other party work through whatever is stated.

Rather than seeking to impose solutions, the mediator assists the parties to *negotiate,* what Daniel Dana says "is the process of seeking settlement or agreement." The ideal result is *conciliation,* which is "a state of mutual good-will between principles."[27] A goal of the mediation process is that the principles begin to understand that just because a situation made them feel a certain way does not mean that the other person meant it to be hurtful.

Emotional intelligence is arrived at in relationships when we learn to interpret each other's actions in ways that do make us feel hurt and defensive. When people gain each other's trust and can say to one another, "Jane, when this occurred, I thought you meant to make me feel this way. Is that how you meant it?" they move into discussions that lead to mutual conciliatory gestures, actions, and agreements that make the workplace harmoniously productive. Time and energy is not spent avoiding each other or having disputes with each other.

Breakthrough is a mutual shift by each person from an attitude of "me against you" to "us against the problem" or the challenge at hand. As breakthrough approaches, facilitate the process by asking the parties, "What do you think you need from your officemates to resolve the challenge? Can you, Mr. X, do what Ms. Y suggests? Mr. Z, what do you need from Mr. X and Ms. Y to comply? Can you, Ms. Y, comply with what Mr. Z suggests?" The goal is to frame an agreement that each party accepts. Ask the parties if they each feel the "deal" is balanced and fair. Amend the agreement if necessary.

Resolution means the agreement is behaviorally specific. Once the "deal" is recorded, set a time and date for a future follow-up meeting to see how the deal is working for all and see if any adjustments are needed. Keep in mind that as the context changes, there may be a need to adjust the deal. The ultimate goal is for the parties to address their challenges by working through them in a state of emotional intelligence, so misunderstandings are limited, and people feel like all the parties involved have the best interest of the others at heart, and they make their own informal agreements to adjust to ongoing circumstances and situations.

Following the mediation, provide feedback by meeting with managers to apprise them of agreements reached that involve work assignments and any changes in process. This can be accomplished over the phone, if time does not allow for a second meeting with them on site that day. Hopefully, immediately following the group session, managers will see a change in the employees' behaviors toward each other, which reflects positively on how they approach their work.

Mediation is not the solution for all issues. If employees are involved with illegal behavior or violations of the employee manual, then counseling and discipline are the appropriate processes. If, following mediation, someone grows entrenched and refuses to follow through on what was agreed, counseling may be a viable next step. The purpose of mediation, however, is not to identify guilty parties and assign blame; neither is it to punish parties for past behaviors. Mediation is designed to determine how to move forward productively. It is not a Band-aid but opens festering wounds and pours in healing salve. Successful mediation provides long-term and lasting foundations for ongoing, healthy working relationships.

Chapter Twenty-one

When and How to Discipline Employees

There are times when mediation is not the appropriate process. I recommend disciplinary action against an employee when he or she stops a team of people from moving forward into a mission-focused process. Because removing people can have psychological, emotional, and legal outcomes for an organization and its remaining members, it is far better to first work with problematic employees to focus them on the unit's mission and fold them in as productive organizational team members rather than to experience high rates of turnover, which entails re-training costs and learning curve-productivity lag times. I like to say that great organizations are built upon love and forgiveness, because everyone makes mistakes and everyone needs chances to bounce back from them.

Both the workers and leaders can (and probably will) make some mistakes. They are not Jesus Christ. As humans, we are bound to make errors. We will not do all things perfectly. Inevitably, we will offend each other. We, therefore, must be quick to extend love and forgiveness to each other in order for our organizations to thrive. This is not to say that you do not discipline poor performance. Any disciplinary or corrective action, however, should be carried out with a desired outcome to restore the employee to focus on the mission by cooperating with the other team members who are working together to accomplish it. Pain, or something unpleasant, like a counseling memo that documents poor performance, temporary loss of pay, or forced time away from the job, can provide powerful learning experiences that will motivate employees to want to perform differently.

Patterns of negative behaviors merit discipline because they provide evidence that the offending party is not changing to conform to organizational standards. If despite two to three counseling episodes where the undesired behaviors were specifically articulated and steps were detailed for how the employee will address and correct them, and there still is no change, you probably have a member who is incompatible with the team. If people are going to be successful within an organization and with its customers and/or clients, they must know and care enough to bear the values that the organization has determined lead to success. If employees repeatedly verify that they cannot provide those behaviors, they will be a drag to other employees, clients, and partners. For the sake of the greater good, it is better to remove them.

Behaviors That Should Be Disciplined

Behaviors that undermine team dynamics merit discipline because their outcomes circumvent and frustrate the processes that accomplish the mission efficiently. The leader's role is crucial in the process of monitoring team dynamics to ensure that each player or member participates in a way that does not impede the progress of other people on the immediate team and those throughout the organization.

Before we can effectively discipline employees, we must know what behaviors contribute positively to dynamic team processes and which ones undermine them. Among one-dimensional people are those who are forceful, overly competing, and downright mean-spirited. They tend to act from an attitude of "you are either for me or against me." This is quite different from being outgoing, outspoken, or passionate. Forcefully competing people respond to the normal ebb and flow of give and take in the workplace as if others are out to get them when they disagree with them. Forcefully competing people tend to assault and attack others rather than negotiate and discuss ideas. Forcefully competing people character assassinate anyone who disagrees with them. Because they are so mean-spirited and aggressive when it comes to any type of process that involves negotiation, many people will have to withdraw from them, shutting down functional team processes, resulting in less work getting accomplished. This is true regardless if the forcefully competing people are peers to those they abuse or are in managerial or leadership roles above them.

Other people are withdrawing and withholding passive-aggressive types who tend to pout when they don't get their way, and, in essence, they put their thumbs in their mouths and refuse to participate appropriately. They don't treat everyone the same. They don't respond to e-mails from certain people; they don't readily share information, or they share partial information, which prevents other gifted employees from being able to see the big operational picture, which limits them from being as effective on their jobs and fulfilling their tasks in a proactive, problem-solving manner.

There are people who really cannot handle position and power and any assignment that they feel gives them importance, status, or cachet in an organization. These people suffer from approbation lust, which is an inordinate desire to be praised and admired. Among these types of people are those who are consumed with "being the boss," or "the leader," or "the one in charge." One-dimensional leaders have a tendency to attract and promote other I-D's. This is because people naturally gravitate toward people who are like them. If I am a I-D person who desires to be on a pedestal with adoring fans surrounding me, I am going to attract, hire, and promote people who will make my ego gratification their priority.

Another challenging phenomenon for organizations is that there are many adults who, emotionally, are in junior high school, and they cannot like someone unless they are joining forces with that person or a faction of others to attack and put down someone else. These people form unhealthy alliances, the negativity from which causes others to seek ways to withdraw from them. The behavior undermines functional organizational process and synergy.

My experience is that forcefully competing people also are withholding people. They tend to be forceful and rude and respond sporadically to those whom they outrank. They lord their authority over others and try to micromanage them, so the employees are never as proactive and productive as they otherwise might be, because they are trained through harsh and rude experience that they had better not take action or breathe without the permission of the leader. The challenge for organizational interaction and workflow processes is that there is often no rhyme or reason to the pattern of the unproductive behaviors of those who are forcefully competing and those who are withdrawing and withholding. Both types of behaviors, in my opinion, should be disciplined, because interdepartmental collaboration, information sharing, and workflow processes are so compromised by them. I address these behaviors whenever I see them. If the behaviors persist, I begin the discipline process after two to three informal discussions and warnings and two to three formal, one-on-one counseling training sessions.

Verifying and Vying with Vampires

What is the difference between 1) a real vampire who enjoys being hominus nocturnus; 2) a person who is a vampire but is in denial about it; and 3) a person who is delusional and thinks he is a vampire but, in fact, is not? To further illustrate, the real vampire enjoys sleeping in a coffin during the day and is invigorated by his night prowling. He truly enjoys the terror his victims experience as he satiates his bloodlust in raptured ecstasy as he drains them of life. The person who is a vampire, but is in denial about it, prowls the night and takes victims. Late the next afternoon, however, he awakens from his blackout and sees the traces of blood on his hands and is repulsed by the vague flashbacks he has of what he did the previous night. He says to himself, *I can't be a vampire!*

The third person is psychotic and self-deceived. He is no vampire but thinks he is one. He is psychologically enthralled and emotionally enticed by the thought of being one of the undead that is very powerful, fast, and treacherous. He thinks of himself as dashing, daring, and dangerous. He sleeps in a coffin and has purchased many other accoutrements one would expect a vampire to have, but he is no vampire. He is just delusional.

What all three of these people have in common is that each of them will bite your neck, so eventually you will have to treat them the same way. They each will force you either to defend yourself against them or be consumed by them in some way. To get their behavior to change, you will have to put a stake through their heart. In other words, you will have to find some painfully effective method to get them to deal with the reality of their situation.

Of the four types of employees discussed earlier, vampires are the "can but won't" types, who are crafty and intentional. They can do things the right way, but because they are vampires, they are doing them so they can find an opportunity to bite your organization in the neck to further their own agenda.

The vampires in denial are the "can't and can't" types of employees. They can't help themselves when they fail to perform. What is in them is beyond their control. They routinely snap and turn into vampires.

The delusional "vampire wannabes" either are "can't and can't" or "can but won't" employees who are hopelessly trapped in their fantasy and cannot hold it together to do the job, regardless of how sincere they are in their intentions to do so. Just when they act normal enough to get you hopeful that this time they will be different, their flight of imagination consumes them, and they behave like a parasite that undermines your initiatives, a tick that gets under the skin of your team members, a social mosquito that annoys others within the organization who call you to ask if there is someone or anyone else you can assign to the process, because no one wants to deal with them.

People who power up on others with rude, excessive behaviors are the vampires who enjoy being so. Vampires tend to be thickheaded brutes whether they are male or female. Vampires are not sophisticated to know that many things are worth fighting (negotiating) for, but few things are worth having a fistfight over. Vampires deal with everything in a way that pushes all others involved into devastating fistfights that destroy working relationships. They don't read the subtle signals that psychologically sophisticated, three-dimensional people readily pick up. Vampires don't get it. They do not understand the subtleties of your organization's mission. They either are clueless or do not care about the constant drain of synergy their behavior has upon the organization. They are oblivious to how they make everyone else in the context feel.

Other vampires are in denial about who they are and never admit to ever doing anything wrong. You can't convince them of what they are. They are masters at denying their personal responsibility in any matter. Interactions with them leave you feeling crazy, as if you did not witness what you saw and experience what actually happened. Too much constant interaction with them sucks you into their distorted alternate reality. Delusional vampires are those who intend to be nice people, but they just can't help themselves. Any bit of cachet or importance that they perceive they've obtained from being assigned a task or role (regardless of how temporary) goes to their heads. They get overwhelmed with their own sense of importance, and they act bizarre. Tasks that should take a few brief phone calls are elevated to full-scale meetings. Instead of sending brief e-mails, they hand deliver volumes of background material to prepare you for the simple e-mail.

"Vampires" suck the life out of organizational synergy through their brutality, denials, manipulations, and delusions of grandeur. They drain a lot of time and energy from many who come in contact with them. The stake you use to deal with them can come in the form of ineffective evaluations if you supervise them. To discipline them, speak to their specific offending behaviors and try to corroborate your observations with the statements of witnesses.

The Appropriate Disciplinary Process

An appropriate disciplinary process tends to start with counseling. A counseling memorandum records a discussion between a supervisor and an employee about specific behaviors that must or must not occur and how the employee agreed or disagreed with the supervisor's analysis of a situation or circumstance that is at issue. The counseling memorandum becomes a formal written record that an action or incident took place between two or more members of an organization, or that a single member undertook an inappropriate action or failed to take an appropriate action in a situation. Because everyone can make mistakes, the focus of the first counseling memorandum gives the employee the benefit of a doubt as a teaching tool. Counseling documents that specific instruction was given to address and resolve a situation that occurred. The specifics assist the employee to identify behavior that is unacceptable and clarify the specific behavior that is acceptable and preferred.

If the undesired behavior continues, and repeated formal counseling fails to curtail it, the supervisor must take steps to formally discipline the employee. Discipline is designed to discourage and restrain undesirable behavior while it encourages positive, appropriate behavior. Discipline can be seen as punishment, reprimand, retribution, or chastisement. Discipline should be progressive to grow in severity when an employee engages in repeated offenses. Supervisors should not be confused about what progressive discipline is. If an employee first does one thing wrong and then does another thing wrong and then another, each of which is addressed by separate counseling memos, progressive appropriate discipline may mean that a fourth memo is given to the employee for continually displaying "poor judgment." References are made to the previous counseling actions, and the employee is perhaps sent home without pay for a few days.

Discipline attempts to obtain appropriate employee behavior through imposing penalties. After receiving mild penalties, it is hoped that in the future the employee will want to avoid the behaviors that caused them. If the mild penalties fail to result in the appropriate employee performance, the discipline becomes progressively more severe. Company policies determine what behaviors are subject to immediate discipline that forgoes the counseling process. Matters for discipline include criminal behavior, misconduct, insubordination, harassment, chronic lateness, and repeated failure to meet adequate job performance (incompetence).

While there are certain offenses, such as falsifying information, stealing, or compromising sensitive data or physically assaulting someone, that are grounds for immediate dismissal, the subtle four behavioral patterns discussed above are far more challenging to deal with because while any one offense may seem minor, the cumulative negative outcomes on job performance tend to be enormous and significant. Because they are subtle, coworkers and supervisors often struggle to define them, and they cannot get the culprit or perpetrator to acknowledge and address them appropriately. When coworkers get fed up and erupt emotionally in response to something that has happened or not happened in the case of a withdrawing and withholding person, the perpetrator often can make them appear to be overreacting. For instance, the perpetrator can say, "It was an oversight that I did not send you an e-mail or notify you."

To the casual observer, it may appear that the perpetrator is being persecuted over an "innocent mistake," but insiders know that so-called "oversight" may mean that a department head does not get notification of specific information that impacts other employees he or she supervises. Repetitive "mistakes" and "oversights" are evidence that someone is not doing his or her job thoroughly and appropriately.

As a supervisor, I do not spend a lot of time trying to determine why people repeatedly fail at tasks. If I have to address the issue more than twice verbally, I begin taking formal counseling action. Once I get to the point where I have to take time away from the main mission to write down what an employee is doing, I don't give the employee much wiggle room. I do not get trapped in discussions about their personal lives, their past history, or how they used to perform; I address the behavior that I want stopped, and I explain and document the behavior and the appropriate job requirements. If there are mitigating circumstances, I try to get the employee to address them by attending education or training programs, or using personal or sick leave or family medical leave if appropriate. I fully expect that the training provided through the counseling memorandum will correct the behavior. If it doesn't, I document it as often as it happens and take progressively stronger actions with a goal of making the poor behavior stop or the employee so uncomfortable that we come to a mutual understanding about shortening his or her longevity with the organization.

Most employees will realize through a properly conducted evaluation and disciplinary process whether or not they have good "job fit" in the current employment situation. If they cannot fulfill the mandates of the position they are in, the well-documented counseling memo trail helps them to identify their strengths and weaknesses and work abilities and preferences. The educational process that could lead to discipline, but which does not have to, is a tool that assists employees to recognize whether or not they have good job fit and at what employment situations they are most suitable for and are happy doing.

360-Degree Evaluations

It is the leader's personal style of interacting with others and how well he or she models appropriate team interaction that determines whether he or she brings out the best in people or causes them to shut down and withdraw, so the organization does not benefit fully from their personal experiences and knowledge— which is the reason they were hired in the first place. One way to ensure that, as a leader, you are conducting yourself in a way that facilitates others being open to provide their input is to provide for 360-degree evaluations, whereby team members anonymously provide feedback about your performance and leadership. This may be the mirror needed to help us become leaders who empower the people within our workplaces to reach their potential to provide the constructive synergy necessary for ultimate mission achievement. We need a mirror to look into that consists of the honest opinions of others.

This process is very humbling and may best be handled as follows: 1) the various department heads and team members help develop evaluation forms that drive at the core actions and activities that facilitate fulfillment of the unit's mission. The forms dive into defining values and behaviors that each employee must act upon within the work setting to achieve the mission. Different forms may be developed for different job titles and roles and responsibilities of the various team members. 2) The completed forms are submitted to the personnel department for approval. 3) The forms are administered by a designee within the personnel department. They are distributed to team members selected by lottery unless all team members evaluate each other. The evaluations are e-mailed to an address that masks the personnel department employees who will compile them, score them, and distribute the results to the person being evaluated and his or her supervisor. This process provides anonymity between the employees providing the evaluations and each person being evaluated. 4) Scoring the forms is accomplished through a rating system that weights the responses provided by various team members. For instance, if the director is being evaluated, the assistant director's evaluation is weighted higher than the evaluation provided by a clerk.

This process gives each team member the potential to have

THE THREE-DIMENSIONAL LEADER

input into evaluating how the team actually functions. It also gives everyone in the organization the opportunity to see that the mission, vision, and values apply to each member of the team. When all the players on a team are not wholeheartedly engaged in fulfilling the mission, the organization loses the benefits of their input. We would not want to use a chain that has a weak or poorly functioning link, yet we do that in people processes all the time. There are behaviors that drain people of their work vitality. These include being forceful, rude, sarcastic, and mean. They also include being passive rather than merely cautious and withdrawing rather than merely being contemplative.

Marshall Goldsmith, after whom the Marshall Goldsmith School of Management is named and who is considered one of today's most successful executive coaches, is renowned for helping successful leaders achieve positive changes in behavior to benefit themselves and their teams. Goldsmith, who has worked with more than eighty Fortune-500 chief executives, speaks about how, as leaders, we need to "quell our inner jerk."[28] Goldsmith promotes four golden behaviors: 1) Care about what your colleagues say and feel about you; 2) don't try to prove you are always right; 3) ask, listen, and follow up; and 4) solicit appraisals from your associates. Goldsmith polls an executive's associates every three months to measure whether his behavior has changed, passing on the results to the executive. Goldman says, "Without the feedback, there's no incentive to change."

Organizations and teams achieve synergy through what I call the three C's: communication, cooperation, and coordination. A disruptive team member is one who negatively impacts the three C's. It is the three C's that determine how well the employees or volunteers interact as a team to rally around the mission, which is the team's reason to exist.

To keep their organizations functioning in healthy ways, leaders need to track process breakdowns to the people who are contributing to them malfunctioning. When people tell me the system is broken, I respond that, as good managers, we will find the actual desk where the paperwork is stalled or not being completed properly, and we will provide instruction to who is sitting there. Quite often what I have found is that it may be due to "factionalism," whereby two or more employees form a subculture of doing things their way as opposed to the organization's way. A faction is a small silo. Those who do not care about interacting as a good corporate citizen within their teams or who fail to understand its importance and tend to continually find ways to work around or outside of the procedures established by the team, including adhering to communication protocols, are those who most frustrate people throughout an organization.

These "jerk mavericks" do not care how many other workers will get into trouble with their bosses or how many other divisions or offices will be impacted by not having a document properly signed, authorized, and put through appropriate channels where checks and balances can be administered properly. Mavericks think their personal agendas override any organizational mission. They say things like, "Rules are made to be broken," and they may be completely uncaring about, or oblivious to, the impact of their failure to comprehend that the larger organization or team has multiple missions to fulfill, including maintaining good records and appropriate documentation.

An Effective Evaluations Program Can Drive Appropriate Behavior

An employee-performance evaluation program should be designed and conducted to achieve employee development for the purpose of mission fulfillment. It should assess whether or not there is job fit between the employee and the tasks he or she has been hired to accomplish. An evaluation process usually is conducted by completing a form. The form should contain at least two parts. One part details the job duties, which are the actions, activities, and behaviors that go into accomplishing the job. The other part defines what the successful accomplishment of those job duties will be, such as so many sales or services per week/month/quarter. The form should define the other parties with whom the employee must coordinate or provide those sales and services.

An effective evaluation program measures the employee's specific levels of performance achievement in relation to the stated job duties and productivity goals. The evaluation should state how the employee's actions, activities, and behaviors met, exceeded, or failed to meet stated goals. Ideally, both the employee and the evaluator should be able to easily identify and agree upon to what degree the employee has accomplished his or her job duties. Regarding any areas in which the employee has fallen short, both the evaluator and the employee should agree upon what steps the employee will take to adjust behavior to improve job performance and/or what the employer will provide to assist the employee to improve performance.

Getting the leadership "who" right so you can get the "do" right requires organizations to identify III-D leaders who really are what Michael S. Hopkins calls anti-heroic leaders.[29] This is in contrast to what we often think about when we think of leadership. Typically, we think the ideal leader is a charismatic, all-powerful, all-knowing individual who has all the answers and is the hinge pin upon which an organization pivots. This style of leadership is poisonous to the leader—who can grow addicted and dependent upon the toxicity of applause and adulation. To be infected by approbation lust opens one up to being led astray by those who want to "suck up" by being a "yes-man" and speaking of only what the leader wants to hear. Egotistical leaders and their "yes-people" easily detach and quarantine themselves from the institutional memory of the organization. Their egos become the trees that blind them to the realities of the contextual forests they are supposed to negotiate for their organizations.

It is very important to be able to attract antiheroic leaders, because if we get the right "who," we get the right "do." To run an organization that obtains the greatest synergy from its people resources, leaders must understand that, first and foremost, leadership is service to employees that helps them succeed at their jobs. Leaders who are healthy spiritually and psychologically are the balanced, well centered, and properly focused individuals who create balanced and healthy organizations.

A properly constructed and conducted employee evaluation system helps employees to have an appropriate assessment of how to make continuous improvements.

Chapter Twenty-two

The Power-Drunk Leader

Power-Drunk Behaviors

What is the difference between a person who is drunk on alcohol versus one who is drunk on his or her own power? The same behaviors are witnessed in both types of drunks. The organizational "I'm the boss" junkies are so consumed with "being in charge" and "having people" work for them and being able to control decisions that they lose their sense of reality about the mission and how to delegate appropriately to achieve it. They cannot learn from those around them. Organizations with "power drunks" at the corporate steering wheel experience the same devastating mishaps that occur on our streets and highways when people drive under the influence of alcohol and other substances.

The organizational mission becomes the casualty when leaders steer the corporation while under the influence of judgment clouded by one-dimensional and two-dimensional egotistical thinking. Most of these people's decisions are filtered through questions they ask themselves, such as, "What will this do for my image, stature, and position? How can this be done in a way that makes others notice that I am the leader?" Their "what's in it for me" point of view is the siphon that consumes the organizational synergy from all of their activities. These leaders never are going to let subordinates accomplish what the leader feels he or she cannot personally control. Thus in a very real sense, people throughout the organization constantly have to put their local activities on hold while they wait for the leader to make decisions that should be delegated to them.

Organizations headed up by those drunk on power suffer from the same erratic behaviors and loss of productivity as families do when substance abusers head up the household. A dear friend of mine, who has overcome the grip of deprivation that alcohol abuse had on his life, says that when you are abusing a substance, everything is wrapped up in selfishness. It's all about you and why you want the substance, and what you are feeling that justifies you wanting and pursuing it. People who are drunk on alcohol and other substances and people who are drunk on their power typically display these behavioral traits:

- Mood swings and emotional overreactions to information.

- Distorted views of reality that ignore the legal or operational context.

- Grandiose delusions; thinking they can force and shape outcomes through the power of their decisions, regardless of how many people try to suggest that another direction is more appropriate.

- Memory loss, as they can't remember who was promised what, when.

- Mean-spirited talk, vendettas against people whose faux pas or mistakes are trivial in relation to the boss's overboard responses to them.

- Loss of mission focus; behaving as if their emotional outbursts and displays of whim are the very reason for their existence and give legitimacy to their position.

- Blame shifting rather than taking personal responsibility for their own actions.

- Protection of their disease and dysfunction rather than acknowledging the need to overcome it.

- Numbness to things that require appropriate action.

- Ignoring essential data, processes, and procedures.

I have witnessed many poor leaders who think their job titles mean they have the power to vent about their personal whims and style preferences, as if the reason the organization exists is for them to be able to exercise undue authority to interfere with and micromanage the activities of everyone around them.

The I-D leader doesn't think about the process steps required for an organization to achieve its mission. The I-D leader only thinks about his or her personal whims at the moment. If he or she feels that someone is out of line (whether it is true or not), they get in that person's face and spout off. They speak abusively and throw around their positional weight. When leaders are drunk on their own power, they waste valuable positional cachet ranting and raving over trivial issues and, while doing so, sacrifice credibility with their subordinates.

Even though many subordinates have much more class than their bosses and never speak back to them in the tones and language choices with which they routinely are assaulted, the subordinates lose respect for the bosses who waste valuable energy and time spouting off about their pet peeves that have little, if anything, to do with the organizational mission. Many I-D bosses actually waste time looking for opportunities to spout off because they believe it gives them legitimacy as a way to display their power.

Leaders who routinely spout off are like the boy who cried wolf so often that people became desensitized to the warnings, so much so that when a real emergency arrives, the organization fails to respond properly. I think many leaders verbally power up on people over trivial matters because they cannot identify what really is important. Others do it out of insecurity. When they feel uncertain about a situation, they resort to ranting about their personal whims or whatever is troubling them at the moment. Instead, they should keep the long-term, big-picture view of the mission in focus and what it is they must ultimately accomplish to achieve it. This will guide them, like a beacon, through times of ambiguity and insecurity.

Another I-D power drunk, loss of mission-focus trait is that they waste meeting time talking more about themselves, their abilities, their ideas, and their greatness at the expense of facilitating the organization's mission. Instead they could use that time to rally their people resources to it and train and prepare them to be empowered to accomplish it. During meetings, if the leader monopolizes everyone's work time with stories of his or her weekend, hobbies, likes and dislikes, you are witnessing sure signs that this person really only cares about himself or herself rather than the organization's mission. The fact that so much meeting time is spent with the leader talking about personal likes and dislikes is also a sure sign that the leader is more than willing to put personal preferences above the needs of the organization and its employees.

Perhaps it could be said that power drunk I-D leaders either are in denial about their shortcomings or are so full of self-adoration that they are convinced of their superiority and rightness, and think that because they are the leaders whatever they do is okay. Their sense of mission and the appropriate behaviors that accomplish it, therefore, completely are overshadowed by self-centeredness and ego. How many leaders waste precious opportunities, as the troops are gathered before them, by spending extensive time in a monologue that is self-ingratiating and full of self-flattery? The tragedy of such talks is that they come at the expense of the incredible team dynamics that could be developed by addressing the challenges the organization faces and focusing everyone's attention to see them in light of the long-term vision and the mission process steps that will overcome them. Meetings are opportunities for the leader to point down the mission path to the vision and say to the team, "Shall we proceed together? Let's lock arms and conquer this thing!"

Such team-building dynamics are forfeited by I-D leaders who verbally boast as if they single-handedly have accomplished everything that the team, unit, or organization has participated in. Such "I do it all" posturing accomplishes little at the expense of discouraging the collective potential of the many who realize they are not appreciated, and their contributions are being co-opted to fuel the leader's egomania.

Those who try to lead with charisma and/or tyranny are open to sabotaging themselves—especially if they grow psychologically and emotionally dependent upon the applause, adulation, and ingratiation of those who want to "suck up" and curry favor by groveling in the aura of the leader's presence. Leaders need to surround themselves with people who are loyal to the mission and who will ask tough questions to help them stay focused on achieving it by appropriately negotiating the context in which it must unfold. Three-dimensional leaders know success is not achieved by being surrounded with "yes-people" who only say what the leader wants to hear. Surrounding oneself with "yes-people" is the ultimate "seeking of self"; only looking at yourself fails to deliver anything close to the level of organizational achievement and satisfaction that is accomplished through team synergy that negotiates the broader context to achieve mission fulfillment.

Chapter Twenty-three
Cultivating a Leadership-Development Culture

The long-term viability of healthy, robust organizations can be achieved when they cultivate a culture that develops deep benches of competent leadership at every level of the organization. To last longer than its current executives, organizations must be intentional about developing its future cadre of leaders. I believe it is essential for organizations to have internal leadership-development programs because by bringing people up through your own ranks, you are raising up leaders who understand the culture, processes, and values that have made the company successful. This institutional memory is a brain trust that is essential for leaders to be able to draw upon to successfully undertake the change initiatives that the organization must undergo to negotiate the future contexts it must perform in, if it is to survive. To develop leaders, senior executives must create opportunities that give those junior to them experience at the art of leadership. The mentoring process I mentioned above is integral to a culture that intentionally develops new crops of leaders.

Longevity should not be the main criteria for promotion and status within an organization. We all know people who have been on the job twenty years yet really only have one year or two years of work experience and still function at the entry or novice level, caring only to engage in tasks and issues that rookies can handle. Yet there are other people who, within a short time on the job, quickly grasp the basic actions and activities that achieve superior job performance, and they rapidly continue learning and growing to understand the larger organization's mission and how to handle the resources to negotiate the context to accomplish it. They see how their roles impact and mesh with the other departments and what needs to happen for the organization to succeed in the larger context. Promote these kinds of people, as they have the capacity to be III-D leaders.

Transitioning Doer-Managers into Effective Leaders

Accountants, lawyers, and other professionals who have been great technicians (good Samson types) can have challenges gaining a mission-focused, ten-thousand-foot view of the context. They may make the II-D mistake of thinking they are getting promoted to do more of what they were good at. As a manager, however, they have to learn to shift their role from doer to coordinator. They have been promoted to provide mission-oriented direction and oversight to the pool of professionals they now oversee, so they can accomplish all that the organization needs from them collectively as a unit.

Consultant Don Giek tells of an accountant who, once promoted, provided little organization and direction for the pool of accountants he oversaw. His II-D mode of leading was to take on the most difficult cases. Those cases were the most time consuming, leaving him little capacity to coordinate the activities of the other accountants and be available to give them guidance on any matter necessary to keep his entire unit on schedule with the concerns of the larger organization.

While I believe it is good for organizations to have doer-managers who stay in touch with what they are supposed to manage by continuing to do some of the work, leaders must strike a balance that allows them to handle oversight responsibilities.

Keeping one's fingers in the actual work being managed helps the coordinator to keep perspective on what he or she actually is tasked to manage. The challenge is that the doer-manager cannot get so engrossed in the "doing" that they have no capacity for the "managing."

Remember, people only can do what they know. Quite typically, people are promoted because they are good at some or all of the technical aspects of their jobs, and the company promotes them, hoping that the new leader will be able to give mission-focused oversight to the technical unit's processes. For that oversight to be achieved, however, the new leader must understand that he or she now is a management-coordinator asset that prioritizes case assignments and workflow to give the greater organization the synergy it needs from the unit as a whole.

To accomplish this synergy, the doer-manager must ascend above the II-D status of being a good lawyer, accountant, or technician and move into the III-D frame of reference of "my mission is to lead by arranging circumstances so employees can succeed at their jobs, so the unit accomplishes its technical services in support of the larger organization's operation." This is accomplished by understanding the overriding needs of the organization to meet its requirements for standards of quantity and quality of output.

Assessing the Capacity for Three-Dimensional Leadership

Too many people who obtain management jobs have little idea what it means to lead other employees to focus upon the organization's mission and to fulfill it by directing, empowering, and supporting them to negotiate the various contexts that emerge and evolve. Their leadership acumen often is a I-D perspective that, *What I am doing is okay because I'm the leader.* I have been with people at leadership-training programs who complain that they do not want to be involved in the training because they are not leaders—even though they are in supervisory and managerial job titles. They say they do not want to tell other people what to do. That these types of people get into leadership, management, and oversight positions becomes a tragedy for their organizations and the people they oversee.

Leadership prospects should be assessed, tested, and interviewed to determine their capacity to perform the management functions of directing, monitoring, planning, and organizing. If people do not like to do these things, they should not be selected for leadership—regardless of how good a technician they are or how much more pay they want to make. One-dimensionals may be good technicians who can get their individual tasks completed, but they are completely unsuited to lead others. Two-dimensional leadership, that understands what multiple technicians do, is required to at least get most of a unit's work accomplished. Three-dimensional leadership will ensure that not only is the one unit functioning well, but that it also coordinates effectively with multiple units to get the enterprise's mission accomplished.

Character and Competence

Putting the wrong people in key leadership positions has tremendous negative outcomes for organizations. To select the right leaders, organizations must look for character and competence. Character means the potential leader has a clean heart about the mission and knows how to work with others in open, honest, and selfless ways and is motivated to do what makes the organization successful. Leadership competence can't be separated from character and is recognized by the following:

- Capacity to Understand MRC (mission, resources, and context). Review teams should place secondary emphasis on specific technical knowledge. Technical knowledge is very important and necessary, as one must understand what employees do and are working with in order to arrange circumstances that are favorable for them to succeed at their jobs. Technical know-how is often far easier to get others to learn, however, than getting them to trust, delegate, cooperate, and coordinate with other members within the organization. These values and behaviors are essential for people to negotiate MRC to operate robustly as III-D leaders.

- Decision-making ability (DMA). Note at different times of people's careers certain parts of their characters come to the fore and guide and overshadow their perceptions and decision-making processes. A person who values job security (the need for which may come with a promotion and more pay and benefits) may be overly risk averse and may begin to fail to make appropriate decisions. Leaders also must be able to make decisions while tolerating some ambiguity. They need to have a grasp on MRC to know how to move the organization forward despite the existence of some emerging factors that create some uncertainty in the context. If leaders wait until all uncertainty has faded and the signals are crystal clear, which actually never may happen, competitors probably have already beaten them to the market. In a competitive environment, "the-right-of-first-passage" goes to the one who has taken some calculated risk based upon a solid understanding of and focus on MRC. The one who gets product out on the market first usually has done so despite some ambiguity, risk, and uncertainty.

- Character attributes to Submit Ego to the Mission (SEM). Many people easily talk mission, but few have the best interest of the organization at heart to walk it out day to day. A person's essential character traits have been formed long ago and make one suitable or unsuitable for leadership within your organization. Those who are suitable can SEM or should be able to demonstrate that they have developed the intellectual, psychological, and spiritual capacity to learn it.

Three-dimensional leadership character and competence are summed up in the capacity to understand MRC and the ability

THE THREE-DIMENSIONAL LEADER

to SEM, which provides one with DMA despite ambiguity and inherent risk.

The process to developing and growing leaders involves the following four steps:

1. Identify potential leaders and nudge them into gradually more significant responsibility. This involves some risk and requires a combination of delegation, mentoring, and intervention when necessary.

2. Build up their leadership gifts through coaching, mentoring, and events and activities that both teach and show how to lead. Teach about power abuse and wielding power appropriately. Teach conflict management and how to deal appropriately with others who may not see clearly the vision, mission, and values now but may grow to do so.

3. Teach and mentor the up-and-coming-leader(s) how to work in such a way that team members are empowered so synergy is achieved from their diversity.

4. Pass on the leadership baton of responsibility. This involves entrusting and empowering the potential leader's "untried virtue." The assumption can be that the virtue is there, lying under the surface, and it must be nurtured, drawn out, and encouraged to step forward and try.

In chapter six of his book, *Courageous Leadership*, Bill Hybels says he looks for the following five leadership traits in people he approaches as potential leaders: [30]

1. Natural Ability to Influence Others: Some people unconsciously exert influence over others as follows:

   • Their wisdom generates or accrues the most respect.

   • Their ideas capture the attention of the group.

   • Their suggestions become the marching orders.

I strongly caution that we must look beyond mere charisma, because a one-dimensional person can be a strong voice, full of sound and fury, attracting a lot of attention and signifying nothing in terms of mission-focused direction and MRC insight.

2. Constructive character that uses influence wisely. These people possess the following character traits:

    - honesty

    - humility

    - stability

    - teachability

    - integrity

3. People Skills or Relational Aptitude:

    - These people must relate well to a broad range of personality types and style preferences, such as people with personality quirks and disorders, power and control issues, and self-esteem deficiencies.

    - They must have great listening skills to be able to take in information provided from diverse sources and presentation styles.

    - They must be able to greet people warmly and accept their input.

    - They must ooze and embody the corporate vision.

4. Drive and Action Orientation: These people are comfortable taking the initiative in challenging situations.

    - Great leaders are people who make it happen, and they energize other people—even though they may do so with a quiet demeanor.

5. Intelligence, mental agility to be problem solvers—as distinguished from merely having degrees or being good test takers.

    - Great leaders possess street smarts, which is why they can effectively deal with so many different types of people and circumstances.

- They must possess a natural curiosity that gives them what Hybels calls "intellectual elasticity"[31] that motivates and keeps them learning over the long haul and the duration of their lives.

- Leaders must be able to process a myriad of information, presented from a multitude of perspectives from the diverse complexities within the context.

- They must be able to decipher it, categorize it, prioritize it, consider the options it presents, and make the right decisions concerning it.

Bill Hybels recommends that once you have identified people with these traits, be intentional about placing them within your orbit. Dialogue with them to eventually arrive at a mutual consensus about their willingness to participate in leadership growth and mentoring, which may take place over several years, with the understanding that there is no guarantee it will result in an actual leadership role or position.

Your bench of leaders will benefit from combinations of on-the-job formal and informal training and mentoring as the catalyst for their growth and development. *It takes a leader to develop a leader.* So be careful about only getting an academician to stand in front of a group and provide "leadership training." Nurture and train your bench both with those who present theory as well as with input from seasoned leaders who have "been there" in the trenches and emerged successful. Apprenticing is learning from an experienced mentor who is a master at the craft. Jack Welch, former CEO of General Electric, said that he spent up to 30 percent of his time in leadership mentoring. Bill Hybels says that he spends ten days each year formally training and mentoring leaders.

Chapter Twenty-four

Leadership Styles and Types

In his book, *Courageous Leadership*, Bill Hybels identifies ten leadership styles.[32] I provide six below, some of which are hybrids and combinations of the ten described by Hybels. Each leadership style is uniquely suitable for different situations or accomplishing different missions or different stages of missions. Different leadership modes and approaches are needed for organizations to move from one stage of their development to the next. Regardless of what phase an organization is in, it needs combinations of the leadership styles listed below to steer all of its various departments to fulfill their parts of the collective corporate mission. Keep in mind as you read below that within each category there are I-D's, II-D's, and III-D's. Described below are the III-D versions of these leadership types.

The Entrepreneurial Leader. Entrepreneurial leaders are great at startups and getting things off the ground. They bring tremendous focus and energy to birth things. They rally and inspire others to the vision and articulate what Jim Collins calls a "BHAG, the big, hairy, audacious goal." Entrepreneurs shape it into a concrete practical mission, lay out the process, and push it down the track. Once things are up and running, however, they tend to get deflated by the day-to-day routine operational and managerial activities required to keep things going. Consequently, they want to move on. The Apostle Paul, who pioneered many churches, is a good example of an entrepreneurial leader. Once the churches were up and running, he appointed elders in each town and turned them over to them.

The Administrative/Strategic Leader. The strategist breaks down the mission into a game plan of easy-to-comprehend process steps that assist employees and volunteers to accomplish the main thing. Leaders gifted in strategy align energies and resources so they are deployed appropriately within their contexts to accomplish the missions that fulfill visions and bring them into reality. Administrators can be very good consensus builders to unite a wide range of constituents into a complex organizational web and focus them upon a common purpose. Administrators love relating to diverse groups of people.

III-D administrators have enormous diplomatic fluidity to negotiate and work with others to help them see how to channel their own styles into the mission effort, to achieve win-wins, without stepping on toes. They are gifted to listen, understand, and think outside the box. Regardless of the contexts they confront, they do not feel confined but determine how to overcome obstacles to move the organization forward. They are gifted at taking new people into the organization and helping them to fit into the group, so their strengths are deployed in ways that are consistent with organizational values to help fulfill the mission and vision.

The Operations/Managerial Leader. Operations leaders need to be good managers. Managerial leadership is the ability to organize processes, people, and resources to implement each step of the mission once an administrator has worked out how to achieve in the context. Managing leaders oversee accomplishing the day-to-day tasks that must be executed proficiently for a mission to unfold in an orderly manner. Managing leaders solve day-to-day problems and set and reach milestones. They have the capacity to implement and carry out the strategy within various departments with the values of the larger organization.

III-D operations leaders are gifted team builders who get the right people skills and chemistry organized around the processes and tasks they are well suited to accomplish to fulfill the mission. Team builders read people and plug them in where they are most effective. (Entrepreneurial and administrative leaders also have varying degrees of this ability.)

The Shepherding Leader. Shepherding leaders build community that enhances the personal experience of each person who belongs and or who participates therein. Shepherding leaders are attracted to Human Resource (HR) and training functions because they like people and want to nurture them and see them develop. A challenge shepherds have, however, is they get so people focused that they tend to forget about the mission to let the people do their own thing rather than the organization's work. Followers tend to be very loyal to shepherding leaders because of the close relationships they forge. III-D shepherding leaders do not allow I-D people to leverage relationships to get away with doing what they want, and getting what they want, from the system but rather keeps them focused on doing what the organization requires to accomplish the mission.

The Motivational Leader. Vince Lombardi was a tremendous motivational leader. These leaders are very encouraging and inspiring. They also know which of their team members need public acknowledgment and which ones prefer private "atta boys." Motivational leaders make workers feel good and important about being part of the process. They tend to be very creative about finding new ways to inspire others. They also know when to give them a break and rest. They know when to challenge the team to take the hill and when it is time to rest at the bottom of it.

The Reengineering Leader. The reengineering leader rescues troubled projects and broken processes. This leadership talent can be seen as strategic both administratively and operationally to resurrect and refocus teams that have lost their way or teams that are at a standstill because contextual changes have caused their previous mode of operation to be ineffective. Reengineering leaders reassign people to the areas and roles in which they are better suited, given the current challenges. They rebuild and re-inspire team resources to focus on accomplishing their missions in the face of an ever-changing context. Reengineering leaders are great detectives at uncovering what went wrong and where the organization, department, or ministry drifted from the mission and how to get back into the right flow. They nudge the team forward while patching it up to heal its wounds. Hybels says that reengineering leaders do not want to start, shepherd, or manage for the long term. They rescue situations, get them up and running, and then want to move on.

Like Bill Hybels, I believe it is essential that organizations have some combination of most of the above leadership styles on its executive team and throughout every level of the company. Internal leadership mentoring and training programs can help organizations identify these various types of leaders who are up and coming throughout the company, so their specific gifts and abilities can be honed and plugged in where the organization needs them at various times to address pressing issues. Organizations need a visionary leader to provide clear and compelling ways to the desired future state. Organizations that are not sustained by a captivating vision eventually die. All teams need a workable, strategic, step-by-step plan that puts feet to the vision. Every group also needs a motivational person to inspire and lift the spirits of its members. An organization's shepherds ensure that all the members feel included and play well in the sandbox.

An organization that has lost its way and is struggling to get back on its feet needs a III-D reengineering leader who can determine how it must restructure to take advantage of emerging opportunities within the context. The reengineering leader, how-ever, needs the support of a III-D strategic administrator who can align the organization's internal operations so its multiple units and divisions are positioned and focused on doing what negotiates the context to achieve success. Once the new processes are up and running and back on track, organization's need III-D shepherding leaders to continue helping people to develop and continually learn the right things, so the company keeps innovating and keeps abreast of the trends. When the leader's styles match the organization's mission strategy, tremendous things can be accomplished. Frustration and failure are more likely to occur when there is a mismatch.

Leadership and team resource chemistry propels organizations to reach their potential. Chemistry is not homogeneity but is achieved when diverse people share a common vision and the core values and philosophy about achieving it. One-dimensional leaders only work well with those with whom they have homogeneity. Multidimensional leaders achieve synergy for their organizations by taking advantage of the cosmic chemistry their diverse peers and coworkers provide as they approach challenges from their varying perspectives.

Homogeneity breeds redundancy. If you and your team members all look alike and think the same, some of you probably are redundant. Redundancy causes organizations to miss out on the opportunities that varying perspectives provide, so they forfeit the robust synergy that can be achieved when diversity is well focused and managed.

Chapter Twenty-five

The Resource of Teams

Love and Forgiveness are the Glues that Hold Teams Together

A team is a group of people who are brought together to achieve a mission, and its members are given different assignments, responsibilities, and tasks for the purpose of accomplishing only what can be achieved through their collaborative efforts. A team is a group of people who undertake the mission to do what none of them can accomplish alone. To repeat what was stated previously, "Teamwork," says Patrick Lencioni, author of *The Five Dysfunctions of a Team,* "is the ultimate competitive advantage, both because it so powerful and so rare!"[33]

Groups of people are the most sophisticated and complicated resources to manage in any organization. Once people congregate, they can get distracted from the mission and begin focusing on each other. Pride and insecurity can cause us to compare ourselves to one another. We can grow jealous of, feel threatened by, and begin to compete with each other when we should be supporting one another to accomplish the mission by coordinating to pull in unison on the same rope. There are many phenomena that can distract us and undermine the mission. Leaders must be proactive to keep teams focused and productive.

Lencioni advises, "Teamwork … comes down to mastering a set of behaviors … that are uncomplicated, but extremely difficult to put into practice day after day."[34] Highly effective leadership develops people resources into outstanding teams that accomplish far more than any mere collection or group of individuals can achieve! Lencioni continues, "Success only comes for groups that overcome … behavioral tendencies that corrupt teams." Because we all can make mistakes, "Love and forgiveness are the glues that hold teams together."

Because teamwork is so powerful, the investments made in forming and developing great ones pay off tremendous long-term dividends. Teaming can obtain synergy by tapping into the talents of diverse people who have various job titles and skill sets to cross-pollinate their ideas to improve problem solving by ensuring all the concerns of constituents and stakeholders are addressed. Team synergy can provide for more efficient and effective project management and outcomes. Team dynamics is especially necessary to achieve change initiatives and organizational cultural shifts.

My ranking of leaders into three categories is based upon my estimation that leadership success and failure hinges largely on the ability to form and obtain synergy from teams. One first must be clear about the team's mission in order to determine the skill sets and job titles required to achieve its purpose. While I-D leaders will place whom they know on a team, a III-D leader will form a team based upon what the team members know in relation to what the mission requires.

Teams can be temporary, such as those that are put together to accomplish a particular project. Project teams should be given a clear goal and provided with an understanding of how management intends to implement the outcomes. If I know the purpose of an assignment, I can more appropriately ensure I have covered all the bases to complete it as thoroughly as possible. I have been assigned to several project teams that were given a particular set of instructions from top management, and midway through pursuing them, it became apparent that top management either was confused about the context and the information that caused it to form the project team in the first place or had changed its mind about how to respond to it. Thus the charter around which the team was formed became invalid, rendering the team's mission and purpose pointless. Yet the team continued to meet and drag on to fulfill its mission, even though it was painfully obvious to the participants that management no longer had any use for the results. Sometimes a change in the context, or a change in the way leaders understand the context, necessitates a change in a project team's focus or mission. When this happens, those who formed the team should be frank about its status and why the change is occurring. They either should refocus the team or cut the losses quickly and get people back to more productive and fruitful activities.

Leadership builds bridges between the *who* and the *do*. Leadership requires the ability to analyze people's skill sets, discern their motivations, and link them to specific task-oriented missions that help an organization succeed. A team-building leadership rule of thumb is: *Do what you love, and get other people to do what they love.* Ask employees and volunteers what they love to do; verify they actually can do it, and then, if possible, plug them into a team where they can do it.

Team Dynamics

The quality of leadership determines the quality of followership. Leadership determines whether or not the followers find their calling, are matched to their capacity, and reach their potential. T. Boone Pickens says, "Leadership is the quality that transforms good intentions into positive action; it turns a group of individuals into a team."[35] When considering people for teams and assignments, consider these dynamics:

1. *Capacity Determines Commitment:* Determine each employee's or volunteer's capacity for time commitment, involvement, and tolerance levels for risk and pressure, and match team assignments to those capacity levels. Service capacity varies from person to person. High-capacity

people like high stakes, high pressure, high time commitment, and significant responsibility and involvement. Others like medium- and low-capacity service opportunities. High-capacity people throw themselves into demanding activities and will be bored and not challenged with anything less. They can handle a volunteer-service opportunity that perhaps would tax a full-time employee. To retain people in work and in volunteer organizations, they must be matched to service opportunities that are compatible with their capacity and tolerances.

2. *Cooperation Determines Community:* Not many people have the capacity to serve in isolation. They often want to serve in an environment that is characterized by what I call "Triple F (FFF) Synergy," which is one that has people who are "friendly, flexible," and enjoy the "fellowship" of other people. Even though team members separate to complete assignments and tasks alone, they frequently congregate to collectively organize and compile the results. "Fellowship" involves people coming together around a mission who serve in camaraderie by working hard in a cooperative spirit of give and take. They also bond and reminisce about the experiences over coffee and/or meals.

3. *Coordination Determines Accomplishment:* Geese get synergy flying in formation. Teams accomplish synergy when each member cooperates to fulfill his or her role while remaining in formation. By cooperating and flying in a "V" formation, each bird in a flock increases its flying range by at least seventy percent more than if it flew alone. The lead goose has the tough job of breaking wind at the point of a V formation of migrating geese. The movement of each bird's wings creates uplift for those behind it. If one falls from formation, it immediately feels the extra resistance and struggles to get back to the advantage of flying in configuration.

The geese rotate taking the lead position, so that as one tires of breaking wind, it retreats into the back of the wing where the team's lift supports it, while another goose takes on the demanding point position. The geese supported by those in front honk to encourage them to keep up their speed. If a goose gets sick or is wounded and cannot stay with the flock, two geese will follow it out of formation to help and protect it. The trio remains together until either the injured companion dies or is able to resume the journey, at which time they work together in formation to catch up with the flock.

Organizations can gain similar synergies from their teams, but they must work at resolving human-interactive challenges so that the members fully cooperate with one another. People who share a common direction and sense of community can get where they are going quicker and more efficiently if they work together. A team working toward the same goal draws strength and support from one another. As each member takes turns doing the hard jobs and skull sweat, all will make it to the finish line healthier and more whole.

When it is our turn to be the point person, we need and deserve the active support and praise of the team. Love and forgiveness provide the lift for team synergy, and we must stand by each other in times when we each need compassion and understanding. This gives us the ability to "agree to disagree" and continue to work together in formation. By giving each other supportive "honks," we help encourage each other as team members who collectively provide what is needed to accomplish the mission.

Because organizational success is determined by how a collection of individuals behave in a group context, I thought about calling this book *The Three Dimensions of Organizational Behavior.* I felt that by doing so, people who are not in official leadership job titles and roles will see that their individual behavior is an essential component to successful organizational process. Though the appropriate behaviors are simple and uncomplicated to understand, many of us know from firsthand experience how extremely difficult it is to get everyone to practice them to provide the collective strength necessary to achieve organizational goals.

Training people according to the following Thomas-Kilman Conflict Mode Instrument, which can be thought of as a "team-behavioral matrix," can help team members better understand how their behavior impacts others and the work processes they have been brought together to accomplish. When people are in a group or team setting, they tend to respond according to the four behavioral patterns in the matrix below.

Team-Behavioral Matrix

People involved in team and group processes tend to conform to one of these four basic categories of behaviors:

1. Collaborating, Conciliatory, Sharing, and Problem Solving

2. Accommodating, Compromising, and Smoothing

3. Forcing and Competing (controlling)

4. Avoiding, Withdrawing and
   Withholding (passive-aggressive)

The following chart, reproduced from the Thomas-Kilman Conflict Mode Instrument,[36] shows a team member cooperation-participation matrix. The goal for our behavior in team contexts is to function in the high-right behavioral quadrant, where there is a good balance between assertiveness and cooperation.

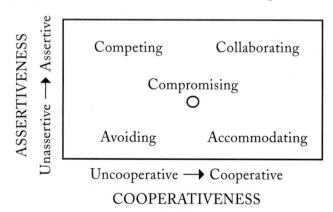

Collaborating, Conciliatory, Sharing, and Problem Solving

The human-interactive dynamics that facilitate appropriate degrees of assertiveness and cooperation to provide for the most productive behavior are displayed on the upper-right quadrant of the matrix. If people are overassertive, aggressive, angry, loud, and forceful, they push away other people who will have a tendency to shut down and withdraw, so their contribution, input, and synergy is lost. Just like a baseball team does not want to lose the input from its shortstop, we should not want to lose the input from any member of a team upon which we participate and lead.

Accommodating, Compromising, and Smoothing

Some people, on the other hand, have an inappropriate aversion to conflict and may fail to share their true feelings and provide their valuable input and withdraw prematurely to avoid what, to them, is an uncomfortable situation. The team and all the processes upon which the team is working suffer as a result. Team members need to be aware of and sensitive to the temperaments of those with whom they work. We should concentrate on being sensitive to others to draw them in by being accommodating and smoothing.

Another challenge for accommodating, compromising, and smoothing people is that they may be willing to purchase peace at a cost that is too high for the team to absorb. For instance, if they allow negative behavior to go on just because they want to avoid conflict, a forceful or dysfunctional person may be allowed to be rude, uncooperative, and divisive, which pushes other people away and thus destroys team synergy and dynamics. Leaders need to have spines to stand up to such people, especially when they are destructive to the people teams whose collaborative input is necessary to accomplish the work at hand.

Forcing and Competing (Controlling)

Being purposely hurtful sends huge negative ripples throughout an organization. It communicates to others that they really cannot trust the leader who allows it or the person perpetrating that behavior. There really is no need for us to be purposely hurtful to other human beings with whom we work and with whom our bosses, coworkers, and stakeholders have the expectation that we will cooperate. Leaders and workers who needlessly have a competitive attitude toward others are those who feel they have to assert themselves as the "est." By that I mean that these people feel they have to be the "best," the "brightest," the "smartest," and the most "knowledgeable." It is not enough for these people to give their input. They feel they must do so at the expense of devaluing anyone else's. To me this is a red flag. The homogeneity that results from only one person's opinion getting to count means that you have allowed a controlling person to suck the synergy out of the process. There will be no benefit realized from the team's diversity.

This behavior really is far worse coming from leaders. Because people have a natural tendency to ingratiate themselves to those in leadership, and, consequently, they easily and readily take on the same negative attitudes about others that the leader exhibits. Three-dimensional members throughout the organization learn that the front office is a place of mean-spirited, backbiting, and sniping personalities, and they increasingly find ways to disassociate themselves from it. Leaders need to be diligent to conduct themselves in a manner that facilitates collaboration, sharing, compromising, and cooperation throughout their organizations. Leaders need to model the behaviors that say, "I respect and value each member of the team because our organization needs our collaborative synergy to be successful."

Avoiding, Withdrawing, and Withholding (Passive-Aggressive)

There is both a positive and negative aspect about people whose tendency is to withdraw. Some people do not need to be pushed away, because their natural inclination is to be shy and hesitant. Instead, they need to be drawn out and encouraged to be full participants. Some people are willing to cooperate but have a natural tendency to hold back until invited to jump in and participate to fully share the load. Some withdrawers are kind and tenderhearted and want to make sure they are not stepping on anyone's toes, so they take a backseat. You must be intentional about drawing them out so the team benefits from their input.

There is a negative type of withdrawing and withholding person, however, who must be dealt with in more dramatic ways—usually by getting him or her off your team. There are some people who are passive-aggressive or who have some sort of personality disorder that makes them withhold, not share, not buy in. Some of these people continually go to the left when the team has decided to go to the right and vice versa. These types of withdrawing people are among the most frustrating to deal with. These are the "can but won't" type of employees. They are capable and sometimes do the work, so you cannot say they totally are incompetent. Passive-aggressive workers may eventually do the work but on their own timetable. This can make it difficult to discipline them without you seeming to be overly fussy. You must document a pattern of such behavior to demonstrate that this person deserves discipline.

Obtaining synergy from a team involves re-inspiring and refocusing people to overcome the challenges that impede them working together smoothly toward mission fulfillment. Those people, however, who systematically demonstrate that they want to force their way, or fail to fully participate, to the detriment of the dynamic team processes, are on a collision course with your team's ability to accomplish its mission. Those who manage the mission are probably going to have to remove those people.

Remember the football team analogy and how people who play various positions approach the game from different psychological perspectives? The different psychological viewpoints that people bring into a team environment can cause misunderstandings in communication and in how team members interpret each other's behaviors. Assisting your team to work through these challenges will help them get to the level of emotional intelligence with each other, so they can go about cooperatively solving problems. The football analogy helps to explain what I mean. For instance, to a running back, "protect the ball" means to wrap an arm and hand around it and press it tightly into the body, so opposing players cannot knock it loose. To an offensive lineman, however, "protect the ball" means to slam into and block or knock down opposing players who are coming to tackle the person who has the ball. The different approaches various types of people take to resolving challenges can cause misunderstandings that can lead to needless conflicts. Wise III-D leaders recognize these challenges as they are developing, and they work to get people to cooperate to focus on the mission and achieve synergy while doing so.

The Forming, Storming, Norming Team Process

Dr. Bruce Wayne Tuckman published one of the most quoted works on team behaviors in 1965, titled *Developmental Sequence in Small Groups.*[37] Dr. Tuckman observed that groups go through a process of forming, storming, and then norming. The leader must work to help the team reach a normal functioning stage. This is achieved by clarifying mission goals during the "forming" part of the process, so people see the vision and will value it to work through the initial hardships that result when they are learning to get along with each other. The leader must help the members work on identifying what impedes their cooperative teamwork during the "storming process" that results when people experience conflicts as they begin misunderstanding each other. The "norming" process involves the team members evolving to where they commit to trusting and relying upon each other to take ownership to collaborate to fulfill the mission. Teams that are operating in the third dimension are those that have normalized relations and defined and rallied around a set of values, goals, and measurements to establish a culture that guides their daily interaction and decisions. Reaching "the third dimension of teamsmanship" involves making the commitment to invest in what it takes to arrive and continue to work at the level of emotional intelligence with each other.

It has been my observation that when a group of people are well focused on a common mission and cooperating to achieve it, each person on the team will see about eighty percent of his or her views and initiatives implemented and moved forward. Because of the various psychological perspectives, people must work through their communication challenges and potential misunderstandings to collaborate with the other team members, so that they approximate the 80/20 postulate, where twenty percent of their ideas are rejected and eighty percent are embraced. The challenge is while people are in the storming process that they don't get so frustrated and angry at each other that they say and do things that cause their relationships to break down before they normalize to work well together in the eighty percent arena.

The mediation process outlined earlier is designed to assist employees to cooperate by bringing down the barriers to them understanding each other. Once they are at the level of emotional intelligence, and they are not being consumed by feeling as if their buttons are being pushed, they have the psychological and emotional capacity to focus and take ownership of the process and follow through to arrive at solutions to solve challenges.

A Case Study that Proves the 80/20 Postulate

Here is how a mediation session resulted in outcomes that were consistent with the 80/20 postulate. One of three employees who had the same job title was to be reassigned to another location. Neither Ms. Y, nor Mr. X, nor Mr. Z wanted the assignment, and a number of the other twenty-seven office personnel formed different factions to support one or two of the three employees, thus establishing "win-lose" dynamics. Because it is possible that, as the organization changes, each of the three employees may be tasked to work together again in the future, making one of them the perceived loser now would injure office relationships and possible working relationships in the future.

Conversations with management, the supervisor, and Mr. X, Ms. Y, and Mr. Z indicated that each of them was performing acceptably. Any of the three employees would do a good job in either location if they, and the offices involved, were free from the stigma that one would "lose" by getting the new assignment and another would "win" by not getting it. I did not needlessly want to cause resentment against our management structure by appearing to come from the "ivory tower" and interfere with a local process to break something that, in the employees' minds, did not need fixing, for there was resentment against management already.

The employees lobbied managers and checked with union reps and our department's personnel and employee-relations offices—all of which are legitimate resource experts that ensure upper managers get their decision right and go about implementing them using appropriate procedures. Office tensions mounted rapidly as all the official parties determined that Mr. X had less seniority and would be forced to make the move.

Local management asked that I do something to alleviate the tension and conflict in the office. I conducted a mediation session as outlined above. The result of the process was that both Mr. X and Ms. Y, with Mr. Z's assistance, arrived at a compromise designed to be a win-win for both of them, their clients in their current office, and the clients in the office to where we wanted one of them to move. They each would go to that office two days per week.

I believe that in any process involving the decision making of team members who are well focused and on a common mission, each will get about eighty percent of what he or she wants. I wanted someone there five days per week. I got someone there for four days per week. That's eighty percent! The two employees worked out an arrangement whereby they each shared responsibility for something they initially did not want to do. Their solution was mission oriented and required a forty percent change in work assignment for each of them. They worked out a win-win for themselves in that they would both get mileage, and they both remained assigned to the original office three days per week, which is where they were emotionally attached. The mileage arrangement cost my organization less than forty dollars per month, which I felt was a small price to pay for the opportunity to keep two employees happy, mission focused, and working from their hearts as opposed to dealing with feelings of resentment toward each other and management for making one of them lose.

The employees arrived at the solution within a week of the intervention. The work arrangement on their terms meant that they both went into the new situation in a better team-oriented frame of mind and emotion than if either perceived that the decision was forced upon them. They gladly fill in for each other when one goes on vacation. I anticipate that one of them will fall in love with the coworkers, managers, and clients in the new office. If that happens, one may decide to be there more days a week.

The situation was so challenging to the employees in the office because it appeared as though someone was going to win and someone was going to lose. Mediating the situation required that I get my emotions out of the way. The employees had been trained well, and the timing of this situation became an opportunity to trust them to demonstrate they were mission focused. I had to invest faith in them and sit back and allow "the process" to be the ultimate arbiter of the outcome. Good processes led to good outcomes. I got an eighty percent favorable outcome—and a win-win situation whereby the employees appeared to be free of the resentment and conflict that prompted the mediation.

Responsible individuals make up responsible teams. Even though we rely upon teams to fulfill missions, we must not lose sight of the fact that teams rely upon collective individual effectiveness. Each employee must handle his/her assignments. Consider how sports teams rely upon individuals to achieve their roles. In baseball, each team member bats individually. Each player, regardless of position, must catch, stop, and throw balls. A football team executes plays by players fulfilling their specific assignments. Team synergy and success is accomplished through the collective individual achievements.

Types of Team Processes

The sports team analogies below can assist your team members to understand how their roles come together in various team processes. The traditional auto industry product-development process is an assembly-line process much like a baseball team functions. In product development, various teams of conscientious individuals fulfill their responsibilities and then successively pass the ball/project to the next team/player in the process. As each team leader collates and completes their part of the project and then passes it on to the next department, the ultimate mission is fulfilled. Designers pass the ball to engineers, who develop the product and its assembly processes, then hand it off to the manufacturing team for mass production. Once the finished product is available, marketing teams begin positioning the product to make it palatable for public consumption.

A basketball team is a cross-functional one that operates in a fast-moving environment, where each player frequently may assume the position of any other player. Unlike baseball teams, where each player remains in a fixed position, basketball players run around and rotate through each other's spot/position. While all the players may rotate around the court and pass through the spaces traditionally occupied by all the other positions, each basketball player has a primary role and assignment.

The taller players—the center and forwards—have the distinct role of getting to the basket to try to get any rebounds. This is actually why they are on the team. The guards tend to be the shorter players who dribble the ball up the court and are adept at shooting from a distance. No one tends to complain, however, if forwards also are good at shooting from a distance, which they often are. No one complains if the guards also pick off a few rebounds. Like a basketball team, business and organizational teams achieve synergy when members are not stuck on job titles but approach projects with a joint, cooperative mind-set to share responsibility for task fulfillment and ultimate team success and mission achievement. For instance, store clerks and fast food workers need to operate by everyone cross-tasking into and out of each other's position on the floor or behind the counter. During busy times and when staffing is short, regardless of job titles, office workers fill in for each other to assist clients.

Teams rely upon individuals to make productive contributions. On any sports team, each player's individual stats are known, studied, and analyzed to determine his or her potential contribution to the team effort. So if you are leading a team, keep in mind that it is what each individual does that determines the team's success.

Mission Determines Team Structure

To assist your teams to obtain synergy, determine if the mission they must fulfill is best achieved if they function like a baseball team, a football team, a basketball team, or like some other analogy not mentioned here. The assembly line-like function of a baseball team, where the ball (product) is thrown from player to player, suits a design and manufacturing mission. If your team must be in a flexible design mode, however, where they constantly are improving existing products, such as computer software, a basketball team model where players interact in a much more interrelated manner may work best to accomplish the mission. The basketball team model is appropriate for teams that must be cross-functionally nimble to make continuous periodic adjustments and improvements.

The football team, because of its sheer size and diversity of roles, is a robust model for organizations that consist of multiple divisions. The linemen make up a department, just as the running backs make up another one. The receivers make up a department that includes the large tight end, the "fleet of foot" wide receiver, and other people who run out to catch passes. The defense can be split into departments that parallel the offense. The defense also has a department of linemen and a department of linebackers, and then there are the defensive backs who are interceptors of the passes meant for the offensive receivers. Like in football, the members from the various departments of a corporation "huddle" to get instructions and assignments to fulfill short-term missions (called plays in football). For work processes to be achieved, the members of the various departments must function in unison. All of them must be out on the field fulfilling their roles and responsibilities.

Team-Resource Makeup Determines Coaching Style

Sometimes a leader must adapt his/her style to obtain synergy from team resources. New York Giants Coach Tom Coughlin, who won Super Bowl XLII, demonstrated the effectiveness of this. Coughlin, who was sixty-one during the 2007 season, has continued to grow and change to appropriately negotiate the context of his mission. Tom Coughlin has changed his style of leading and coaching. Previously, he was inflexible about his rules. As the 2007 pro football season was getting under way, defensive lineman Michael Strahan did not show up for the Giants training camp. In years past, a Coughlin player would be cut from the team for this behavior, but Strahan was accepted back. The team wanted him back. In years past, Coach Coughlin would not have considered what was going on within a player's head and heart that might contribute to him not being at camp. Things were black and white, cut and dry; if you did not do what the coach wanted when he wanted it, you were done.

Coughlin had always been a winner. He proved that at Boston College and had taken the AFC Jaguars to the playoffs prior to coming to lead the Giants. Coach Coughlin, however, adjusted his leadership style to suit the times and the mix of the personalities of the player resources he had. Reconciling with Strahan was good for the New York Giants. It was good for the other players, and it was good for the team's fans. Changing was not easy for Tom, who says he has had to learn to bite his tongue in order to build relationships with his players. Prior to the change, Coughlin was known to fine players for not adhering to rules regarding pregame dress codes. Changing, however, allowed the coach and the players to come together in the true spirit of what it means to collaborate as team members.

The three-dimensional Tom Coughlin says that winning the right way involves putting human relationships into the professional aspects of the mission of football. Tom realizes that his players want to win; they want to do things well on the field. The coach has arrived to understand how to win with the mix of player resources he has, and the players appreciate him for this. The words "respect" and "love" between players and coach is not uncommon to hear when the New York Giants coaches and players speak about each other.

Love is what unites people who come together to work hard to accomplish something great and achieve a mission, like win a sports game or championship, or to accomplish business success and provide decent paychecks for lots of people to feed, clothe, and house their families. Great teams are able to commit to each other and work through their challenges. First, they will work through their interpersonal challenges, and then they present a united front to the world to conquer the mission at hand. Such a united front is hard to stop. In the Iliad, Homer said, "There is strength in the union even of very sorry men."

Leaders most likely only will get team members to rise to the level of commitment necessary to achieve a great cause by elevating that mission in importance and significance in their minds and hearts. The cause must be elevated in the minds of employees so they have a reason to invest in the hard work of establishing good working relations with those whom they are tasked to collaborate.

Another excellent model and analogy for team forming,

development, growth, and collaboration is a musical band. The different musicians represent a cross-functional team that comes together to rally around the common goal of performing songs. The various musicians also approach the same song from the varying perspectives of their instruments' sound dynamics and capabilities and the parts they play and sing, much like how people from the finance, human resources, marketing, and operations departments bring different perspectives to the same body of information. Music is produced through the process of the musicians learning how to rehearse together in ways that facilitate effective collaboration and cooperation. The musicians collaborate to decide who is going to take the lead and who is going to provide filler parts and grace notes during various parts of the song. All band members must cooperate to achieve the mission of producing great music.

As a musician and songwriter, I have had the privilege of seeing new groups of musicians come together as new teams to form into some dynamic bands whose mission is to collaborate to create an original sound. The most dynamic band I have had to date is called Earl Wallace and The Flood. It took two years to find, audition, and assimilate the right group of musicians into what became known as The Flood. When we first came together, we all brought our backgrounds of the various types of music we had played in the past. The past, however, threatened to shape the ideas that musicians had of what we would sound like in the future. When a musician would hear a song and say, "This is cool! Let's make it sound like … " and they would name a well-known band or song, I would say, "That indeed is great music, but why don't we make our own great music and not try to become a copy of what someone else has done?" The key for me was to get musicians to break with trying to sound like something they had heard or which was familiar to them in the past.

Once musicians understood I was trying to get them to create an original sound, they would ask, "Well, what is that going to sound like?" I would be honest with them and say, "I am not quite sure, but when we get there, we certainly will hear and feel that we are getting it right. Our musical mission is to arrive at a marriage between melody and message. Our mission is to tell some very neat stories with music that accentuates, supports, and conveys the meaning of the lyrics." We eventually settled into a style of music I called "rhythm 'n' roll"—a blend of rhythm and blues and rock and roll.

After two years of forming and two more years of evolving (only rehearsing one night a week), we arrived at our musical destination. The stylings of the core musicians comprised the group sound. Once we knew who we were musically, we could recruit other musicians who were compatible with our newfound sound. We eventually cut a CD of nine original songs entitled "The Finished Work," after the song that became the inspiration for the title of the work.

There was more to our mission, however, than just music. As part-time musicians who had full-time careers and businesses, we set out on a mission to play good music without neglecting our families or burning ourselves out by trying to take on too much. I developed a motto to which I could rally the members and obtain the support of their spouses and children: *Families First and Music Too.* This motto captured our value system, which led us to hold one rehearsal a week (on average) and to play one concert a month (usually). We would schedule concerts as much as eight months in advance, so there were no surprises to spring on our families. This helped us be good moms and dads and get to our children's school, sports, and our other family activities. We would play only one concert a month or a series of concerts over one weekend a month, and thus we would be responsible employees, managers, and business owners.

Chapter Twenty-six

Leading Change

In *The Seven Habits of Highly Successful People,* Stephen R. Covey says there is a difference between managing and leading. Managing ensures that people are engaged in the activities that get them to climb the ladder of operational achievement and corporate success. Leadership ensures that "the ladder is leaning against the right wall" in the first place.

For people to work within a mission-oriented framework, they need to know that this ladder is leaned against this wall for these particular reasons. Thus they get to see the larger context of the overall mission purpose to which they are contributing each day on the job. This helps people to buy in and more fully cooperate as effective organizational members. It helps them to understand why the operation is set up the way it is and why a particular set of values is conducive to providing products and services effectively. Thus they not only understand why the ladder is leaning against a particular wall, but also why it has not been leaned against a different wall.

If you know why climbing the other walls is not essential to mission fulfillment, you more readily discern which ideas, values, and activities are important, and you can avoid wasting time pursuing those that are not. It is this understanding that separates the mission oriented from those who are distracted by numerous, seemingly good ideas that come along each day but which are not conducive to mission fulfillment. Part of a good manager's and leader's learning curve is to siphon through all those "good ideas" to determine which ones are best for accomplishing the mission given the operational environment or context in which they work.

Three-dimensional leaders have people coming to work who are directed to activities that help them to achieve collectively what the corporation needs. They avoid pursing initiatives that do not actually support their core mission. III-D leaders discern and avoid those initiatives that, on the surface, look like they are part of the core mission but, in actuality, really are not. III-D leaders know which initiatives waste time and suck attention span, functional capacity, and resources into a vacuum from which no positive production, service, or mission-related outcome can emerge.

Understanding why the ladders are leaned against certain walls helps employees to understand the arena and paradigm in which they work to achieve their mission. Thus the people resources can use their individual ingenuity to reach their individual potential for achievement to accomplish collective greatness for the organization. The understanding of the larger context empowers them as team members. They know why the team exists, what it is to accomplish, and how to do the work within the organization's larger framework given particular sets of circumstances.

Rallying Resources to Change Requires the Right Motivation, Map, and Message

Rallying resources to wholeheartedly participate in change initiatives requires leaders to have and present the right motivation, map, and message. To rally people to a mission involving significant change, you first must make sure that you have the right change initiatives that actually will lead to the desired outcome. Don't act upon presuppositions. If you set out to solve a problem by using false premises, you will not solve the problem, and you will appear foolish in the eyes of your employees. You only will end up with style-preference changes, such as the wording of slogans and the colors of posters, which will not address the root of the matter or the heart of the issue, which is adjusting operations to actually impact how a mission is fulfilled. If you set out based on ill-targeted assumptions, more tragically, you will not meet your customers' needs nor satisfy your employees' expectations that you are there to help them meet their clients' and customers' needs.

Mission-Motivated Messages

The right motivation means that you actually are implementing a change that really is directed toward accomplishing the mission. Remember, great leadership negotiates a set of circumstances that are favorable for employees to succeed at their jobs. Don't go hunting down a trail that is detached from or does not lead to better employee job performance or organizational success. Your motive must be connected to how your organization will accomplish its core missions. Your motivational focus must be on your customers and how your employees interact with them. This is especially true for government and service organizations. Product manufacturers must be motivated to focus on what customers are willing to purchase and what your employees do that delivers it.

The right map means that you are analyzing the right data that gives you enough information about the performance of your organization, so you can determine down what paths it has gone, where the synergy is, where it is being lost, what is falling short, what is succeeding, and what direction must be taken to bridge the gap between failing performance initiatives and mission accomplishment. The goal of your data analysis is to help you define a process map that helps your employees walk down the path to their organizational job success.

The right message means that you must present your findings and explain your initiatives in language and terms that are compatible with the organization's culture. You do not want to sound like an alien who has just landed from another planet by

THE THREE-DIMENSIONAL LEADER

using language that says, "I am the new leader, and this is the new foreign culture. Everyone has to adjust to me." You do not want to communicate to employees that you have not taken the time, or that you do not care enough, to understand the culture of their work environment. Doing so alienates them and fails to achieve their buy-in, or it causes them to ignore you. People must know how much you care before they will care about how much you know. Taking care to demonstrate that you understand and appreciate the employees' perspective by addressing them in terms that show you comprehend and relate to their work culture is essential to earning credibility.

Change must be carried out in appropriate language and terms that the team understands. When a quarterback is traded to a new football team, he cannot expect to call out plays using language from his old team environment. The quarterback has to learn the new team's offensive system. Because the context always is changing, leaders often must make adjustments, but they must do so using the team's appropriate language and terms.

In a football game, if it is third and long, in the huddle the quarterback calls a pass play that requires all the ends and backs to go out as receivers. When the QB is on the line of scrimmage, however, the middle linebacker calls the defense into a blitz formation, which moves an additional man up to the line, so now there is one more defensive rusher than there are offensive blockers. To fulfill its mission the offense must make an adjustment in its play calling. So the QB calls an audible that brings one of the ends in to block the extra defensive player who has moved up to the line. The audible signals only are effective if everyone understands them. Each team has its own audible signal language. As a wise quarterback, you must learn and call out the audible signals in terms that are appropriate for each team you lead.

There is much talk today about leaders "finding and expressing their own voices." The challenge with many leaders is they believe that because they are in the leadership role, whatever crazy thing comes out of their mouths is worth hearing. Leaders need to express what resonates with employees in terms of mission fulfillment and context negotiation. I once heard a leader trying to inspire an audience of employees by telling a story of how he tied a rubber chicken around his leg and walked through an office to see if anyone was paying attention, and he said that no one noticed. Later I heard other employees asking, "So what does wearing a chicken around your ankle have to do with us working more effectively? Why would I want to pay attention to or acknowledge something like that?" The leader had a loud and clear voice, but the message was not resonating with and making sense to the employees. Unlike the quarterback above, his audible signals were not getting the team to appropriately adjust to what they felt they were facing. Many team members did not even think he was calling the right plays for the game they were in. They felt the message revealed that the leader did not have a clear grasp of how to fulfill the mission.

Appropriate Data and Analysis
Maps the Mission Pathway

Changes within organizations need to be undertaken from an organizational inner-contextual perspective. Initiatives that change the way employees work require not only training workers, supervisors, and managers, but also requires integration of the finance, management information systems (MIS), and research and statistics departments that ensure transactions are recorded, captured, and reported out in ways that are useful for the organization to map and track trends. Data consistency helps give leaders the opportunity to see outcomes as clearly as possible. Data interpretation consistency also is important. We must be careful not to implement the recording and reporting of data to answer particular questions and then later use it to try to answer different questions. Of course, there are times when, after reviewing requested data, we realize that we did not ask enough questions or the specific questions we need answered. In those cases we realize that understanding our business, and services, and what we are tasked to manage can be somewhat of an evolutionary process, and we have to work with our MIS data-production branches and teams to tweak what we capture and report.

While people may tend to get frustrated with working and then re-working to get to the right data, if members throughout the organization realize that we have the right motivation, map, and message, they will feel we actually are making progress in understanding the employee and customer transactions and the dynamics that drive our businesses, and everyone will feel there is forward progress. Computer technology is making data capturing and reporting processes less cumbersome, but it still is a lot of work for programmers and coders to accomplish these things. Leaders need to work with a broad spectrum of knowledgeable people throughout an organization to ensure that they request what the organization really needs. This may reduce the learning curve and the evolutionary data request and analysis processes.

Change Requires Learning, and Learning Is Stressful

Change is stressful because learning is stressful. My theory is that what one-dimensional leaders don't understand, they fear, and whatever they fear, they try to ignore or kill. Three-dimensional leaders are not change averse because they see the ten-thousand-foot view of the context and why the adjustments are necessary to achieve desired outcomes, given the emerging or new environment. Change is tough on us all because it requires work and learning, or skull sweat, to obtain and digest new information and respond to it appropriately. Learning is stressful because it involves processing new and unfamiliar material; it requires assimilation of information that may not be similar in format, structure, or in computer software that is familiar to us.

Few of us like being in situations that make us feel uncomfortable—like we are the proverbial "fish out of water." Learning is like that. To learn often requires us to leave the comfort zone of the pond we are familiar swimming in to cross over unfamiliar territory to get into the next body of water. To stretch my analogy a bit further, since fish don't have legs, we can feel like we're flopping around over the information and context until we make progress in understanding and negotiating them to feel like we are swimming comfortably again. We tend not to like change, because it is fraught with uncertainty. It is emotionally and psychologically painful for us to change.

It is often the leader's responsibility, nonetheless, to get an organization to change not necessarily what it does, but how it does it. Often organizations do not need to change their missions to remain competitive. They do, however, have to do it with different technology that provides the means to accomplish the processes of manufacturing or service delivery. If manufacturing, the workers have to learn to operate new machines and equipment. If service delivery, the workers have to learn to operate new computer-information processing systems.

Generally, people do not change willingly. They change only when the pain of staying the same is perceived to be greater than the pain of changing. Pain can be red ink that stems from dissatisfied customers, decreased sales, loss of market share, and inefficient operations that fail to provide products at competitive prices or deliver them in timely and cost-efficient ways. Pain can be high employee turnover, so synergy is never obtained from ranks of experienced people, resulting in institutional memory loss. The organization begins to act like a stroke victim who cannot remember many functional activities and processes. If companies do not respond to these pain messages that should be sending signals to their headquarters' central nervous systems, they will fail to obtain adequate funding that is the air and blood supply that keeps the organization alive.

Leading Change by Achieving a Balanced Inside-Outside Approach

Leadership or consultation that comes from outside an organization can provide some insights about how to operate within a context that those in the proverbial "forest" cannot see because they are blinded by the trees of the challenges immediately before them. One must get above the forest—of daily pressures and "the way we always have done things"—to be able to think out of the box and make new connections between seemingly disparate pieces of information within the context to achieve new synergies. While an "astute outsider" may be able to recognize opportunities for change, he or she needs to rely upon "astute insiders" for strategic process implementation to go about the changes in a way that makes the most sense to people within the organization.

Wise leaders must be humble enough to learn from those within the organization with whom they must partner to accomplish job changes. It is extremely important that new leaders go around their learning curves gracefully. The appropriate process for accomplishing change is that the leader must get others to see what must be done, and then he or she must listen to the experienced employees about how to go about it. The leader may compel some changes, but buy-in is necessary for employees to own the changes and franchise them throughout each department and to successive generations of the organization. If followers shut down, the leader will lose the valuable input they can provide that ensures the long-term success of new initiatives.

To find a starting point for change, realize that within failing and struggling organizations there are people and possibly whole units that are achieving at a very high level or rate. Identify them and conduct fact-finding interviews to raise the hood of the organizational vehicle to determine why their engines are running smoothly down the roadway to success when others are stalled and failing to do so. You also should identify and interview those who are not achieving as highly, or who are failing in performance, to determine if the various units' success and/ or failures are rooted in personality or some unusually high level of individual effort and personal achievement, or a lack of basic motivation, or if it is related to leadership, job design, or process issues. You are looking for elements of those operations that can be replicated and transported to other sections of the organization. If you identify what contributes to failure, you can work to change or eliminate its occurrence in other places throughout the organization.

Three-dimensional leaders will identify what contributes to success and will try to "bottle it" to mix it into the organizational strategy. III-D's will keep those success factors in mind and will make sure that each little decision is consistent with the identified strategy that ultimately drives organizational success. If the organization is in disrepair, perhaps it needs a deep values overhaul to redefine and put some heart and soul into its mission, and/or it must restructure and reorganize its resources to strategically redeploy them in the context to fuel long-term success.

Getting others to change requires people skills, which are summed up in the Golden Rule, in Matthew 7:12, "So in everything, do to others what you would have them do to you."[38] Treat people like you want to be treated. Do not think that because you are a leader you are on a higher plane than others and can treat them any differently than you treat your boss if you want his/her collaboration. If you want similar heartfelt teamwork from your employees, treat them as if what is in their hearts is important to you.

I once put together a performance plan for an organization that was marginally performing. Of its eighty people, five or six were identified as achieving superior results, while most achieved what was adequate, and a dozen definitely were underperforming. We identified what those super-achieving people were doing, which included the number of clients they serviced, what services they actually provided them, and the number of services on average they provided each client. I bottled that formula and then made a three-tier client service-achievement model to motivate employees to reach for goals. The rates of services and performance outcomes from the top achievers were identified as the top tier. I extrapolated from those figures to create a middle tier and a bottom or minimum tier of performance. Scalable incentives were designed to encourage employees to reach for achieving the next higher tier of performance. We designed and rolled out training modules to show employees what we discovered about their performance; how we modeled their best processes to construct the performance model; and how readily accessible to them was the performance that would get us to achieve our organizational goals. Within three quarters we hit our targets, and by two quarters later, we were exceeding them by ten to fifteen percent in most categories!

Negotiating the Risk of Change

Bill Hybels, in his book *Courageous Leadership,* talks about handling downside risks, which have tremendous potential for upside gains. Hybels notes,

> There are all kinds of risk takers. On one end of the spectrum are the extravagant risk takers, who bet the farm repeatedly. They usually end up losing the farm. At the other extreme are leaders who are risk adverse. They wouldn't take a risk if their lives depended on it. My dad was not like either of these extremes. He provided steady, consistent oversight of his core businesses, but he wasn't opposed to taking an occasional risk. He used to say ... if you don't take a flyer once in a while, you'll never learn anything new, and life will get very boring.

> When pilots take a new aircraft for a test flight, they are taking a flyer. My dad believed in flyers, and he took his share. He tested new ideas in business, and experimented with new strategies, and tried new products. He took a certain number of risks with people and with investments. Some flyers worked out well for him and paid off handsomely. Others crashed and burned and he paid dearly. But when a crash occurred, he would tell me about the lessons he'd learned and about the joy he had during the adventure. "It's only money," he'd say. "It's not the end of the world."

> It didn't faze him a bit if people rolled their eyes at one of his long shots. He seemed almost impervious to naysayers. When

people told him he was nuts for considering some new venture or flyer, he would just smile broadly and reply from some secure interior place, "You're probably right. We're going to find out in a few months, aren't we?" But he never let the approval ratings of his peers affect his risk-assessment capability. He was neither a careless risk-taker, nor was he risk-averse. He just believed that a calculated flyer here and there would keep him on the cutting edge of growth.[39]

Progress often requires taking risks. If we don't take the risk—especially in the areas that require us to venture out to where we have not been before, progress is unlikely to occur. Leaders need to take a certain amount of risks with people and investments. Even when they don't turn out well, sometimes the lessons we gain from the experience is the learning process upon which future success is launched.

There is always the risk of possible failure from any change or new venture. Hybels' Willow Creek Church took a risk on a ministry branch to Generation-X, ages eighteen through twenty-eight. Today there are about two thousand people in that ministry. A few years ago the church ventured into a $70 million building project. They had $20 million in cash but took a risk and did obtain the other $50 million needed. Hybels recommends that when your organization is facing a new challenge that you review its list of advisers and mentors to determine if you need to raise or lower their risk profile to address the issues at hand.

Remember, the formula to get people into a mode that is more acceptable to change includes getting them to see the options that are open to them. You have to inspire them to have the confidence that they can learn what needs to be learned to overcome what needs to be overcome. The leaders must have a broad view of the context in which the mission unfolds, and they must have knowledge or be able to obtain enough information about the context to determine the process steps to take to get to the new operational state and outcomes that change is supposed to achieve.

Since "mission matters most," leaders need to express themselves to employees in terms that make the most sense to them as they go about fulfilling it. Leaders should use language that is consistent with the cultural context in which the organization operates. It matters what you say and how you say it to be aligned with the internal context that will make the most sense to employees. If you are rolling out a change program, show its relationship to the performance goals or customer-service goals or operational context that provides the most synergy for people to work well together to achieve the company's mission. Your employees have to implement the changes, so they need to fully comprehend why the organization needs them to go through what it takes to make the adjustments successfully. When you demonstrate that you have the right motivation, map, and message, you will gain credibility with subordinates and not come across as the "new person" or "hack outsider" who does not understand the organization's institutional historical context and mission and how it must unfold within the community, industry, and market context.

Part Four

Negotiating the Context

Chapter Twenty-seven

Converting within the Context

Leadership is negotiating to arrange and organize a set of circumstances that are favorable for employees to succeed at their jobs. This cannot be accomplished unless you understand three things: the organization's mission, the context in which it unfolds, and what job roles and responsibilities your employees should perform within it. Understanding the context of your unit and organization is what separates three-dimensional leaders from the others. III-D's "convert within the context." To be successful ultimately means that you understand your mission, the resources available to accomplish it, and that you deploy those resources within a changing context in such a way that they continually function to fulfill the mission.

The *context* is the arena, the paradigm, the social and economic environments, the culture and its rise and fall of fads, and its taboos, trends. The context includes the competition, market cycles, available and emerging technologies. The context consists of the factors that contribute to the costs of doing business, including supply-chain dynamics, procurement procedures, budgets, interest rates, inflationary and deflationary factors, union and civil service rules, other workplace policies and company guidelines, current and proposed laws and government policies and regulations. The context involves the political landscape that may cause other government policies to emerge or change. The context is what makes up the environment in which your resources are deployed to fulfill the mission. The context is the circumstance, the situation, the background, the past relevant history, current laws, social norms, emerging developments, and the operational framework in which the mission-work must unfold. How consumers respond to your products and your competitors' products also make up a context in which your resources must be deployed and positioned to fulfill your organization's mission. The context has to be negotiated to overcome every challenge to accomplish the mission.

As we saw with the football analogy, the context can be the physical environment, landscape, and the weather when the mission calls for humans to exert energy on a sports field in varying climates. Earth's physical environment is a context to negotiate when one considers energy policies designed to address the challenges to harness the wind, solar power, and other renewable resources. Natural phenomenon such as earthquakes, hurricanes, tornados, drought, floods, and volcanic eruptions are considered disasters based upon the degree to which they disrupt human activity, such as commerce. These factors are a context to negotiate when determining how to fulfill a mission.

All organizations have both an internal and an external context. Both contexts have to be understood and negotiated to overcome every challenge to accomplish the mission. The various players and personalities in the finance unit or the engineering department and those on a project team all are contexts that must be negotiated successfully to achieve a mission. Negotiating the context ultimately means networking with the relationships, the other people in the arena in which your mission unfolds. These include those in your organization and those in external organizations with whom your organization must coordinate.

The external context comprises the immediate and the remote or extended environmental phenomenon and circumstances in which the mission must unfold. The immediate external context comprises the local community wherein the business or organization is located and from where the workforce most likely is to come. The local community is from where the most damaging criticism can start that can have the most far-reaching negative impact on the company. Companies do well over the long term when they keep their immediate backyards clean and pollution and scandal free.

Suppliers are part of an organization's context, and the company's relationship and dependency upon them determines whether they should be viewed as part of the internal or external operation. A few years back an earthquake in Indonesia damaged an Intel chip-fabrication factory, the result of which was stalled production for those who relied upon supplies of those chips. That plant was a close partner for information-technology manufacturers. Auto manufacturers also have close relationships with parts manufacturers and suppliers. From conglomerate to small contract manufacturers and local machine shops, networks of relationships are forged into partnerships that provide the synergies that make businesses successful.

Negotiating the extended external context can provide you with a perspective to develop your business across regional, national, and international boundaries. Because the laws that impact raw materials procurement and product distribution and use vary from one location to another, you will need local professional knowledge to arrange circumstances favorable for your business operations.

To understand and negotiate your operational context, you must get an objective ten thousand-foot view of the extended operational paradigm in which your employees, partners, and contractors must work to achieve the mission. The resources must be deployed strategically to "convert within the larger context" that can include suppliers, partners, and consultants. This requires leaders to negotiate with those parties to achieve win-wins, so the larger network of associations benefits from arrangements that are favorable to both their employees and yours succeeding at their jobs. Thus every operation concerned wins by fulfilling the joint mission.

Negotiation Nexus

To negotiate is to interact with others to reach agreed-upon courses of action. Negotiation is not manipulation. It is bargaining, consulting, and discussing to reach settlements where mutual, collective advantage or outcomes occur that satisfy the various interests represented. Negotiation is a continuous process that parties must engage and reengage in as the context changes. A change in context requires renegotiation to arrive at or maintain the circumstances that facilitate mutual organizational success.

The opportunity for negotiation occurs when two or more parties have missions that converge in such a way that requires their agreement, cooperation, or participation to be successful. The goal of negotiation is to keep the mutual agendas and missions moving forward in a win-win manner, thus ensuring they do not collide.

The basis for negotiation is for parties and the people who represent them to at least be willing to see each other's viewpoints. Negotiation only can be effective with people who think as we think and who feel like we feel. This does not mean that only homogeneous clones can arrive at harmonious accords. Satisfactory outcomes from negotiations require that there is agreement of basic terminology, which demonstrates that diverse perspectives are willing to organize around an agreed-upon set of distinctions, parameters, and values. The people at the table must have an agreed-upon common understanding of the terms and issues that are being parleyed. This means that when they say the word "deficit," or "blue," or "truth," they are talking about the same thing. Thus you have the basis for win-win. When one party misunderstands what the other means, the potential increases for win-lose. Effective, long-lasting outcomes from negotiation occur when both parties obtain wins.

When people from varying viewpoints come together to discuss an issue of mutual interest and concern, the potential "storming" that can occur must be managed tactfully, so the participants relax enough to work through any initial misunderstandings, perceived insults, and threats so they can move on to be the high-right-quadrant participants on the "Team Behavioral Matrix." While the negotiations are underway, the worst thing that can happen is for people to put their marbles in their pocket and withdraw from the process, although temporary breaks may be necessary to ease tensions so that later cooler heads can prevail. Sometimes temporary breaks are advisable to give the negotiating parties the opportunity to digest information divulged, learned, and received during a negotiation.

The "Team Behavioral Matrix" provides a template for what is required for effective negotiation to take place. If when negotiating, one party or more is overly forceful, an agreement may be struck, but if one party feels forced into it, or feels he was not fully heard, or feels he was run over or through when trying to express resistance, before he leaves the room and the door quits swinging shut he is working on ways to break the agreement or resist its initiatives.

Sometimes the ideas or initiatives actually are good, but if those involved in the processes, however, feel they were not afforded the appropriate time to take the information back to their organizations to determine how the initiative can be implemented in a way that works best for them, they will feel forced into the decision. In such cases, the right thing implemented in the wrong ways and at the wrong times become the wrong thing for them.

Negotiating with Vampires, Real or Delusional

People who are manipulative, self-centered, and self-aggrandizing only see initiatives from their own one-dimensional perspective. They may think they are being proactive movers and shakers when they violate the integrity of other people or organizations in the context by conniving, making side deals, and forcing pacts on others. In reality, however, they are poor negotiators of the context. Proverbs 15:22 says, "Plans fail for lack of counsel, but with many advisers they succeed." When manipulators make side deals that rope other parties into agreements they are uncomfortable with, the initiatives are pushed forward without the full benefit of the input of all the other units and organizations whose wholehearted participation would guarantee long-term success.

Remember the three types of vampires? Vampires include people who act naïvely about the negative impact their behavior has when they turn what should be negotiable processes into manipulative campaigns of backroom deals that steamroll others into settlements that are bad for them. When you reach out to vampires, whether they are real or delusional, and explain the negative impact their behavior is having, they say, "Well, I do not mean it that way," and they do not change their behavior. Regardless if the vampires are in denial about being so or are intentional about and/or proud of their deceptive, life-sucking behavior, the end results are the same. Vampires rope people into deals that they feel are inappropriate for them and their organizations.

The people who are being overly forceful are demonstrating that they do not have the ability to think as the others think and feel like the others feel. Many bad feelings and consequent strained and fractured relationships result from forceful behavior by a participant who, for some reason, feels he or she has the mandate to be a dictator instead of a negotiator. Effective negotiation gives people appropriate time to digest and respond in their own way to the information presented. Forcing an issue can cause a passive-aggressive response. Compelling others to go along with your initiatives may get slight nods and lip service, but it rankles the soul and pushes the heart far away, and true collaboration will not be forthcoming. Rather than completely ruining relationships, it is better to agree to disagree, while engaging in fair, open, and honest processes.

The Three-Legged Stool of Understanding

I have a theory about how people absorb, understand, and internalize new information. I call it the three-legged stool of understanding. I once told a lobbyist whose customers included Lockheed Martin that I believe that on average people must hear new information three times before they fully assimilate it and act upon it appropriately. What often is required is that they also hear it from three different perspectives. He said he has the same concept and also calls it the "three-legged stool of understanding." He said that when he is lobbying for a particular outcome, he believes that he must explain the data, the circumstances, and the issues from the perspective of the union workforce, the corporations, or employers involved and also from the perspective of the senate and congressional legislatures who are looking out for the interest of the people, which includes constituents, workers, and employers. Incidentally, viewing issues from all these perspectives generally helps one to arrive at a position where at least everybody wins something.

Each branch of information, and/or the perspective from which it must be viewed, is like a leg of the stool. Experience has led me to see that people tend to have a negative or knee-jerk reaction when they are confronted with new information for the first time. I know that it sounds redundant to say that people hear new information for the first time, because if it is "new" it also is "first," but there is a difference between hearing and understanding. What tends to happen when new information is presented, people often try to figure out how to reject it, as their own presuppositions compel them to challenge it. When people hear new information for the first time, it feels uncomfortable to them, as if they are sitting on a one-legged stool. When the stool tips over and they fall off, because the information does not satisfy or work for them, they tend to attack the person who sat them on that stool. They attack the person who is providing the information. Proverbially, they shoot the messenger.

When people hear new information for the second time, it

still feels uncomfortable to them, as if they are sitting on a two-legged stool. It is still very challenging for them to balance on that stool, and it too does tip over—just not as vigorously as did the one-legged stool. When the two-legged stool tips over, however, the people attack the information. They pick up the stool to examine why it fell over. They snatch papers from the one delivering the information, and they say, "Give me that! I don't believe that! I am going to research that, and you'll see that I am right!" As they interact with the information, they actually are engaging in the process that builds the third leg of the stool.

I have been in meetings where my leadership team and I have had to deliver some pretty challenging news to employees, and when we are at stage two and people storm out of the room, attacking the information, I generally have other subordinates saying, "Don't let them talk to us like that and leave that way." I respond, "No, let them go. It is the information they are attacking, not us. They now are going to do some research and interact with the same information that led us to the conclusions we presented to them. The first time we heard the information, we did not like it either. We've interacted with the information several times before we accepted the conclusions and took appropriate action. Now let's give them time to get through the same knee-jerk reactions we experienced."

By the way, if you have credibility with people and they trust that you have their best interest at heart, they immediately will move to stage two and will not attack you for delivering the new information.

The third time people hear the new information, they are much more comfortable with it, as if they are sitting on a three-legged stool. The information now is "actionable" for them. They are now poised and capable of taking appropriate action in relation to the information.

People who have learned how to learn are aware of this three-tiered information reception tendency, and so they develop techniques to try to objectively assimilate new information to get on a three-legged stool as quickly as possible.

One- and two-dimensional leaders fail to build three-legged stools of understanding because they often are afraid to provide information they anticipate others will react to negatively. They may lack the people skills to negotiate the initial emotional responses, or they may feel so uncomfortable with conflict that they want to avoid its potential and so put off sharing information. I anticipate the negative reaction to new information and so have learned not to take it personally. What I do know is that if three months from now I have to act upon an unfolding situation, I am going to try to prepare you well in advance for the change by giving you as much of the new information that is appropriate as far in advance as possible. This allows people to get over their knee jerk early in the process, which allows time for them to build the capacity to act appropriately as the contextual deadlines approach.

Using the three-legged stool concept provides the most humane approach to dealing with employees. It best enables them to appropriately absorb information and act upon it. Because employees tend to be emotionally attached to the physical location where they work, it is better to tell them as far in advance as possible (at least three months) of any potential office move. During the first conversation where the move is presented, people tend to get very upset and may even say some things that perhaps should not be said to or about management. People may even suggest that the messenger *"stick the information in a place where the sun does not shine,* leave the office immediately, and never return." My experience has been, however, that usually no longer than a day to a week of that initial conversation, and sometimes on my cell phone within ten to twenty minutes of leaving, the employees have picked up themselves from falling off the one-legged stool and have assimilated the information and are ready to talk about it in a more rational way.

The employee usually calls me and apologizes for the knee-jerk reaction. Sometimes he or she will explain all the reasons why what I have suggested is a terrible idea, and why no one in their right mind would inflict such a decision upon good, hard-working employees whose clients are accustomed to this particular office location. I may find out that the employee's family situation requires that he or she work within proximity to child-care, a sick parent who requires attention during the employee's lunchtime, or any other multiple sets of issues that the employee feels requires his or her presence at the current physical office location.

The second conversation actually is where we build the second leg of the stool of understanding, upon which both the employer and employee must sit to arrive at a win-win solution. I might say something to the employee like, "Have you spoken to your wife about what I said?" Sometimes the employee will say, "No, I do not want to upset her about a possible move." I usually say something like, "Well, what does it look and feel like for you and your family to make this change?" During the second phase, I do not try to give or suggest answers. I just try to nudge the employee to consider speaking to all the parties involved, including his or her family, and I invite the employee to participate in the process of advising our local partner organizations about the possibility of what will take place.

The third leg of the stool of understanding and cooperation gets built when the employee says to me, "Well, this move can work if we do it this way..." Sometimes "this way" means that the employee requests that certain things be done on a particular two days a week as opposed to the days that I have suggested. In these cases the employee has very good mission-essential reasons why something should happen on a particular day versus another. The employee knows the local environment and context and why one day is better than another for particular functions or processes to take place. Sometimes the employee will say, "This can work if we do it during a particular month as opposed to another month, for various reasons."

It is important to realize that there are many ways to go about achieving a work-related mission, while giving as much attention as possible to an employee's family situation. This is why employers offer family health insurance plans. In exchange for an employee handling the work-related mission, the employer provides a quid pro quo that includes salary and family health coverage. As an employer, when I make a move or a change work for the employee's family, I am contributing to that employee's long-term loyalty and job satisfaction, because the happier family means I have a happier employee who is going to be more loyal to the company and be a more cooperative office teammate.

I once worked for one-dimensional bosses who forbade me to say anything to employees about office moves until we were two weeks from the scheduled change. Their reason was that this would give the employee less time to resist it. At one point I told them, "You are making a coward out of me by requiring me to tell employees on Friday that their offices are being moved two Mondays from now." This does not give them time to assimilate the information appropriately, nor properly arrange childcare issues, how they will continue getting their kids to and from school, and extracurricular activities.

I also often was taken by surprise because the bosses presented the information to me as if it were going to happen sometime in the distant future. They forbade me to talk to employees about what possibly cold transpire and would say, "Don't tell them yet and upset them needlessly, as we are not sure yet when the move will take place and to where the office will be relocated." What I subsequently found out, however, was that these bosses, these "men without chests," already knew the exact date and the details but were too cowardly to want to deal with the knee-jerk first response employees would have to the information.

One move was handled in an exceptionally poor manner. An employee was to move across town to an office in a facility that a partner organization was renovating. Our bosses kept the move so secretive from people who were overseeing the local context that they terminated the lease and shut down the employee's office two weeks before the partner organization had completed the renovation of the new location. The employee received a phone call from our central headquarters on Friday that he was to report across town to the new location the following Monday. When he reported to the new location, members of the partner organization showed him that his office was not yet ready and assured him that they had not received any notice that he was arriving today. Building managers advised him that it would be about two weeks before the space he was to occupy would be habitable. In response to this, our regional and central management told the employee to work from home for two weeks.

Since our business was providing services to walk-in clients, which could not be accomplished from the employee's home, which was in a remote location, far away from the community's business district, both the employee and his wife concluded that this was the agency's way of firing him. The employee told me the situation placed so much stress on him that he experienced nausea, had many sleepless nights, sought psychological counseling, and ended up on ulcer mediation. Three-dimensional leaders avoid front-loading stress on employees and embarrassment with partners through such clumsily handled situations.

Developing a Decision-Making and Implementation Rhythm Based on the Three-Legged Stool Concept

I once worked for a government organization that was experiencing significant downsizing that included the closing of numerous branch offices. I advised upper management that my prerogative was to notify offices and partner organizations within them as early as possible in the process by advising them, "We are thinking about not renewing our lease to either downsize the local operation or close it to consolidate it with a neighboring community's operation." I advised that giving even a year's notice, if possible, would allow the following scenario to unfold: Those in the local offices would disseminate the news throughout their local communities that the office might close. Local politicians and the media invariably would get involved. When calls would come into our headquarters, because we had a long lead time and only stated that we were thinking about making a change, we could deal with the leg-one reaction from employees and the local community by saying, "No final decisions have been made, but we are experiencing significant budget challenges that require some very tough decisions to be made over the next several months. We are more than happy to share the information that we have at this time, if you would like it."

Some people on leg-one mode would be angry and hang up on us. Others would give us their opinion but would not want to have any real discussion. Others would try to get as much accurate information as possible and would want to absorb it before getting back to us for comment and discussion. Because we have not stated that we were going to do anything definitively, we could deal with building leg one of the three-legged stool of understanding very early in the process, with people feeling less threatened because the change was not imminent. We also would be giving a long time to build trust through appropriate information sharing and give-and-take informational exchanges.

Leg two of understanding would take place as people got back to us and requested and reviewed the information that led us to our conclusions. Leg two would continue to be built as people called us to get additional answers to questions regarding the information and to discuss appropriate options in response to it. Leg three would be built when the community representatives would get back to us, providing suggestions as to what we might possibly accomplish together as we jointly worked on the challenge.

When the public felt an announcement was sudden or had caught them by surprise, people felt cheated and deceived, as this information was sprung on them at the eleventh-and-a-half hour in the process. This especially was true for people who lived in small communities, where the relationships were tighter knit. People would confront our employees with the information in the local shopping plazas and put them on the spot about it. Our employees who lived in the community would see themselves as partners and community resources and would advocate for the office not to close. I would anticipate advocacy for the community from employees who lived within them. We had been training them to advocate for the public; why would they not do so now? When employees had ample time to process the information, however, they became the best resources to work through it with their local communities. Often they were forbidden to do so because I-D control freaks in a central office somewhere felt the community should not rely upon the employees but upon them because they had the job titles that said they are the only ones to deal with responses to the information.

We attempted to close two offices in small communities but failed to do so when there was so much uproar about it. In both instances we placed small ads in the newspaper announcing the changes, giving the communities as little time to react as we felt legally was necessary. Our methods did not build trust nor gain the communities' confidence that government knew what it was doing or had their best interest at heart. One of the offices remained opened and unchanged in any way, because we could not negotiate the political context of the storm of protest that ensued. In the other community, once the word was out that we could not afford to keep the office open, the community rallied around our mission and obtained free office space for us.

We did not learn any lessons from these two experiences, where the empirical knowledge of recent history indicated that in fifty percent of the cases, the community actually would assist us with our challenges by helping us to obtain free or low-cost office space. Instead, we continued to keep our cards close to our vests, sharing as little information as possible, and withholding from those who probably would have helped us a great deal.

Good Process Is Good Context Negotiation

Highly competent leaders recognize that how we go about our leadership activity is equally as important as what we are trying to accomplish. This means paying attention to the rules and conducting business in ways that help others to feel as comfortable about it as reasonably is possible. A good quarterback pays attention to the rules and the game clock, or else any gains his team makes immediately are removed because the referees call a delay-of-game penalty and yardage is taken away. Good process leads to good outcomes. How we go about leading our operations actually determines how effective, far reaching, and long lasting the impact of our initiatives will be. If we go about our missions the right way, we should get the right results that many people in the system will feel good about supporting and implementing. The leaders of government-run public service organizations need to treat as partners the people within the communities wherein the operations are located. Three-dimensional leaders are committed to converting within the context in a way that honors the organization, its employees, and its partners and encourages and supports them to be the best facilitators and representatives of the mission they can be. The timely sharing of appropriate information that gives consideration to how people digest and adjust to changes is part of good process.

Leading in ways that are effective for the external as well as the internal context facilitates how workers are trusted and treated as associates and integrated into the overall mission orientation of the business or organization as a whole. Through the appropriate training and timing of delegation that I explained previously, leaders and employees learn to trust each other to negotiate to convert the organization's mission effectively within the context. This encompasses orienting workers to the internal structures, procedures, controls, and processes that help the organization to manage its resources to ensure they effectively are deployed to achieve their intended purposes. These good leadership processes support the mission to benefit and add value to both the internal and external customer.

Appropriate Organizational Structure
Negotiates Local Information

"Changing circumstances would almost inevitably be known first to the local managers on the scene, and often much later, if at all, to the central planners, who had far too many industries and products to oversee to be able to keep up with day-to-day changes for them all."

Thomas Sowell, *Basic Economics* [40]

Information that is vital for an organization's survival often is found at the customer-service end of the operation. It is only actionable for the corporation to take advantage of it, however, once it is brought to the top of the organization and disseminated down internal informational highways that network to all the various branches. Many organizations suffer from an administrative structure that does not provide mechanisms to learn and respond efficiently to what local agents and employees observe about customer preferences and the competitive environment that must be negotiated to succeed at its mission to provide goods and services.

For example, imagine you are the salesperson in a shoe store, and on Monday a couple of people walk in asking for a particular type of yellow footwear. Your store, however, does not provide yellow shoes, only blue, red, black, brown, and grey. On Tuesday six people walk in and ask for yellow shoes. On Wednesday a dozen and a half people come into the store asking for yellow shoes. You are now rather concerned by what you perceive as a cultural phenomenon that has significant economic implications for your organization. Of the more than two dozen people who have come into your store over the last three days and asked for yellow shoes, upon learning that you do not carry them, all of them but one left without making any other purchase. The others were not interested in any other product you offer. You observe, however, that those same shoppers later passed by your store carrying bags of items from the stores of your competitors.

You go out into the mall hallway and start a friendly chat with one such shopper by stating, "I'm sorry we did not have the item you requested. I hope you found what you were looking for." The patron smiles and holds up her bags and says, "Yes, I did, and I got several other bargains at the same time!"

You advise your store manager that sales are being lost because the store does not carry yellow shoes, and you ask, "How quickly can we get some?" The manager replies that decisions about what color shoes the store carries are made by the regional office. Over the next six days more and more people come into the store, make a request for yellow shoes, and, upon learning that you do not carry them, leave without making any other purchases. Your manager sees the trend and speaks to other area store managers who are experiencing the same phenomenon. The store managers agree they must convince the regional manager that their stores are experiencing an alarming phenomenon where each day more than a dozen people enter them trying to locate and purchase the yellow footwear. After several calls, the skeptical regional manager finally calls corporate headquarters and is told that other regions also have called in, requesting an immediate delivery of yellow shoes, but executive decision makers from their central company headquarters believe this will be a short-lived trend, and soon people will come into the stores asking for the traditional shoe colors, which have been the flagship products that in the past have made the company what it is today. They decide, therefore, to take no action.

The trend grows and endures for more than a year, however, as more and more people continue to join the fad of wearing yellow shoes. The shoe store chain now is on the brink of bankruptcy, having lost significant market share by not carrying the product that could have led its sales during this time. All this could have been avoided, however, if centralized executive management had responded to the request of its local stores, which were the first segments of the operation to become aware of the market development.

The challenge is for central bureaucrats to learn and respond in a timely manner to front-line employees as situations are unfolding. The future of all manufacturing-retail industries depends upon how timely they respond to consumer preferences that often first are realized by front-line store employees.

In his book *Basic Economics,* Thomas Sowell explains why the centrally planned and controlled Russian economy failed, even though it has approximately the same land mass, natural resources, and population as does America. His points are illustrated below through how gas stations are supplied in Russia versus how one is operated in America. In Russia a centralized government organization determines which stations receive how much of various types of fuel.[41] For instance, a centralized government agency determines that a station on the corner of East Avenue and Maine Street is going to receive a predetermined number of gallons of diesel fuel. A tractor-trailer truck pulls into the station in search of diesel fuel, only for the driver to find that he has guessed wrong because that station ran out of diesel a couple of days ago and is not scheduled to receive any more for several more days. The driver of the tractor-trailer truck attempts to back out of the station onto the street, as he has precious little fuel left to drive around and look for a station that has diesel fuel. But he can't move because there is another tractor-trailer truck also in search of diesel fuel that has pulled into the station behind him. The second driver cannot back up because there are several cars bunched up behind him that also are blocking part of the street. The traffic jam spreads as more and more cars get jammed up at and around the corner of East Avenue and Main Street. This is a microcosm of how the Russian economy failed due to central bureaucratic planning and control.

What happens in the American economy, by contrast, is that the gas station owner, operator, or manager notices in the morning newspaper that over the next several days there is going to be construction out on Route 442, which means that for each of those days hundreds of vehicles will be detoured right past his station. He uses that local knowledge to take a risk by ordering more diesel fuel in anticipation of the number of additional trucks and vehicles that will pass by his establishment in need of a refill. The parent company of the gas station may be in a very faraway state yet trusts the local knowledge of the service station operator and immediately dispatches the requested diesel fuel. The end result is that the local station sells thousands of dollars worth of extra diesel fuel that week, and both the parent company and the local station manager make good profits. There are obvious benefits from trusting local knowledge and not hampering the individual ingenuity and initiative of those who must negotiate the local context.

I know there are some leaders reading this who are asking, "How can you trust local management to do the right thing with the operation entrusted to them?" The risk involved in the managing or parent company's relationship with a subsidiary is a necessary part of the dynamic business and operational environment. There is risk involved in every human relationship where one must trust another to do the right thing. Husbands and wives must trust each other to be faithful every day. Business owners must trust employees and managers to handle the company's resources appropriately. Employees must trust that the managers and owners are doing the right things with company resources so they all can be paid accurately and on time. Even though a percentage of individuals in the local operations will violate what is entrusted to them (just as a percentage of those who work in central headquarters also will), organizations must strike a balance between central bureaucratic oversight and controls and empowerment of local initiative.

Let's say the company supplying diesel fuel is a parent to ten thousand local gas stations nationwide. Of those ten thousand stations, 9,850 will be engaged in appropriate and profitable activity on any given day. The other 150 are getting into trouble due to employees, managers, and/or operators who have gambling or substance abuse and addiction problems. Or those stations will get into financial difficulty because the managers and employees working within them will have domestic strife issues or spending compulsions that they will try to cope with by stealing from the company. Some managers will have personal problems, and they will choose to spend their time at work focusing on them rather than on the business.

In each of the situations above, the parent company's business is going to suffer. To deal with the 150 aberrant stations, however, the parent company will not make blanket rules and policies that hinder the operation of the other 9,850. It will initiate controls to assist the operators of the struggling outlets to regain financial solvency and profitability. If those controls are resisted or fail, the parent company will allow or force the poorly performing entities into bankruptcy, so it can regain the rights to those stations and hire new management and/or locate new buyers who may do better with the operations in the future.

All types of organizations are challenged to come up with the right balance of bureaucratic procedures that provide enough structure to achieve operational integrity and the synergy that results from the efficiency and nimbleness that employees need to appropriately respond to local market and situational dynamics. This is as true for churches and not-for-profit organizations whose central bureaucracies are tasked to oversee local congregations as it is for corporations that oversee their outlets.

Negotiating the Local Context

Leadership Profile:
Oscar's Beverage Franchise Saga

"We shall be unable to turn natural advantage to account unless we make use of local guides."

Sun Tzu[42]

One- and two-dimensional leaders tend to fear the unknown and often reject new ideas and initiatives because their lack of understanding of the context prevents them from seeing the relevance of the information. What follows is the story of Oscar (not his real name), who works for a Fortune-500 beverage-retail company. I met Oscar at a party. After I learned that he worked for the company, I commented, "Of the last five bottles of the beverage I purchased, three of them were flat. What is going on with your distribution? I am a lifelong, loyal customer, but I am only going to try a few more bottles. If this sixty percent-flat average continues, I will cease buying the product," which I eventually did for several months. Oscar told me the following: He had grown increasingly frustrated with his new leaders. Oscar went to work for the company and learned the business from the ground up, working under a gifted franchise owner who grew his operation from one regional distribution center to more than a dozen over a twenty-five-year period. The three-dimensional franchiser was successful because he invested heavily in his employees by paying them well but also by structuring job roles so that they would grow based upon increased employee productivity and achievement.

Among the strategies that accomplished this was that he insisted that route drivers had college degrees, because he intended that each of them would become sales managers of their own routes to grow the company's business by expanding into more markets and territory.

To entice entry-level route drivers who had college degrees, he paid them handsome wages that adequately compensated white-collar types for doing blue-collar work. The strategy worked, and the franchise owner's employees began conquering new territory by outselling all their competitors in their ever-expanding market spaces.

The new sales had to be supported by on-time deliveries that had to be supported by more production and more and larger warehouses in which superior organization of inventory management had to be achieved. The college graduate route drivers who had learned the business from the ground up got promoted into management roles in production and within warehouses. Those former route drivers had firsthand field experience as to why the organization of production and inventory was essential to on-time deliveries so storeowners could obtain timely deliveries of products to sell that had a finite shelf life. These newly promoted employees had grown the company by developing sales experience and saturating their individual local markets with product by getting it into more and more stores throughout the territories along their original routes. These new sales led to new routes.

The route drivers actually managed their own routes. Because they intimately knew the territory in which they were selling new accounts, they knew how to organize their schedules and structure their deliveries to ensure that stores received product on rotations that were consistent with sales volumes. Commissions were based upon sales, and sales were based upon the storeowners' confidence that if they made the investment in display cases and signage, the sales route drivers could provide the customer service on-time deliveries that would make both the store and the sales drivers profitable. The relationship between the storeowners and the route drivers, therefore, was an intertwined partnership in which both took some risks to provide what the end-user consumer would purchase.

The franchiser's strategy to negotiate the local context by investing in and relying upon sales route drivers paid off, as his operation outsold its main national competitor about thirteen to one in the territories into which he expanded. Quadruple wins were achieved between the franchiser, the sales drivers, the storeowners, and the consumers who received great-tasting, thirst-quenching, and refreshing beverages. What appeared to be a simple proposition actually was a skillful construct of interrelated human interactions promulgated by the III-D franchiser understanding how important sales and service were to his operation and then figuring out a way to attract the right types of employees by treating them with respect and dignity by compensating them appropriately for who they were and what he expected of them.

This success was being undermined, however, because the franchiser decided to retire and sold the now thirteen times-larger franchise back to the corporation. The new generation of corporate managers, hired by the central corporate headquarters, implemented cost-savings measures and textbook policies that were designed to increase profits but had the opposite outcomes because they resulted in reduced sales, more production waste, inefficient warehousing and distribution, and faulty supply and deliveries to stores. These foibles led to greatly reduced sales route driver morale and job satisfaction. If the corporation fails to negotiate its internal context by dealing with its production and inventory-management problems, it never will solve its external contextual challenges to meet customer needs by appropriately supplying stores with quality on-time deliveries to meet sales demand. The corporation also began failing to handle its part of the equation that supports sales drivers to fulfill their expectations for their salaries and commissions.

The corporation arrived at these deplorable circumstances through a typical series of I-D decisions and processes. The corporate cost-cutting measure reduced the sales drivers' commissions per unit by half. This immediately meant that sales drivers could do the same amount of work and earn only half the income incentive for doing so.

The next thing the corporation did was to centralize operations so that local drivers no longer were negotiating their local sales and delivery context. These decisions now are made from another region, who hired its own salespeople to work those markets—taking the work away from the drivers who actually had been successful doing both the sales and delivery job by making relationships with the storeowners they drove by every day. Consequently, on Mondays sales drivers now are given their routes that have been designed the week before by an office at regional headquarters. Those assigning the routes lack the intimate territorial knowledge of traffic patterns, including one-way streets and other nuances that can impact delivery time. Drivers never know what route they are getting and now routinely travel along unfamiliar streets to stores with which they have no long-term, intimate relationship.

Delivery times are increased because the drivers are spending more functional capacity to read maps and road signs and figuring ways around one-way streets and other routing obstacles. Accidents actually have increased because of driver distraction. On-time deliveries have been compromised both because of the driver challenges cited above and the fact that those in remote regional locations do not always know the most efficient route to deliver product logically from one store to the next. Drivers are spending more time on the road to accomplish less than they could when they controlled their familiar routes.

The corporate culture has further complicated its challenges because more and more managers have been hired from the particular alma maters from which senior managers have graduated, increasing "groupthink" by replicating corporate layers of homogenous people who have the same textbook knowledge. This is typical I-D and II-D leadership activity that hires people based on who is known rather than what is known. One such hire is in charge of a huge warehouse. The warehouse manager's previous experience was with a commodity that had unlimited shelf life, so it was not as critical to stock product to facilitate first-in, first-out inventory distribution. Significant amounts of product have had to be disposed of because of past-due expiration dates. These errors, however, often were discovered by route drivers as they were making the deliveries.

Store manager and owner frustration has increased because not only were deliveries no longer on time, but the product no longer had the same quality as before, and customers have let the storeowners know their dissatisfaction. The poor product quality can jeopardize a store manager's relationship with regular customers who may go elsewhere to purchase the product and will do their other shopping at that location as well. Oscar said that some storeowners have advised the drivers and the corporation that they no longer even want the display cases in their stores because their store's reputation has been compromised by having an empty display that, even when it does get filled, contains product that can't be sold.

Oscar said that it has taken several years for the national office to finally get around to thinking that something may be amiss at the regional office. Many of the I-D and II-D regional leaders who have hired their former college and graduate school classmates have protected one another by not passing along to the national office the employee complaints about faulty product leaving the warehouse and storeowner and customer dissatisfaction with the delivered product. Employees have tried to work with the new wave of regional managers because they want to protect the business they built up and upon which their livelihoods depend. The employees, however, have been rebuffed and forced to watch regional decisions and processes compromise product quality and timely deliveries, while being told that those regional decision makers have graduate degrees and know what they are doing. Real-time experience on the streets, however, continues to tell front-end employees that those within the regional office are not doing what makes the storeowners and consumers happy.

Oscar also observed that his company's stock dropped while the general stock market was climbing. Oscar said that because he can observe firsthand that his corporation is on a path of decline, he has sold off his stock. Employee morale continues to decline as the I-D and II-D regional managers continue to do things that do not make sense to the employees, storeowners, and consumers in the local context. The national office, however, recently has implemented an employee-comment process that is supposed to bypass the region. Oscar is waiting to see if it helps salvage sales within a territory that had outperformed many others for the company. Oscar's expectation was that the distributorship would be considered a model to replicate rather than an experiment for untried, unproven methods that are a departure from what had been working, was not broken, and did not need fixing.

Many frustrated employees who had constituted the institutional brain trust and memory of the local operation have bailed out and taken other jobs. By the time the company comes out of its stupor, there may not be enough of those with historical institutional knowledge to provide the information necessary to reclaim the lost ground.

For Oscar's sake, and because I would enjoy partaking of the beverage he delivers, I hope the managers get their act together. Or perhaps they will be replaced by gifted III-D leaders who are effective managers who can accomplish the tasks that are required for product to reach me satisfactorily.

Chapter Twenty-eight

Maintaining Leadership Focus through Growth and Change

"The natural formation of the country is the soldier's best ally; but a power of estimating ... and of shrewdly calculating difficulties, dangers and distances, constitutes the test of a great general."

Sun Tzu[43]

You effectively negotiate your context by aligning your employee and partner resources to pursue your mission according to the values that have been established as the foundation of good working relationships and efficient operations. When your operations expand, your particular internal and external contexts must be analyzed and negotiated to achieve efficiencies in supply chain, product distribution, and/or service delivery. With a proper blend of centralized controls and local empowerment to initiate purchasing, you can achieve a balance that takes advantage of economies of scale while ensuring each local branch is supplied appropriately to respond to regional variances and idiosyncrasies in consumer choices. You must "filter" to discern, recognize, trap, discard, and resist initiatives that seem on target with your core competitive product offering or service but which really are off track from accomplishing it. You avoid doing merely what is good to ensure you have the capacity to do what is best to accomplish organizational goals.

The Hedgehog and Fox

In *Good to Great,* author Jim Collins provides a metaphor of two types of companies. One organization is led in such a way that it is like the fox. The other organization is led in such a way that it is like the hedgehog. The fox is swiftly moving and is sure-footed. It has great eyesight, and its hearing is superb. Overall, it has many gifts to perceive the complexity of its environment, but it fails to organize the data into a unified response that assists it to conquer its mission. Foxes are solitary animals and only live on average two to three years, which is short compared to more than double that for wolves, which have learned to get along in teams/packs to survive in the wild. The fox is an agile, complex strategist. He bounds over objects and crawls under others in search of ways to conquer his prey. Complexity without unity equals confusion. Simplification of complexity reduces confusion so one can efficiently achieve what is required for survival.

The hedgehog, in contrast to the fox, though very simple, is by no means stupid. It has only one competitive advantage in its defense against the fox. It rolls into a tight ball—leaving only sharp and unyielding bristles to confront its enemy. That simple strategy allows the hedgehog to actualize its life—search for food, build its den, and rear its young. Hedgehogs routinely live four to seven years in the wild, more than double that of the fox. Because it deploys this one strategy effectively, it wards off predators and obtains a steady diet to contribute to its relative longevity and its bequeathing to the next generation of its successors.

Collins notes that the hedgehog leaders of our society are not simpletons. Successful companies, says Jim Collins, are like the hedgehog; they have identified the one or two or a few things that differentiate them in the marketplace that they can do better or nearly better than anyone else to achieve competitive advantage. This one activity, or few essential ones, makes possible all their other functions. It is companies led by leaders who focus on their core competitive product offering or service strategy that are the most successful over the long term.

Being a hedgehog does not mean that you are "functionally fixed," so that you can't adapt and are locked into a narrow, precarious existence. It means you understand the one thing or the few things you can do better than anyone else, and you focus on and continue improving, innovating, and strengthening that offering. Collins says that "hedgehogs see what is essential and ignore the rest. Leader foxes, by contrast, never gain clarifying advantage, but are scattered, diffused, and inconsistent."[44] To understand your hedgehog concept means that you know you are in the business of transporting people and goods as opposed to being a railroad company. Had railroad companies understood this, rather than thinking they were merely in the rail-travel business, they perhaps would be major airline companies today instead of being out of business or having greatly reduced business through competition by planes and truckers.

The current high price of diesel fuel, however, that is making trucking less cost efficient and competitive may be opening new opportunity for those in the rail industry. Perhaps to negotiate the context of high fuel prices truckers will adapt from a long-haul to a short-haul mission, which will be to get products to and from the train freight yards. Soon trains may move huge volumes of product that recently were hauled overland by trucks. Upon arrival to a distant train freight yard, however, trucks will take on the short-haul mission and get the products to local distribution warehouses and stores. Another phenomenon that can make sense to many businesses to adjust their operations in response to the high price of fuel is to build warehouses adjacent to where sales are taking place. It may be more cost effective to store more products on site than to utilize just-in-time delivery models that require frequent over-the-road hauling expenses. Since the price of fuel continues to fluctuate, like many variables in the context, operational models continually must be evaluated in relation to the changing environment to determine their efficiency.

Collins cites that Hewlett Packard's company mission is not limited by the nomenclature of any technology it currently makes, because HP knows it is a manufacture of "business and office machines." HP is poised to hedgehog and utilize whatever technology emerges that will change the efficiency, effectiveness, and the nature of business and office machinery. If the advent of new technology pushes a style of printer into extinction tomorrow, HP will move forward to utilize and deploy it to provide a fresh line of office machines using the latest available technological resources.

Consolidation seems imminent for the auto industry. Perhaps automakers may hedgehog with fewer models that are designed to serve narrower market niches. Chrysler Corporation's acquisition of Maserati lacked synergy because it took both companies out of their hedgehog concept. Maserati now makes a profit through pre-ordered sales that customize its exclusive vehicles to suit the specific requests of the individuals who can afford them. Chrysler is more of a commodity product for middle-class families. By both focusing on its core offering, Chrysler can work to differentiate itself and achieve its share of a specific market segment. This will be more efficient and effective than trying to be all things to all drivers.

For organizations to excel at their overriding purpose, they must be led by leaders who understand and embrace their hedgehog concept. Organizations that know their core competitive advantage tend to outperform fox-like organizations over the long run. Three-dimensional leaders help their organizations to thrive by cultivating and fine-tuning what gives them their main competitive advantage. These same leaders also provide a filtering function for their organizations, so they keep the main thing the main thing. They are not distracted by all the sights and smells in the environment as an inexperienced hunter fox is.

Leaders steer their organizations into their hedgehog concept by answering these questions: "What is the organization's mission, what are the resources available to achieve it, and what is the context that must be negotiated for resources to be deployed to successfully fulfill the mission?" Mission is determined by asking: "Why does our organization exist? What is the thing we can do or provide better or nearly better than anyone else? What is the main purpose our organization serves in the competitive marketplace? What is the main thing that we do that matters to people?" Resources are understood by asking: "What do we have and what is required to accomplish our mission? What core product or service offerings do we provide that customers will choose over our competitors?" You understand how to negotiate the context by asking: "What motivates customers to desire our products and seek our services?" Leaders of service organizations also need to ask "Why do customers walk through our doors and ask for our assistance? How do we add value and contribute to the community, customers, visitors, and our volunteers?"

Leaders get their organizations focused on their main competitive advantages by answering these questions and elevating the answers as the organization's mission statement rallying cry. The organizational vision is articulated as the state of ultimate mission fulfillment if the organization is wildly successful. Three-dimensional leaders arrange their organizations' internal operations' work environments to accomplish the missions that fulfill that vision.

Leaders Must Keep the Main Thing the Main Thing

To "keep the main thing the main thing" may sound like a trite expression, but it really is difficult for leaders within organizations to keep focused on their missions. There are so many distractions to which our egos can get attached that it really is challenging for us to keep the main thing the main thing. Leaders must emulate the focus they need to provide their organizations. Bill Minchin, an administrator of a large church in Upstate New York, notes,

A key for leaders is to recognize that you can't do it all, and that it perhaps is better for the organization that you don't need to do it all. Identify what you are best gifted in and focus on that, and then identify the gifts in some of the other leaders and empower them to take on some of the other responsibilities. If these types of changes can be implemented within the organization, this is a good thing. But one must make an assessment and often must hand over to others things you personally can do very well if you are going to best utilize your time and talents.[45]

Structure Needs to Support the People Who Are Doing the Work

Organizational structure either facilitates or hinders productivity and growth. Organizational productivity growth cannot be sustained unless it is supported by appropriate structure. Structure is needed to support ongoing, continued growth. Here's why: Growth causes change, and to accommodate that change may require a change in organizational structure. Growth will tend to cause changes in the way people work. They will have additional responsibilities. If you add fifty more table settings, or three more convention room changeovers per week, or three hundred more services to provide, or five hundred more envelopes to be stuffed, or a thousand more products to produce and deliver, additional resources of time, materials, supplies, people, and money will be required. Structure will have to be adjusted to facilitate new volumes of information, resources, and workflows.

The process of growth and the corresponding structural changes that should accommodate and facilitate it, involves freezing and unfreezing and then refreezing. How this works is your structure is in place, and as growth occurs, you unfreeze and adjust to change your structure to handle the new environment that you must negotiate as a result of the growth or success. Then you refreeze while you continue scanning the context to discern where and when you must unfreeze again to accommodate additional increase or achievement within your organization. Without appropriate changes, people will feel frustrated in their work and inefficiency and ineffectiveness will be the outcomes. Gains may not be sustainable unless they are at the great personal expense of some hapless soul or souls who are left to flounder and deal with insufficiently organized and/or undermanned operations.

Negotiating your internal context involves orienting the workers' focus so they see how they fit in with the organization as a whole in relation to its internal structure, controls, and procedures, and how those are designed to help the organization keep track of its resources and to ensure they are deployed effectively and appropriately to the mission.

Organizational Structure Must Be a Vehicle for Transferring Organizational Values

Effective organizational structure facilitates people working within the company's stated values system. As organizations grow, structure has to be put in place. An employee handbook and procedural manuals must be developed regarding how resources are procured and allocated, and there must be checks and balances that provide oversight for how accounts payable and receivables are administered. Ideal structure and procedures facilitate the core values and strategies of the organization.

Pastor Rex Keener, whose organization experienced rapid acceleration of growth in the past five years, notes,

> Structures need to be such that they allow you to deliver your core competencies and strategies without compromising your values, so that others [employees and volunteers] can live them out. Because if leaders are not careful to proceed with well thought out, balanced approaches to how you administer your organization, your policies and rules become a straightjacket for the future.[46]

A challenge for any mission-focused leader is to interact with human resources so they get onboard with the main mission and devote themselves to what essentially will make the organization successful. An organization is a social body of people who need to be focused on mission, resources, and negotiating the context. People must leave their egos at the door for this to happen. None of us is completely free of the desire for self-promotion and thinking we are something great or better than the next person. All of us are tempted to make unhealthy comparisons of ourselves with others, thinking that we have this or that thing that a coworker does not that makes us better. When we are focused upon thinking like this, we lose sight of how those people also are the actual resources the organization is relying on to implement the mission. Not all of us have the same gifts, nor are we supposed to be exactly alike. Remember that a football team is the most dynamic when it utilizes the various body sizes, playing styles, and psychologies of its players to obtain the maximum synergy their diversity can provide.

Effective leadership requires the ability to be humble to model how all must submit to the mission that matters most. Whether you are appointed to a position regarding which you have had little or no experience, or if you have obtained it by rising through the ranks, you will need to continue to learn if you want to succeed. The new position of leadership requires a different perspective because perhaps now, in addition to being a peer worker, you also are the person tasked to make sure the work gets done, that it is properly accounted for, and that both customer and employee needs are met.

The book of Proverbs tells the dangers of a leader or anyone who thinks he or she is greater than others and fails to have a learning attitude. Proverbs 26:12 says, "Do you see a man wise in his own eyes? There is more hope for a fool than for him." Leadership requires accountability, and accountability requires vulnerability, openness, and honesty. If we are open to share with our teams the areas in which we most need growth, we can empower their strengths to help us succeed as leaders. These values and behaviors are hard to fake for any period of time. Growing in them helps us to be suitably transparent to form and work with a team that is the greatest resource for mission fulfillment.

Chapter Twenty-nine

Core Operational Success Dynamics

"He will win whose army is animated by the same spirit throughout all its ranks."[47]

Sun Tzu

Successful organizations have a core operational success dynamic (COSD).[48] These factors are what give organizations their unique status. Understanding your COSD is a primary step to achieving organizational integrity. Articulating your COSD (pronounced "Cos-Dee") expresses your organization's heart and soul. Your organizational COSD exists where its heart of values converge with its soul of mission. These dynamics are related to your hedgehog concept. They are imbedded in why the corporation exists, such as "to manufacture products x, y, and z, or provide x, y, and z services, which have these certain attributes that customers value." If adhered to and worked out well, these dynamics provide your organization with the most potential for success and achievement of growth.

Your COSD can be thought of as core value proposition dynamics and relate to the heart of your organization's mission and why people join your club, select your products, or choose to work in your shop in the first place. Your operational dynamics relate to the internal processes, relationships, and controls that are the engine of your company, fueled by your values stated in your mission, vision, and values statement. Your growth dynamics stem from how your organization's offerings are perceived by the public, including consumers, partner organizations and distributors, analysts, government auditors, and others within your external context. These all contribute to the fulfillment of your strategic mission within your organization's larger contexts.

The core operational success dynamics (COSD) are the essential parts of an organization's culture that underlie its success in achieving its reason to exist. These are the aspects and components of the internal context that make it successful in designing, engineering, manufacturing, and marketing what consumers want. The COSD is about how people work together to cross-pollinate their ideas and efforts to accomplish essential functions and tasks.

Your COSD articulates what makes your operations successful in realizing cooperative effort from your workers to obtain synergy from their diversity. Your COSD captures how you have attracted, organized, and empowered people to do what makes your organization an attractive and desirable place to work or belong to. The quality of your products, outputs, and service delivery conveys the success of your COSD and are a reflection of how many people you have attracted, organized, and empowered. Your sales and services are a reflection of how much cooperative effort and synergy from diversity have been achieved as a result.

The What and How of COSD

What you are producing or providing are your products, outputs, or services. *How* you arrange your internal operations to successfully provide them (if done well) is your COSD. A COSD statement is a motto that captures what you do and how you do it. It is a shorthand articulation of your strategic plan. Your core operational and success dynamic (COSD) consists of the distinct leader and employee behaviors that make up your organization's "way" of doing things. So a COSD statement articulates the "HP way," the "Stewart's way," the "Beverage Distributorship way."

- For the Hewlett Packard Company, the COSD might be stated as: "At HP we design office machines with the latest technology in an environment that is as upbeat, creative, cooperative, fun, and as practical as the products we provide."

- At Proctor and Gamble (P&G) a COSD might be stated as: "At P&G we unleash creativity and empower initiative to provide products that make a difference in the everyday lives of people throughout the world's communities."

- At the General Electric Company (GE) a COSD might be stated as: "At GE we put imagination to work to solve tough global challenges in ways that are economically successful within the world's markets."

- Stewart's might state its COSD this way: "At Stewart's we support each other through horizontally and vertically integrated relationships that provide our customers with the highest quality products at great prices."

- Another version of the Stewart's COSD statement might be: "At Stewart's, because we are closer to each other, we are closer to you."

Your organization's COSD articulates the internal corporate culture that facilitates people working cooperatively together so processes flow smoothly to efficiently produce, effectively provide, and successfully deliver the information, product, and/or services for which it ultimately exists.

Internal operations need to be aligned to facilitate your core operational success dynamics. When you can understand your desired internal organizational context well enough to articulate your core operational success dynamics, which incorporate your critical success factors that are driven by your values, you can instruct your leaders in how they contribute to operational success and why employees, clients, customers, and volunteers appreciate and find them meaningful. You can rally your people resources and teams to the mission(s) imbedded within and which make up those dynamics. You can train your human resources in the values, actions, activities, and behaviors that contribute to achieving the COSD. Employees and volunteers can be evaluated based upon how well they comply with, contribute to, and support the COSD standards. The best corporate citizens personify their organization's COSD.

Effective internal operations are those that specifically and intentionally are arranged to facilitate achieving the mission's COSD. Values (good and bad) acted upon consistently form the organizational culture. The appropriate values that contribute to effective operations make up what I call the "Core Cultural Dynamics" (CCD) that give the organization the most potential to succeed. You and your employees cannot violate your values without, in most instances, disrupting your processes. When leaders and employees act out the organization's stated values, the core cultural dynamics (CCD) prevail to fulfill the core operational success dynamic (COSD). If your organization's COSD is undermined or subverted, it is because leaders and/or employees have disregarded or violated the values. Employee expectations are frustrated, and job satisfaction declines. Employees start asking themselves and each other, "What is the leader or are the leaders thinking?" This is because what is taking place does not make sense to those who are trying to do the mission. People will feel "that is not the way it is supposed to be." A sign of employee frustration over violations of the core cultural dynamics (CCD) is that people will leave the organization. If the organization's COSD is healthy, then its processes are aligned to accomplish its mission. The COSD is composed of the reasons people continue to gather to and want to join or remain with your organization. These happy employees are working out the values that make for an effective CCD that fuels a vibrant COSD operating environment.

Franchising Replicates the Core Organizational Success Dynamics

You do not want your organization to become a fractured, loosely associated string of silos that are cults (or victims) of the individuals leading them. You want your leaders to franchise within each sub-organization the values that infuse the core dynamics that make the overall parent organization successful. "Organizational franchising" is my concept whereby the parent company tasks its managers to carry out values. The parent organization needs to see its relationship with its officers and managers as a franchiser to franchisee. The employer is contracting with the employee as a licensee who is authorized and held accountable to carry on the work the tried and true mission-oriented way imbedded in the core operational and success dynamics. Since those values are the cornerstone of a highly collaborative winning culture, managers need to be held accountable to carry them forth.

A key to the success of franchising is the transference to employees and operational structure the value system that generates the culture that makes the parent organization successful. Companies must expect their leaders to transfer within their employees the values that make up the culture that facilitates mission fulfillment. Companies should expect their employees to adhere to the values that support the culture just like franchisers expect that when owners purchase franchise rights they have signed on to participate in the parent company's successful value system and business model.

I believe that many mergers and acquisitions fail to provide synergy for the parent company because organizational cohesiveness, integrity, and unity is not achieved between it and the acquired or adopted entity. Through specific training, the core operational success dynamics (COSD) needs to be blueprinted in the hearts and minds of the adopted family of leaders and employees. The model is how the McDonald's fast-food blueprint provides for a profitable, replicable system that maps out the minutest details to facilitate an easy-to-run restaurant that can be operated virtually anywhere in the world—providing people cooperate and follow the parent company's template, while adjusting for local cultural idiosyncrasies in taste and decor.

Data analysis of the effectiveness of operations can include assessments of how your leaders and employees are doing in adhering to your core operational success dynamic (COSD).

Chapter Thirty

Analyzing Your Context

The Balanced Scorecard (BSC)

The Balanced Scorecard (BSC) is a tool to assess how an organization is handling its mission-success factors, the relationships with which it must coordinate, and the context that must be negotiated to achieve its strategy. A scorecard provides a template for categorizing the elements of an organization's internal and external contexts. Set up properly, a scorecard can provide organizations with an overall strategic view of their internal and external landscapes to get a balanced perspective of the success factors within the context that are necessary to fulfill their strategic plan. The card scores how well you are doing in relation to all that must be considered to operate effectively. It can be adapted to assess elements that feed your core operational success dynamics (COSD).

Robert S. Kaplan and David P. Norton introduced the concept of the Balanced Scorecard in 1992 as a tool to provide organizations with an overall strategic view. Analyzing quarterly financial reports provides an incomplete picture of all the information needed for an organization to negotiate its context. Kaplan and Norton's model highlights the non-financial, intangible assets and resources available to an organization. Kaplan, a professor of leadership and development at Harvard Business School, was concerned with "activity-based costing." Norton is the founder of the Balanced Scorecard Collaborative in Lincoln, Massachusetts. Their seminal work, *The Balanced Scorecard: Measures That Drive Performance,* published in the *Harvard Business Review,* led to the coining of the phrase "what gets measured gets done." In other words, "People will do what leaders count." The Kaplan and Norton model determines how to assess your organization from its financial, customer, internal business process, learning, and innovation perspectives.[49]

The balanced scorecard (BSC) is a template that describes the organization's strategy to help ensure you are taking into account all the appropriate elements and entities that need to be considered when conducting your business. You can budget for all the strategic activities, control, and operational systems that contribute to your organization's overall performance. Change-management initiatives should include a BSC to ensure they are implemented in ways that are palatable to and obtain synergy from the parties with whom your organization coordinates. Their buy-in is necessary because changes must be implemented in conjunction with those other organization's strategies. The BSC can be used to implement what Charles W.L. Hill and Gareth R. Jones call strategic controls,[50] which are performance measures that evaluate how well managers have considered and utilized organizational resources to create value and to sense new opportunities for the future.

Constructing Your BSC Template

Understanding your mission, resources, and context (MRC) tells you what to score. Your "mission" and how the "resources" are utilized to fulfill it within the "context" determine what your card needs to consider. Scanning your operational landscape in light of your MRC will help in constructing a BSC that counts what has strategic value for achieving your organization's goals. It will indicate where challenges exist because it shows the interrelationships between goals and the activities that are linked to their achievement. While some of the data and information on the intangibles definitely will be soft, it is very important because most business and organizational challenges are rooted in people relationships. It is those human elements and issues that make up your COSD. Effectively communicating the issues that have strategic value provides managers with what they need to have a positive effect upon both the internal and external contexts of your operation. This understanding, when communicated appropriately to employees, gives them the ability to see how their everyday work contributes to fulfilling the organization's overall strategic mission.

Organizations tend to struggle with arriving at meaningful measurements that realistically relate to how their employees contribute to strategic outcomes. For employees to buy in and adequately understand and appreciate how their roles and responsibilities directly contribute to the overall success, there must be a marriage between what they know and must do and what the organization is counting. If the marriage is a congenial one, the employees will find that what is being counted actually is directly related to what they do (or need to do). They thus will feel that what management counts relates meaningfully to what they contribute or produce. If the organization successfully replicates this process throughout all of its departments, it will get a handle on what is happening throughout its various units and will direct, redirect, and reinforce the actions, activities, behaviors, and processes that contribute to fulfillment of the overall strategic mission of its balanced scorecard.

Employees who are educated in this way can perform more intelligently. If they can see the big-picture strategy in relation to what they do, they can make better suggestions and are more adaptable to changes in their jobs that are necessary for the organization to remain competitive in an evolving context. Employees who grasp these concepts become proactive in making recommendations that will improve their job performance to assist the organization to better negotiate both its internal and external environments.

A BSC is a method for understanding what your leaders must do to organize resources and employees, coordinate with partners and suppliers, and interface with constituents to tailor operations and services to the needs of customers, while achieving satisfactory win-wins for all involved. Each branch of your operation must be balanced to meet the concerns of the front-end service-providing employees who also must be good members of your organizational family and cooperate with one another as a factor of internal control accountability. The organization achieves "balance" in its context when employees coordinate by serving well the primary customer while also doing what makes sense to all your external constituencies that have a stake in and an impact on your strategic mission.

Variations of the Balanced Scorecard (BSC)

Customize a BSC to suit your market situation, products, and competitive environment. To meaningfully score an organization, you must choose a coherent set of variables that translate into the performance measures that most contribute to the success of its strategic style and organizational culture that pulls the operational levers that achieves its mission. The different perspectives depend upon an organization's internal and external customers, how it must align with strategic partners, other organizations, suppliers, and distributors, and how it must interact within the current (and changing) external market or operating environment to remain relevant and competitive. A company is relevant to consumers when they choose its products or services. Consumer choice ultimately determines how competitive a company is. A scorecard can help measure the synergies that achieve competitiveness.

The balanced scorecard (BSC) provides a template to measure organizational effectiveness from at least four perspectives that can vary depending on what requires attention:

- customers (both internal and external), stakeholders and strategic partners
- financial accountability and profitability
- operational or internal business processes
- innovation and learning

A *stakeholders' or strategic partners' performance scorecard* can track "the satisfaction of various constituencies who have a significant interest in and impact on the company's behavior and performance." These can include employees, suppliers, distributors, and vendors, stockholders, elected officials representing the communities wherein operations are located, and federal agencies that provide oversight of the industry, mission or program, public service partners, and the client's family members and special-interest groups advocating for them. "Norms should be set for each group and management should take action when one or more stakeholder group registers increased levels of dissatisfaction."[51]

Balanced scorecards can be used to assess an organization's new initiative to ensure it is rolled out appropriately for all the parties it will impact. I provided an organization with a variation of the BSC to assess how its information technology (IT) could support its key business and customer-service processes. Consideration was given to how employees worked and how IT could support those functions. Networking capabilities in those days were not quite giving us the functionality they do now, and many leaders were slow learners, but the process helped the organization see where it needed to go and how it could move forward. Because IT continues to evolve to provide more synergy, assessing how those processes can enable and support operations should be an ongoing initiative. My IT BSC assessed the following:

IT BSC:

1. *The Operational and Financial Perspective* determined how IT-enabled customer service processes would capture and report out on employee individual-performance

outcomes. IT not only supported back-end reporting but also the front-end core competencies of employees to help them do their work by disseminating their knowledge, skills, and activities into competitive service advantages that customers value, such as speedy transfers of data while reducing errors. IT also captures data and translates it for reports on outcomes of employee productivity. Data also helps organizations better understand their customers' preferences.

2. *The Internal Stakeholder and Partner Perspective* involved ensuring front-end employees found the IT systems user friendly to provide value-added functionality that assisted them to deliver services, record transactions, and then recall data in a timely manner. The IT system should be shared to provide smooth information transfers with coordinating partner organizations. Appropriate coordination is facilitated through sharing agreements that allow certain employees regardless of organization to participate and subscribe to gain access. Thus members of all parties can gather and process all the supporting data necessary to make quick, intelligent, and appropriate decisions and responses for clients.

3. *The External Customer Perspective* assessed how IT initiatives meet customer expectations in the e-business age. This includes providing services with the speed, efficiency, and accuracy that customers value. It also focuses on allowing customers to access services provided through e-mail and Web-based portals.

4. *The Learning and Innovation Perspective* recommended the use of e-based training initiatives that employees could access on demand and customize by entering at various learning points. It also provided how IT initiatives would empower and achieve maximum value from employee suggestions. Ideas—even good ones—are just

ideas while they remain in an employee's head or on pieces of paper stuffed inside desks or file drawers. They become tools when they are captured in digital formats and can be worked into spreadsheet analyses and presentations that are disseminated throughout the entire organization where knowledgeable people at all levels can rework, focus, and fine-tune them. These idea tools contribute to sending rational recommendations up proper channels for review that become well-thought-out initiatives that disseminate down communication networks throughout an organization like rain runs down an umbrella to refresh parched ground.

BSC models can have many variations that provide perspectives or paradigms with which to view your operations. There is no set appropriate number of critical indicators within each perspective. Some say between fifteen and twenty objectives are appropriate. The last time I looked, FedEx was using twelve. Still, others say three to five critical success factors are ideal. Here are some considerations regarding various factors:

The Financial Perspective can provide an operation with more synergy than bookkeeping done only to achieve reduced tax liability. Viewing financial data from a customer-stakeholder perspective helps determine the cost of doing business with definable categories of clients, segregated by their profitability. By reporting what the customer gets in relation to what it costs you to build, manufacture, provide, and/or deliver it, you can determine what certain customers mean to your business. This helps you see your business from an enterprise profit-and-loss perspective rather than simply getting financial status reports that provide feedback about the results of past decisions that did not take these factors into consideration. Assessing finances more robustly may require readjusting the books to input data a bit differently, but better outcomes, such as knowing your rolling cash flow to determine appropriate levels of inventory to purchase and carry, are worth the effort. Consulting firms, such as International Profit Associates, can help small businesses with organizing these financial analytical tools.

Including break-even and profit-and-loss analyses provide a strategic business picture that informs managers what contracts and deals are worth pursuing and the various margins they provide. They reveal how profits improve after certain returns on investment have been achieved. Arranging accounting accurately to track and obtain appropriate feedback provides the building blocks to make informed decisions. The financial perspective can include measurements of your goals for survival, growth, return on capital, liquidity, revenue, cost reduction, project profitability, and performance reliability.

The Customer Perspective includes goals for customer acquisition, retention, profitability, and satisfaction and are measured by market share, transaction cost ratios, customer profile, loyalty, and satisfaction surveys/indexes. Supplier and relationships with key accounts also are important.

Philip Kotler, in *Marketing Management, Analysis, Planning, Implementation, and Control,* notes,

> Most company measurement systems amount to preparing a financial-performance scorecard at the expense of more qualitative measures showing the company's health. Companies would do well to prepare "market-based scorecards" that reflect company performance and provide possible early warning signals. A Customer Performance scorecard records how well the company is doing year after year on customer-based measures, such as the following:
>
> - new customers
> - dissatisfied customers
> - lost customers
> - target market awareness
> - target market preference
> - relative product quality
> - relative service quality

The Internal Business Perspective incorporates the core operational success dynamics (COSD). These include goals for core competencies, critical technologies, business processes, key skills, and are measured by efficiency of working practices and production processes, cycle times, unit costs, defect rates, and time to market.

The Learning and Innovative Perspective is a factor of your COSD and includes goals for continuous improvement and new product development and are measured by productivity, entrepreneurship, new ideas and suggestions from employees, employee satisfaction, skill levels, rate of improvement, achievement of performance goals, staff attitude, retention, and profitability.

Do your leaders understand what is new in the industry that can change the context of the business or how it operates? There could be new inventions/technologies that will lead to the development of new products that provide more features or processes that will facilitate making it faster, better, and cheaper. There could be new legislation that opens doors to new markets, expands existing ones, or closes them by making your product illegal or obsolete. Are there technologies on the horizon that might change the way your customers do business, which in turn will have an impact on your current ability to supply them? The companies that are quickest to adapt to these changes will be on the competitive cusps of success.

To be effective, BSC measures must be matched to the strategy that is identified to achieve success. Government and service organizations must be extra diligent here. Leaders must identify the critical success factors that are the actions, activities, and behaviors employees must engage in to provide the services that customers value. Most importantly, leaders must have the appropriate measures that determine strategic success. It is essential to design from the customer's view to ensure that what you think your employees should do to achieve success are those things the customer values.

I consulted with more than one business owner whose operation was in dire financial straits, and the leadership explained that they made certain decisions based upon a social value they were trying to achieve, such as to hire people of a certain ethnicity or have their products be successful among a particular socioeconomic demographic that they felt was underserved. There usually was a strong correlation between the business owner's background and the demographic the organization desired to reach either through hiring or sales. This is because people tend to do what they know and want to work with what is familiar to them. I advised each of them that the primary goal of a business that intends to do great social good, such as supporting jobs for people in poor neighborhoods, is to first be concerned with the color green (money). Without monetary profit from your goods and services, you can't sustain your business long enough or robustly enough to help it, yourself, or anybody else. Of primary significance to any business is the financial perspective. Are you making a profit from your goods and services? If not, then you cannot negotiate your context to do social good. Location often is linked to profitability. You must get your business to a location that is accessible to the customer while also ensuring it is in an environment that the customer will feel safe coming to.

The Three-Dimensional Leader's Balanced Scorecard Assesses Competitive Advantage

The ultimate goal of your BSC is to measure and assess competitive advantage. A thorough and accurate picture of organizational performance requires that financial information is supplemented with other performance indicators. An organization's BSC can help to assess how well it has been achieving the four building blocks of competitive advantage: 1) efficiency, 2) quality, 3) innovation, and 4) responsiveness to customers.

Since people provide potential, watch out for managers who are misrepresenting your core values, because they probably are mishandling your human resources, which embody the spirit of your organization. They probably are mishandling or misdirecting other resources as well. If your leaders are not focused on your organization's mission, a BSC can help redirect them into the appropriate activities that achieve effective operations. Leadership is the key to organizational success. The BSC can help assess your leaders' performance at orienting, directing, facilitating, and achieving your organization's strategy.

The BSC can help you define what your company is uniquely qualified to do and why customers seek what you provide. Focusing your organization's efforts on these deliverables will have the greatest impact on achieving strategic goals. You must understand your "hedgehog concept" to develop and engage in only those initiatives and projects that correlate to the variants you need to score, which are those that feed your competitive advantage.

Two processes are equally important: a) identifying the right objectives and b) drafting appropriate measures for each of them. Selecting the appropriate objectives and measurements will help your managers throughout all levels of your organization better understand their critical success factors. The appropriate score for each measure sets targets that department-level initiatives should be designed to hit. A meaningful, balanced scorecard initiative helps managers and workers to understand the interrelationship between what is being scored (goals) and the specific activities (jobs) that are linked to achieving them. Each department can know how what it does contributes to the scores and the company's competitive advantage.

The balanced scorecard captures the organization's institutional memory by linking data to information that shows how what employees do on the shop floor and at their office desktops contributes to fulfilling the reasons the organization exists. Employee-evaluation forms detail the measured actions, activities, and behaviors they should accomplish to achieve the defined successful outcomes. Managers are brought into the process by being held accountable for ensuring employees follow through with their jobs in the prescribed manner, working within the stated values. Thus the organization institutionalizes essential elements of the what, why, where, and who information that is the backbone of its strategy.

Below is the story of another three-dimensional leader who knew the score and led his organization to excel at negotiating its context to meet the needs of its customers.

Chapter Thirty-one

Negotiating the Sales Context: Community, Commodity, Calendar, and Cost

Leadership Profile:
Eivion Williams
Former CEO Mohawk Trailer Supply
Former Director Schenectady City Mission

Eivion Williams is a three-dimensional leader who has fulfilled his organizations' missions in business and running a not-for-profit men's shelter. In both ventures, he effectively rallied and deployed resources to successfully negotiate the contexts. The business was "Mohawk Trailer Supply, Inc." that grew to gross $14 million in annual sales and employed sixty-four people. The company sold recreational vehicles (RV) and mobile home parts and accessories to distributors. Its sales territory covered north and south from the Canadian border to Baltimore, Maryland, and spanned east to west from Cape Cod, Massachusetts to Buffalo, New York. Mohawk dispatched service and delivery vehicles throughout this territory to deliver 95 percent of the products the company sold.

Eivion got into this business after college, working first as a welder in a mobile home repair shop, where he worked on trailers and RVs and became intimately familiar with every part of the homes and vehicles. Eivion transitioned from mechanic repairman to an owner when a customer couldn't get certain parts for his RV and decided he would become the solution to how there was no local distribution in the area. He decided to open a distributorship and asked Eivion help him determine what to buy.

Eivion spent a couple of weekends going through trade magazines, circling items that were most in demand for the entrepreneur, who then asked Williams to come work for him as a salesman. Because Eivion only saw himself as a mechanic, not a sales guy, it took a little convincing. The new position doubled his pay, and they started the distributorship business. Two years later they incorporated, and Eivion was invited to be part of the corporation, and he bought in and became vice president. Of his employee-to-owner story, Eivion says, "I can't believe my boss had been so gracious and so kind!" Nine years later the principal partner retired, and Eivion took over with seven employees. Four years later their sales had quintupled to about $5 million annually, and the number of employees had increased proportionately to about thirty-five. The company eventually grew to employ as many as sixty-four workers, including seven to eight full-time outside salespeople and seven to eight full-time inside salespeople and seven to eight full-time warehouse personnel. Eivion says, "Year-round we probably had forty, and then we would add twenty to twenty-five additional workers every summer."

The Win-Win-Wins of Sales

Eivion once wanted to be a schoolteacher, but life led him down different paths. He reflects that "sales is teaching." He continues, "I think I channeled my gifts in the right way by becoming a mentor to many people as a trainer in the business world. God didn't want me to be a teacher; I wanted to be a teacher."

"When you are a salesman, you are a teacher," I comment. "You teach people about the product; why it's good for them and how to use it."

Eivion nods approvingly and explains his sales philosophy:

We developed a philosophy early on in the business that there were three parties that had to be connected. We have to have a connection between

1. our suppliers,

2. us as the distributor, and

3. the customer (dealer) who sells to the end user.

If all three people don't remain in the relationship, then there is something wrong. If two win and one loses, you break the relationship and it's not going to continue.

Community, Commodity, Calendar, and Cost

"If they are going to buy it, you need to determine where it needs to be for them to get it."

Eivion Williams

To be successful in sales, Eivion understood that his network of business associates, that included suppliers, distributors, and individual customers, were part of a community that he trained his sales force to coordinate with in a tight relationship.

Eivion relates:

I would constantly go to my suppliers and say, "If I buy five hundred of those and I get them shipped one hundred per month for the next five months and you bill me at thirty, sixty, ninety-day billing, I can pass this price on to my customers." The dealer might buy them because he can schedule their arrival and may not have to pay for them out-of-pocket all at once. This arrangement really can increase both our businesses. Perhaps the distributor would say, "I want to work with you, but we can't give you the thirty, sixty, ninety-day billing, but only thirty and sixty." We would negotiate that, and my customers then could buy air conditioners early in the season in April, and they would have them in their businesses when the hot weather came. They didn't have to wait two weeks or a week to get them. They didn't have to pay for them right away either but could wait thirty to sixty days and everybody would win.

Eivion says he made deals that provided him with cash before he had to part with it to make payments and notes, "I always had cash. I always got my money. If the vendor gave me thirty, sixty, ninety days to pay, I billed my customer to pay me within fifteen to forty-five days. I always got the money."

To be successful in a sales environment, you need to know your community of customers and the commodity or products they want to purchase and which you sell. You must respond to the timing cycles of those customer purchases and how you will restock and resupply to have products available for them. You need to determine the cost customers are willing to pay. Doing this is getting the pulse of the operational components within your sales context.

Eivion Williams figured out the entire context of his business environment, which included meeting demand through understanding buying patterns and product-use rates that drove his retailers' inventory and supply needs. He says, "If they are going to buy it, you need to determine where it needs to be for them to get it." It was a win for me because I didn't need to worry if I was going to get enough air conditioners on the lot to take care of my dealers' needs. I got my warehouse stocked, and I got a better price because I bought them by the truckload in advance.

Eivion explains how his skill at negotiating his business context included managing the calendar to ensure products were available in the supply chain early each season.

We developed an early order system. In January through February I would contact all my major customers and would put together a package that included all of the "A" items, such as hitch balls, hitches, mirrors, sewer hoses, water hoses, jacks, air filters. We then would put together a list and would offer special pricing. "A" items also included parts that dealers needed to buy all the time, such as break controls, resisters, wire for wiring cars, spray paints for painting the covers, about forty to fifty consumable items. To take advantage of the early order list we put out, dealers had to order by February; had to take delivery in March; and they got thirty, sixty, or ninety days to pay for those orders.

Within our target market I had accumulated purchasing data from all of my customers for almost ten years. So I knew what each customer was buying on a monthly basis. Based on their statistics for any quarter or a two-month period, I could tell within ten percent what they were going to need in June. We put together a pre-automatic ordering system, so on the first of June we would mail our customers an order option that would cover them for the next thirty days. Seventy-five percent of what they used the year before was going to be in that audit. That helped me because I just could pre-order months ahead. It helped them because they didn't have to worry about phoning orders in; we'd have all of the buckets of shipments already done.

Eivion explains how he responded to his "community" of customers.

We always did what our customers needed us to do. In a business relationship, most of the time, somebody is telling customers what they need to do, rather than to listen to the customer saying, "This is what I need." So we would have regular meetings with our customers, whether they were buying five hundred dollars per month or five thousand dollars per month from us. At these meetings, I would say to customers, "I want you to put together a wish list that includes what you are distributing and what you want us to do first for you. What are those areas where we can help you be more successful?"

I asked, "Doesn't that make more stress for you as the seller because you have to meet those expectations? Isn't that why salespeople come in with their agenda and try to sell particular items?"

Eivion says that wanting to be as responsive as possible to his customers is what drove him to innovate by using computers more than a decade before it became popular to do so. He says,

Having customers explain to us their needs actually made my life easier. My customers could not call on Friday to place specific orders that would fill their needs for the coming week, because over the weekend they'd sell so much stuff but had no way of guessing what that actually would be on Friday. So they would all try to call in and place orders first thing Monday morning. I wanted to overcome this cycle. So I got my computer people together and explained what the customers were telling me. They needed to be able to place orders quicker, which meant not waiting until Monday morning. So we developed a computer system that was interactive. This was fifteen years before anyone else was doing this stuff. We voice activated a computer call-in ordering system. Customers would call a number and could talk to my computer 24/7.

I was spending forty thousand to fifty thousand dollars a year on software. It was second to none. Nobody could do what our company could. My salesman actually would go out and stand with our distributors and their employees as they entered their orders to show them how simple it really was to use the system.

Not only that, but when a customer came into a distributorship and said, "I need a 13,500 BTU air conditioner. Do you have any?" a distributor could say, "No, I don't, but my supplier does!" A company could call right then and ask my computer if there is any in stock. It wouldn't tell you how many we had, but it would tell if at least one was in stock, and the distributor could press 2 and order it for the next shipment. So we had all kinds of dialogue going on with the customer, and believe me, the customer was willing to pay a bit of a premium for the service, as our prices were always five to six percent higher than my competitors'. There is a price breaking point, however, above which you cannot go before the customer-loyalty factor begins to fade, which is about over six percent. If your costs are five percent above your competitors', customers will buy your products with no questions.

We set the standards, and one of the philosophies that we always had was "if you do what everybody else does, what good is that?" We want to be ahead of the curve. We want to be the industry pacesetter. We want everybody to chase us, so we have to be able to do things that the competition can't do. We did that. We delivered with our own trucks. Competition had a very hard time when they had to deliver by common carrier. They had no control over a common carrier. I had control over every single product that went out of my warehouse. My drivers had the goods, and I knew exactly where they were day and night. Our drivers were considered to be our salespeople. Everybody wore uniforms and had on them their name and the name of our company.

I trained my drivers, "You deliver the goods. They sign the paperwork. They say, 'I have a problem,' what do you do?" They said, "I come back and tell you." I said, "No. You go in the office, and you call and you tell us what the problem is over the phone. The customer doesn't know if you tell me when you get back here, so you do it right in front of them, and we will fix it." The customer always tells you what to do.

Eivion's sales driver customer-service relationship built such a strong sense of community that distributors looked out for them as if they were their own employees.

Williams relates:

My drivers were loved by our customers. We had set routes that we did every day. If a driver was late, by two o'clock a customer calls and says, "Billy's not here. Is he on the way?" We'd say, "Yes, he is." They'd say, "Well, he is normally here by eleven. I'm afraid he may be broken down." They were more concerned with our driver than they were concerned with getting their product. So, we knew the route and would call two customers back to see if

Billy had been there. We'd find out that he had some problems with some stuff that he was taking care of, so he was running late. We'd have him call the concerned customer from his next stop. We trained our guys and then we trusted them.

Eivion says,

Transitioning customers to a new delivery person was tough, because our customers got used to the same guy. We had a hard time doing the handoff. I hated calling the customer and saying, "Billy's not delivering to you next week. I got George, a new guy, and he is great. Give him an opportunity. If you have any issues, call me. Trust me, he will take good care of you." I would tell my delivery guy, "Don't ever walk out of a customer's operation if you have not resolved the problem. If you haven't resolved it before you leave, you have not done your job." We took care of our customers. I had a customer from Burlington, Vermont, a big customer, a $100,000-a-year customer. He paid his bill like clockwork. He was the best payer I ever saw. Our competition would go in and offer him the item for ten percent, fifteen percent, twenty-five percent under market value; he wasn't interested. He'd say, "We buy everything from Mohawk!"

Eivion acknowledges that the worst way to compete in business is on price. The best way to compete is on quality. "Quality, service and trust," says Eivion, who continues.

Our early-order system met a real business need for the dealers by giving them the ability to stock up in advance of their busiest season. If they didn't buy at that time, then later I would not be able to keep up with my ordering and deliveries. I couldn't move the stuff fast enough to keep up with demand. Once the season hits, dealers are going straight out and can't wait for supplies. My early-order system gave them the opportunity to stock their warehouses in advance. They didn't have to worry about getting behind on ordering. I didn't have to worry about rushing as many deliveries.

Eivion notes that his early-ordering system allowed Mohawk to catch up on inventory control: "In fact, stuff that we would think was stolen would be found in the warehouse as we inventoried each early December. We would organize the warehouse, and things that previously were counted as stolen would be found, as it just had been put in the wrong spot."

Mohawk's Community Context

Eivion says, "We were supplying approximately 1,600 RV and mobile home customer-dealers in this vast territory. We supplied them with about 6,500 items. We started out with two hundred customers and gained about fifty annually over the years as we continued to grow."

Negotiating Downturns by Making Quick Adjustments by Getting Help from Your Friends

Eivion told me about how the company got into financial difficulty and how he negotiated that context with the help of a loyal employee force. He relates:

> We were approached by two of my frequent vendors. One was an awning manufacturer in Massachusetts, and we were selling about $1 million to $1.5 million of his product. The other vendor was a major manufacturer of hitch lines. They asked us to open up a branch distribution outlet in Pennsylvania.
>
> Industry developments made the timing of this venture ill fated. The industry was consolidating. Mohawk Trailer Supply had experienced its growth when the industry was in an adolescent stage. Once an industry reaches maturity, it no longer is rapidly expanding and taking in more and more customers. To continue to grow, companies start buying other companies. The consolidations give the larger companies more profits as they take advantage of economies of scale.

Eivion notes how this impacted his decision to attempt the expansion.

A major player in the market was beginning to buy up distributorships. They purchased a distributor down in Allentown, Pennsylvania. They closed down the operation and moved it to Manchester, Pennsylvania. My suppliers and vendors thought that there was now a hole that we could fill in the Allentown area. The plan was to open a branch to service that area, because there is no competition there. So I got my accountant, and he looked over the situation to determine how much would be required to be invested. I talked to some people in that area who had lost their jobs because of the consolidation when the competitor purchased the organization they worked for and moved it. I hired eleven of those people and went into the venture with a full warehouse financed by a loan from my banker. The inventory alone was over $1 million dollars more than two decades ago. On top of this expense was the other infrastructure, the computers we had to have. The investment was well over a million dollars.

I lost all of it in about six months. The competitor, now out of Manchester, decided we were not going to sell anything in that territory. So if we sold something for ten dollars, they would sell it for nine dollars. If I tried selling that same product for eight dollars, they sold it for seven dollars. If I sold it for five dollars, they sold it for three dollars (even though they paid nine dollars)! They just determined that they were not going to be kicked out of their market. Their practices may have been predatory or illegal—I'm not sure. When I realized what was happening, I just stopped. We couldn't sell and be profitable. There was no way I could survive that. I didn't have the staying power. It would have taken about two years to break the other company, and I couldn't survive that long.

I had payments due. I bit the bullet, and we closed the warehouse and pulled the entire inventory back to Schenectady, New York. I negotiated with all my vendors to do one of two things: a) ship back the product with the vendor paying the freight, or b) the vendor could extend credit, and I'd pay them off at a particular rate on the dollar. Every one of them let me pay them off. My mortgage vendor said, "You pay everybody else first, then pay me."

Through that whole process I can't tell you how emotionally devastating this was; the company basically was bankrupt. Our net worth was a negative number. The banker I was doing business with actually loaned me more money to make sure we could complete our withdrawal transition. In total I think he loaned me $1.5 million. We brought in a consultant. He was very sarcastic. He was terrible with people, but he knew business. I had the people skills, but I didn't understand exactly what I needed to do on the business side. Between the two of us we made a great team.

Closing down the new operation was a very emotional decision. I didn't want to fail. The smart business guy decided to help me extract what we could and to get out of there. He was a Christian, and we became good friends. He was a difficult man to deal with because he saw things in black and white. He didn't see any areas of gray. I was not a Christian, so he would come into the office and say, "Here is what you have to do," and I would swear. He'd say, "Hey, you can't be talking like that." I would tell him, "I'm paying you seventy-five dollars an hour and you are telling me I can't swear!" So I am sitting there one day and I took the Lord's name in vain, as I did on a regular basis, and he said, "I'm really offended. I wish you wouldn't take the Lord's name in vain!" I looked at this guy, and the first thing that came to my mind was, "Get out!" But then I thought he may still be of some use, and I could always kill him later! This led to discussions about Jesus Christ, and I gave him my heart and received forgiveness for my sins. I became a believer and a devoted Bible reader. The consultant and I eventually did become friends, and we turned the company around. It was an amazing turnaround!

During that time he said, "For the company to survive you need to fire twenty-five percent of your employees." I said, "I can't do that!" At that time we probably had twenty to twenty-two people working for us. He said, "You are going to go broke, so you have to cut your expenses by twenty-five percent, so you have to do it!" So I decided, "I will tell the employees where we are, and I will give them all the opportunity to take a twenty-five percent cut in pay." He said, "Okay. That might work, but what will happen is twenty-five percent of them will quit, so you will end up with the same result." I told him that I didn't think anyone would quit. He said, "At least twenty-five percent of your people are going to quit, and you had better hope it is the right twenty-five percent, because if you lose some of your key people, you are in a heap of trouble!" I brought the entire chain to our central office and told them where we were.

"Here is the deal," I said. "I can fire one-fourth of you, or we can all stay and everyone takes a twenty-five percent cut in pay, except my wife and me, who will take a fifty percent cut in pay. We can't pay our bills at a fifty percent cut. We will have to figure something out, but that is what we'll do. I don't want an answer now. It's Friday afternoon, so go home, talk to your husbands and wives, and tell them what has happened. Monday morning at eight o'clock we'll meet right here."

Everybody came in Monday morning, and I learned the employees had gotten together Friday night and talked about what was happening, and every one of them decided that they would take the twenty-five percent cut in pay, except two people. My receptionist (whom I had known since I was four years old) said, "You can lay me off because I don't need the money. I'm here because of you, and I like what I'm doing. My husband makes all kinds of money. Lay me off, and I will collect unemployment. A year from now, if you want me back, we'll talk." I said, "Okay, but I don't want to lose you." She said, "Do it!" The other guy was one of our truck drivers who said, "I can't live on twenty-five percent less pay. Is there some way you can cut my pay ten percent? I can live if you cut my pay ten percent, not twenty-five percent." So I went to my four managers and said, "Here is what he said. Do you want to keep him, or do you want to let him go?" They said, "Let's keep him. Cut his pay ten percent, and we will see what happens." So we did, and he stayed.

A year later they all were making ten percent more than they were before we made the cut. Paying them thirty-five percent more one year later tells you what the company profit was. It was an amazing turnaround!

A few years later, after everything was fixed, business was up to seven or eight million dollars a year. Everybody was excited about what we were doing. I kept the consultant on a retainer and paid him every month for things he did for us. He also kept talking to me about Jesus. I wasn't anti-religious; I believed in God. He was persistent. I started going to a community church, and the first time I walked in I immediately felt, *This is something*. I felt like I was home; I felt very, very comfortable.

New Owners Can Change the Business Dynamics and the Team

Eivion eventually sold Mohawk Trailer Supply Company to a national firm because he thought that would give him the opportunity to replicate throughout America the supplier-to-dealer-to-customer win-win-win synergies and tremendous regional impact Mohawk had achieved. What he discovered, however, was how difficult and rare it is to build a team of managers and employees who can adopt the same winning philosophy and work together to negotiate it.

Mohawk continued to flourish and grow until sales were about $14 million a year, and others were taking notice. Eivion recounts, "The company that had driven me out of Pennsylvania was after me constantly to buy my company. I kept saying no. It was about seven years after our turnaround." Eivion says he was not angry at the larger company for what had happened in Pennsylvania. He explains how the situation unfolded that motivated him to sell:

> We were impossible to beat in our market area. They couldn't figure it out. The only way to get me out was to buy me out. We just took such good care of our customers that they wouldn't talk to any other suppliers. My main competitor thought that I was buying my customers' loyalty by paying a kickback under the table to keep them, because the customers were so adamant that they wouldn't buy from any of our competitors.

The CEO of the larger organization kept knocking on my door and flew in and made me an offer, and it was a very fair offer. I said, "No, I'm not interested." He said, "I just don't understand this. You can be an extremely wealthy guy and not have any responsibilities." I told him, "I like what I do. I'm not going to sell the company."

A couple of years later, however, the industry took a dip. We had been through some dips before, but I could see that this one was different. We saw a leveling out of sales growth throughout our entire territory. This was not a dip but signs of growth stagnation in the entire industry.

For a company to be successful, it needs to continue to grow. It's just an economic thing. You can't continue along as if nothing is happening. All employees need wage increases on a regular basis. You can tweak prices by percentages to take in more money only so often. Companies that are growing don't need to try to overly tweak their prices to achieve business synergy, but can maintain and stabilize them, because they are always making extra profit from additional sales growth. So we saw stagnation and thought the industry had reached a saturation point. Not enough new buyers were looking to purchase RVs. Companies like ours either had to sell, or we had to make some other decisions that would help to expand our marketing territory, like buying other distribution points. So I explored all three options at the same time.

Eivion explains that because he could not reach potential new customers from his existing location, he was going to have to acquire or open new distributorships from which points he could cover more territory while keeping up the excellent customer service that had made him regionally successful.

We looked at purchasing a Mid-Atlantic location in the Baltimore area and then one in the Georgia area. With these acquisitions we could cover the whole East Coast. We were already covering from Baltimore up, which was a hard two-day trip that made it very tough to keep up the quality customer service delivery from where we were in Upstate New York in

Schenectady. We looked at the distribution in the Midwest and on the West Coast. We were pursuing all avenues. At the same time, I was looking at new ways to attract other customers within our target market, which was not promising to do.

The market did not look good, and we were having difficulty finding capital for a four to five million-dollar expansion to open up two more locations. After thoroughly analyzing the situation, we thought that if this guy offers us a particular number, the best thing to do is sell the company. The CEO of the larger organization calls as we were on our way back from a business trip, and I met him during a layover in Chicago, and he made an offer that was a million dollars more than we were targeting. Gene, my consultant, advised, "Take the offer." So we accepted it.

Can two walk together, except they be agreed? [52]

Eivion explains how team synergy is built upon each member seeing what the others see and feeling what the others feel, which, as stated earlier, are the dynamics for effective negotiations, the outcomes of which are the triple-C synergy of communication, cooperation, and coordination. Eivion says, "They wanted me to stay on as the COO of the company they had just purchased from me, and I did so against my better judgment. The CEO of the parent company was a deceiver. He and I were like oil and water, 180 degrees apart!"

Eivion's next obligation and challenge became to assist his loyal customers to make the transition to a distributorship that now was under new ownership. Since his customers would not talk to the organization that had just purchased his company, Eivion wanted to ensure the loyal and fruitful relationship would continue in the win-win-win tradition that had made Mohawk and its distributors so successful up to that point.

Eivion says,

Our customers trusted us. It was necessary for me to tell my customers face-to-face that we sold the company, and the new owners would take over operations on January 2 the coming year.

So we put together a traveling road show and did five locations in six days in late December. I called all my dealers, and we met in Connecticut, Long Island, Albany, Syracuse, and a Boston location. We had all of our dealers meet us in rented dining areas in hotels. "We advised we have some industry news to share with you, and it is real important that you come." Eighty-five to ninety percent of the people we invited showed up.

Long Island probably had been our most difficult territory to crack. It took us two years to crack that territory. When we'd go down and make promises, they thought we were just like everybody else that came along. We just had to prove ourselves. So we called them every week. Our trucks went down every week whether it was one hundred dollars or five thousand dollars. It didn't matter, the truck went. Over time we ended up with ninety percent of the RV business on Long Island. We just got them all. When we went down to make the presentation that we were selling the company to a competitor, a guy named Bobby was distraught. Bobby was a guy that never got out of the 1950s. He always wore a T-shirt with a pack of Camels rolled up in his sleeve, and his hair was greased back. Bobby was a real tough character. He talked tough too. Every sentence out of his mouth had a swear word.

We made a slide presentation at lunch, and afterwards, at every meeting, people stood up and said, "I can't believe you are doing this. Why are you doing this?" I told them, "We see trouble ahead in the industry. We don't think we can be what we want to be in the new environment. Things are changing, and I think it's time for us also to make a change." Tough Bobby stands up and tries to talk and starts to cry! He said, "You can't do this. Do you know how much we count on you?" I had to stop the meeting and take Bobby aside. He's sobbing on my chest, and I'm patting him on the back and saying, "Bobby, it's going to be okay." Bobby is saying, "You don't understand how hard it's been to do this!" That was the relationship we had built with our customers!

Eivion explains what happens when a parent company fails to rely upon people to negotiate their local context.

We sold the company, and I went to work as the chief operating officer and immediately ran into conflict with the chief executive officer. I was traveling back and forth between Schenectady and San Jose, California, and we'd agree upon some decisions. I'd go home and realize a week later that the decisions were not implemented, or they were changed so radically that it didn't make any sense from our local perspective. The CEO and I were in constant conflict. At one point I actually threatened him with physical bodily harm. "You keep doing this and you and I are going to fight, and I mean fight!" But I knew that it was senseless to let things get that bad. I had a two-year contract. I worked about a year and a quarter, and I knew it wasn't going to last.

About two weeks later he called and asked me to come out. He had a managers meeting with about fourteen managers. The meeting was terrible! He berated everybody. He had grown men in tears; called them all kinds of names. "You're not doing this right, and you're not doing that right!" At noontime he got up, and everyone just scattered. The room cleared out, and I just sat there. I walked toward the door, and I said, "God, I'm sorry. My Schenectady operation is in this mess because it was my idea. I thought this was a good plan, but this is not about me; it's about you and I'm sorry. Forgive me. Get me out of this." I walked to the elevator, and the owner of the company and the CEO were standing at the elevator. I said, "This isn't going to work. You and I are oil and water. It's not going to work. What are we going to do?" He said, "Why don't I buy your contract?" I said, "Okay. Make me an offer." He made me an offer. I said, "Add twenty-five percent to that and you have a deal." He said, "Done!" I asked him if I had asked for fifty percent more would he have given it to me. He said yes. I hate to leave money on the table. He paid me, I worked for four months, and he paid me for eighteen more, so I got twenty-two months. I basically retired for the first time at that point at forty-six years old.

The Leadership Journey

Although Eivion's first success was with a start-up venture when an entrepreneur gave him his first leadership start as CEO of a new company, he believes he is a reengineering leader whose specialty is rescuing troubled projects and broken processes. Eivion has strong operations abilities to focus people and arrange processes to accomplish a mission, but his passion is to strategically resurrect, turn around, and get things up and running again once the context has changed and things that were working no longer are working. He says,

> I don't think I am a startup guy. I can do that, but I'd rather be a fixer. I like to take something that is broken and make it work or take something that is not working as well as it should and make it better. In the ministries that God has called me to lead, which is basically what I have done since I retired from my previous business, he has equipped me to do exactly that. I just go in and fix struggling operations and take them to the next level.

After enjoying his retirement for a few years, Eivion says he felt God's call and began fixing up not-for-profit ventures. Eivion's first not-for-profit leadership venture was a Christian ministry called the Schenectady City Mission (SCM), which is a rescue shelter for men. When Eivion assumed leadership of that organization, he knew the main goal was to get the various ministries to function well to achieve their departmental missions, which combined to fulfill the larger mission. Eivion says, "I did not think I was equipped to do Christian ministry work. I thought that my call was to be a witness for God in a lot of ways. I was growing in my walk with the Lord. I was in all kinds of Bible studies and doing a lot of things. I just never saw myself being a kind of minister."

Lead Something that Is New to You—
Not by Being a Know-It-All,
but a Humble Learner

I asked Eivion how he had the courage to take the plunge into his next leadership venture at the Schenectady City Mission (SCM). He relates how he transitioned into working his hobby.

During the time that I was retired, I kept looking for other businesses. Every time my wife and I found a business we thought we could do, a door would slam in our face. I had the money to buy businesses; we just couldn't make a deal. In hindsight, what God did was put me on ice for a year and a half, where I had a lot of time to study and fellowship with the Christian community.

The Mission had always been one of my favorite charities. I had a good relationship with one of its directors for years. I didn't know it at the time when I was in business, but I was one of the largest donors to the ministry, which I discovered after I went to work there and started looking at some of the old records. I always had felt gratified giving to the Mission. It was near and dear to my heart.

The Mission was between directors, and two of its board members asked to meet for lunch. At the meeting, I am thinking that I will give them some money, and I was growing a little anxious because the longer it takes to ask, the bigger the number will be. These guys were not asking, so I started getting nervous, and finally I said, "Okay, guys, how much do you need?" They said, "What do you mean?"

"I figure this meeting is about you needing a big donation, so just ask me, and if I can do it I will; if I can't, I can't.'

They said, "Oh no, no. That's not why we are talking to you. We want you to come and be the director of the Mission." I laughed and said, "You must be crazy. Why would I want to do that? Look around you. We're at a place where I can play twenty-seven holes of golf any time I want. I can see the first tee from this table. Look at the way my life is. Why would I want to go down to the Mission?" They said, "We thought you loved the Mission." I said, "I do from a distance. I don't want to get up close and personal with that ministry. There is no way I can go into ministry. There is no way my wife would allow me to go into ministry. She has told me over and over again, she didn't marry a guy in ministry, and she isn't being married to a guy in ministry, whether it is a pastor or anything else." They asked, "Well, would you ask her?"

"That's a no-brainer. Sure, I will ask her!"

I went home, and my wife asked, "How much did they want, Eivion?" I said, "They didn't want money. They want me to go to work at the Mission." My wife asked, "What did you tell them?" and I said, "I told them no way!" I asked her, "What do you think?" To my surprise, she said, "I don't know. Let's think about it." Then I was thinking, *Okay, this is not good.*

As the previous meeting was ending, the chairman of the Mission's board asked how much time I needed to determine my answer. I asked if the Mission was functioning, and he said it was, as he was actually acting as the director temporarily and was anxious to bring someone on board soon. I asked for thirty days to make a decision, and we set a date for me to be at his house for dinner. Thirty days came and went; my wife and I kept talking about it, and I hadn't made a decision.

My wife and I went over to the chairman's house, and she asked, "What are you going to tell him? We have to make a decision on whether you take this job or not." All the way to his house I actually was silently praying to God, *Have her say no. Have her say no.* As we were pulling up to his house, I said to her, "What do you think I should do?" She says, "I don't know," and I sped up a little and drove right past the house. She said, "You missed the house," and I said, "I'm not going in." She said, "You are going to be late." I said, "I am not going in until I have a decision." She said, "You know what? I think we would be okay if you took the position." I said, kind of talking to both her and God, "That's not good enough. It's either got to be, 'Yes, Eivion, take the position,' or, 'No, Eivion, don't take the position.' I'm not going to go on 'I think it would be okay to take the position.' It's got to either be a solid yes or a solid no. I'm not moving until I have a clear answer." She said, "Yes, take the position." We went in, and I accepted the position. We agreed that I would start the day after Labor Day.

I went to the Mission the morning of my first day on the job, and I parked my truck and felt a twinge of panic inside, and I grabbed hold of the steering wheel, said to God, "Okay, you got me this far, but you are not getting me one step farther. I am not going in this building!" Needless to say, he got me in the building. When I walked in the building, I knew I was doing exactly what I was supposed to do with no question in my mind and heart. It was a tough road, but I learned more in the five years I spent at that Mission than God had taught me in the ten years prior to that.

Stretching and Achieving

Eivion says that being the director of the Schenectady City Mission stretched him tremendously. He says it taught him about human relationships and what is required of a man of God. He says he would go into the office every morning about 7:30 or a little before and would spend a half hour on his knees in the chapel. Eivion says he knew he could not do what was required, but that he kept hearing a little inner voice saying, "I know you can't, but I can. Just get up and go." So Eivion said, "I'd go."

Eivion got connected to the organization from end to end by "managing by walking around." Every morning he would walk through each ministry to talk to each department head. He'd go to chapel and would spend time with the men. He says, "It was a great process!"

The Mission had many diverse facets, and I never had a down day. Six months after I started, all of my second-line officers came to me. The managers, the person who headed up men's ministry, and the chaplain all came into my office and closed the door. I said, "Okay, why are we having this meeting?" The spokesperson said, "We just had a meeting and want you to know that six months ago, when you came here, we all had our letters of resignation written and were ready to resign. Things were just really bad here. When you came on board, we decided to give you six months and we'd see how things were going. We just want to show you something." They took the letters out and ripped them up.

Eivion's perspective is that a combination of things was troubling them that stemmed from poor leadership.

They had been in the ministry and had good experience and knew what needed to be done, but they were not being allowed to do it. They felt they each were being led by God to make the ministry work better, and there was no doubt in my mind that they were right. There had been a spiritual permeation that had stemmed from the last leader that just wasn't good and had run throughout the entire organization. A lot of backbiting politics had taken place. The managers could not get any support from the previous CEO.

While I felt we could do some things differently, I also did not bring out a gun and say, "My way or the highway." As we talked about these things, I would suggest, "What if you do this, would that improve your communication and improve your success rate with our clients?" We would work through things over time.

During the first six months, we had what I call "wish-list meetings." We met once a week at seven a.m., and every department head would make up a list of what he or she wanted the department to look like a year and five years from now. We did this every Monday morning for three months. We met and charted out the visions. We would say, "If you could do everything, and you had no money concerns, what would your wish list look like?" Then we prioritized every list. It took us three to four months to get that done. Then we started the implementation process. We started working on doing the most important things on those lists.

Eivion and his team's plans were successful because they developed concrete tactics for their vision. When money came in, they knew exactly what to do with it. They had planned their work, and they then worked their plan. Fundraising became more dynamic because they could solicit money with a purpose in mind, and people like to give to a vision that is connected to a tangible purpose or cause.

Eivion's leadership at the Mission was a mixture of vision, faith, and economics. The Mission's economic model includes a thrift business. The items sold are provided by free in-kind donations. He says,

> Let me tell you some of the things that God gave to our ministry in ways that we could not have planned them any better. We had two thrift stores, one in the main complex, and one out of town in a rented building that was costing us at that time $2,500 per month. We sold donated items and had no inventory costs. We made money at our thrift stores, but the rent was exorbitant. I went on a mission to buy a building we could own and save the rent and actually build some equity in the property. We located a building, and the Board of Directors approved. We bought a building that was fifty percent larger than the one we were renting, and the cost per month was half of what our rental costs were. We bought it, and our sales went up twenty-five percent the first year!
>
> What would it have been like if I went to my salespeople and said, "We have to cut our expenses by fifty percent, increase our inventory and our square footage by another fifty percent, and you've got to add twenty-five percent to the bottom line. They would have said, "You had better get someone else to do it because it's impossible." And it was. But that is exactly what God did. Why? Our part was to be obedient and step out and do what we were led to do.

Eivion's vision and leadership expanded the ministry of the Schenectady City Mission to provide services for all genders.

> The mission had no women's ministry to speak of when I started, and I said to the board that we need to deal with women. Within a year we had a women's ministry. We had no money, but God provided it. We bought a building and started the women's ministry.
>
> There are a few ways one might approach starting that ministry. One way would be to first find the person who would run it.

Another way is to start by determining how much it would cost to run the ministry and seeing if you can raise the money first. Here is Eivion's story of what took place.

> The first thing we had to do was get an agreement from the Board of Directors to approve women's ministry. There was a building next door to us for sale. At first the owners wanted sixty-five thousand dollars for it, and for more than a year (1992–1993) it was obvious that there were no purchasers in this area. We were the only ones that would buy the building. So I kept talking to the owners every three to four months, asking, "Have you decided on a price that we can afford?" Finally, she showed up one day and said, "Thirty-five thousand dollars." I said, "Okay, sounds fair. I have to talk to the Board of Directors."
>
> At a board meeting I presented that we needed to buy this building for thirty-five thousand dollars for a women's ministry. We got into a big fight. One side of the room was dead-set against it; the other side of the room was for it. We had no money. We had about thirteen thousand dollars in a checking account. One of the Board of Directors was a real hard-nosed business guy. He said, "We can't afford this. We have nothing to start with. I believe it's a good ministry, and we ought to be able to do this eventually, but there is no way we can do this now!" People were yelling back and forth.
>
> I prayed, *Okay, God, I'm going to call for a vote. If the vote is not unanimous, I'm taking this thing off the table. Everyone has to be in agreement.* I got everyone calmed down. I said, "I believe this is necessary. I just want to see a show of hands as a vote." I said, "Should we go through with this and try to buy this building?" Every hand went up.
>
> So I look at this guy who had been yelling that this is not good business, and I said, "Why are you doing this?" He said, "Well, somebody has to be the bad guy. Somebody has to ask the tough questions. We need to do a ministry." I said to him, "How are we going to get the money?" He said, "I don't know;

we will figure it out." This was amazing. A half hour later we broke up the meeting, and as I am walking out of the conference room, there is a message over the PA system: "Eivion, there is a phone call." So I go to the warehouse phone, and it's an attorney. He said, "Mr. Williams, I have a few questions for you. We have a person who has left a legacy to the mission, and if you answer the questions correctly, we can send you out a check." I said, "Oh, that's nice. What are the questions?"

"Are you a Christian ministry?" I said, "Yes."

"Are you affiliated with a national organization, or are you a standalone ministry for this community?" I said, "We are a standalone." The attorney said, "Those are the two questions my client wanted answered, and we will be sending out a check in about a week." I said, "Can you tell me how much the check is for?"

"Sure, thirty-five thousand dollars."

So I just got on my knees and thanked God for what he had done. A couple of the board members were still hanging around. I went to them and said, "You are not going to believe this, but an attorney is sending us a check for thirty-five thousand dollars!" They said, "Come on, Eivion. This isn't funny!" I said, "I am not kidding!" Just like that, God took care of it.

When Eivion left the mission, it was a better organization by every measurable standard. They were serving more clients, were in a better financial state, and had better working relationships between the board members, employees, and clients. Eivion says,

Revenues were up fifty to sixty percent. The donor base had increased by about the same amount. The ministries that were working well when I got there were still working well. The Women's Ministry and the Youth Ministry were started and greatly expanded. The Counseling Ministry improved in quality as we brought in an MSW to do counseling.

Eivion also says, "I didn't do that. It was God, not me. I am just a tool."

Currently, Eivion is serving as the executive director of the Alpha Pregnancy Center in Albany, New York. That organization also is expanding to fulfill its mission under Eivion's leadership.

Chapter Thirty-two

Negotiating the Patterns to Convert within the Context

Community Patterns

Bill Dake and Eivion Williams talk about seeing the patterns as a key to success. If the organizational mission is client service, then front-line workers have the most firsthand knowledge about what is taking place throughout the community that is having an impact on clients. If several clients experience or observe the same phenomenon, none of them may even talk to each other to realize they all are experiencing the same thing. Eivion says, "A client may not be able to say, 'This is what is going on in my community or environment.' But if five clients come to you, you can see the pattern of what is going on. The front-line people see the patterns." Both Dake and Williams train front-line managers and employees to identify the patterns. These three-dimensional leaders empower employees to take action about what they perceive to have an impact on customers and clients. When the patterns are brought to the executive leaders' attentions, they work with department managers to respond appropriately and timely.

In business everyone knows that numbers matter. It does not take large numbers for astute people to quickly recognize a development that could indicate a trend. The challenge for many operations, however, is determining what numbers matter, how they matter, and what to do about them. For Bill Dake of the Stewart's Corporation, numbers have the most meaning when they are considered in relationship to the context in which they occur. He says,

> I would describe my personal mantra as "relationships versus absolutes." After 'do not lie,' 'do not cheat,' and 'do not steal,' I don't think there are many absolutes out there. We deal with relationships versus absolutes because all numbers are only meaningful relatively. I am six feet tall. If I was in grade school, I would be big. If I was a professional basketball player, I would be small. We do all our numbers and our counting, our deviations, from the company context. In other words, if you told me how much business you did, that wouldn't tell me much; it would be like telling me the weather. If you said you were fifteen percent below the company average last week and the week before you were twenty percent below, I now know your performance in relation to something that is meaningful.

Sales do not tell a complete story about the health of a business. Dake says this is "because you have items such as lottery that provide only a six percent margin. Gas is only five percent. You have other items that are thirty percent, forty percent, fifty percent, so the gross profit dollars are what you have to spend, and so we analyze everything on gross profit and on deviation on the average of 325 stores. But it is all about relationships; so our numbers are in relationship." Dake says that patterns and trends are revealed in seeing relationships.

> The reason we use the word "relationships" is because we want to keep focused on seeing patterns. Business intellect is the ability to see patterns or trends. If you see patterns in numbers, you can see marketing trends. Some people only see absolutes. Absolutists can't see patterns. So they can't see the trends. The absolute person wants one person, one solution, one point of view. So the primary issue I spend my time dealing with is the

intangible variables of trying to get people to think about the relationships versus the absolutes.

Three-dimensional leaders have a robust perspective as a lens through which they view their contexts so they see information in relation to what is most meaningful to the mission and in relation to the other people with whom the mission must be coordinated. Bill Dake says seeing "relationships versus absolutes certainly is critical." For him the specialists of the business world, who deal only in absolutes, lose perspective on the patterns within the context. The Dake model cuts through a lot of the peripheral noise variables, such as a store's location, the community market it is in, and the traffic patterns around it, to drive at how this store is performing today versus how it performed yesterday. Dake says the comparison is "relative to the previous week, month, year, or thirteen-month period. It's simply a question of relatively are you getting better or worse?"

General Electric under Jack Welsh had an evaluation program that compelled managers every year to deal with employees who performed within the bottom five percent of achievers. One outcome of this strategy could be that, in time, your bottom five percent are those who used to be in the thirty-fifth to fortieth percentile of performance and are people who actually are doing a good job. In relation to this concept, Dake says the Stewart's strategic issue is "how much can you continue to grow [an individual store], and does our process squeeze people out?" Dake believes that with the manager obtaining one-third of the profit of the shop he or she has an incentive to do well.

The model seems to be functioning fine for Stewart's, which, in 2006, hit a billion dollars in annual sales. Since the Stewart's incentive system has been motivating managers for thirty years to achieve steady corporate growth, there seems to be no need to fix what indeed is not broken. Dake says, "Most incentive systems get totally changed within five years because they have flaws in them. This one has lasted a long time." From my perspective this is proof it was constructed from an accurate view of the context and considered the right patterns.

People Make Conversion Possible by Making the Best Decisions in Bad Circumstances

Seeing patterns in the big picture also puts mistakes in context so they are dealt with appropriately before they become fatal errors. Getting your organization on track requires leaders to be oriented to their mission, resources, and context (MRC) concepts. Thus both Eivion Williams and Joe Sluszka, of the Albany Housing Coalition (AHC), were successful in leading their organizations out of disastrous situations, and both did so with their core teams intact. To overcome, one must recognize the reality in the context and face it with accountability.

Eivion accurately assessed the context and made appropriate three-dimensional decisions in the middle of bad circumstances. While he says that "closing down the new operation was a very emotional decision" that carried the stigma of failure, he knew what he had to do, and he did it decisively. The three-dimensional Williams knew he "had the people skills" to handle his resources to fulfill the mission, and he was astute and humble enough to get the business expertise he needed when he needed it. Eivion at first did not see eye-to-eye with his new team member, the consultant, but he remained mission focused enough to work through the storming phase of team building, so the relationship progressed to where he says, "Between the two of us, we made a great team!"

A testament to Eivion's people skills and the credibility he had with his employees is how they all decided to work out ways for the company to survive and achieve the best win-wins possible in the middle of circumstances that were painful to both themselves and the company. Eivion led the way and set the example by taking a fifty percent pay cut when he was asking his employees to take a twenty-five percent cut. Had Eivion been insincere about the value he placed on his employees and had treated them poorly, routinely withheld information from them, and repeatedly demonstrated that he did not respect their input throughout his tenure as CEO of Mohawk Trailer and Supply, when the "chips were down" and their backs were against the proverbial wall, he would have had no credibility with them. They would have doubted his sincerity and not have trusted the information he provided, or they would not have believed that he had their best interest at heart. They would not have trusted that Eivion desired to save the company for their sakes as well as his own. They would not have responded to his leadership and have collaborated effectively.

Continuous improvement requires that an organization has the ability to correct mistakes before they become errors that are accompanied by insurmountable penalties. A mistake is an oversight or a slip or a blunder. An error stems from a longer-term inaccuracy and has greater negative outcomes for the organization. Mistakes that are not owned up to or which are ignored become errors! Whether the organizations above were making great turnarounds or continuously improving, it was the people, both employees and leaders, who were making the differences together. People provide the greatest potential for an organization to negotiate its context.

Three-dimensional leaders live by depositing the "reality check." They dissect the context and review data to assess the patterns and deploy, reassign, and redirect their resources into mission-focused initiatives. III-D leaders see problems as "challenges" that are overcome through negotiating the MRC concept to systematically move forward by making the best decisions possible in the middle of less-than-desirable circumstances. Once managers and front-line employees understand the organization's MRC concept, they can be unleashed in powerful ways to bring to bear their focused skill sets and brainpower upon any situation or challenge in their local context. Because they have a clear sense of the mission they are tasked to accomplish, and they understand the resources available to be deployed into the effort, they have a clearer ability to process and sort information to determine how to achieve the mission rather than be overwhelmed by any complexities confronting them.

Once, while on a flight to Atlanta, Georgia, I sat next to Kevin, the CEO of a ninety-employee company in Upstate New York. He had started his own venture after gaining experience with two very large corporations in the industry wherein his company now competed. He told me about an experience that occurred in his previous organization. He was promoted, and during his orientation meeting his new boss told him to fire a friend of his who was a general manager in another state. He did not want to fire the manager because he felt the market situation in which that office had to function was depressed and difficult for anyone to hit sales targets at that time. Kevin was focused on the context. The company, however, wanted to get another "personality" in the managerial role that oversaw the performance of seventeen people. I asked Kevin what would have happened had an analysis been done of the actual context in which the entire office was underperforming. Kevin says he does not know, because the company's sole focus was on the manager. Kevin left the company before he could monitor the performance of the new manager.

But what would have been the outcome had the company had faith in the manager as Kevin did and come alongside him to analyze the context and then to negotiate it by orienting the manager and the employees to redeploy their marketing and sales efforts? Of course, some would say that it was the manager's job to negotiate the local context and redeploy the resources so sales employees could hit targets, but who knows if leaders higher up in the organization had placed restrictions on doing so. Sometimes the only way to negotiate maintaining or increasing sales in a market where the economy is shrinking is to expand the territory, which could mean that adjacent territories have to be consolidated. Companies can have controls on adjacent territories that may limit one sales region expanding into another one. There may be other factors that prevent efficient expansion, such as population density (or lack thereof) and environmental factors, such as great travel distances that add to the time and cost of achieving sales, offsetting some of the real benefits or positive outcomes, such as profit margins.

Kevin's former employer had to train another manager, forfeiting future return from its investment in the first manager. Kevin believed he could have turned around the situation if given the opportunity. The manager also told Kevin that he did not understand why he was being let go. Assuming the manager was telling the truth, he probably felt there was more to the issue than bottom line sales figures. Training and discreet analysis based upon the MRC concept could have provided the manager and the company with a mutual understanding of the context and how to best negotiate it with existing resources. The manager and the company would have had a better understanding of how to gauge success and failure. Perhaps they both would have had a better understanding and agreement of the relationship between past performance, current outcomes, and future expectations.

A leader's job is to make sense of data and use it to implement decisions that make the best use of resources to accomplish a mission given a particular context. One-dimensional leaders are not focused on the mission, so data and the reality it reflects generally do not even enter into their frame of reference. Two-dimensional leaders, who tend to fail at negotiating the context, cannot make complete sense of the data and determine appropriate responses because they have difficulty seeing its relevance in relation to the operational context and all the other people and partners with whom the mission must be coordinated. II-D's may talk a good game of "we have this information and this is what it is showing us." They only will cite, however, what supports their premise(s) and will be blind to the total reality of the data's relationship within the greater context. II-D's do not have an accurate value of their human resources, and they tend to lack a genuine appreciation for the front-line employees who actually do the work. II-D's, therefore, do not tend to make decisions that actually facilitate and empower employees to do their jobs, so they ignore data that supports the value of what employees do.

By contrast, III-D's act appropriately on available information and implement decisions in ways that actually help employees throughout all strata of the organization to collectively accomplish the mission.

Dependable Data-Driven Decisions

Leaders make inappropriate decisions and fail to relate data to the realities within the context when they have agendas that compel them to have presuppositions and make particular interpretations. When the agenda is hidden from others or they are unaware of it, they end up scratching their heads, wondering, *How did the leaders arrive at that decision?* This is because an objective view of the data does not support the leader's action.

Other times leaders may sense that they don't have all the data, so they hesitate taking action, fearing they are missing something in the context. We can get bogged down in "analysis paralysis" by overscrutinizing every piece of information before making a decision. It is reasonable to be apprehensive about taking action because we sense that there are unknown factors in the context that may undermine or sidetrack a decision or new initiative or venture. While making decisions requires an understanding of the particular context from which the data is drawn or generated, you probably never will have every possible piece of information related to the context. As leaders we need strategies to deal appropriately with ambiguity so we are not paralyzed by it.

Colin Powell uses what he calls the "P=40 to 70" ratio to make decisions. To avoid letting any shred of ambiguity paralyze you, Powell says follow this principle.

> P = the *Probability* of Success and the numbers are the percentage of information required for it. If the information puts P in the 40 to 70 range, go with your gut instinct. Don't take action if you only have enough information to give you less than a 40 percent chance of being right, but don't wait until you have enough facts to be 100 percent sure, because by then it is almost always too late. Excessive delays in the name of information

gathering breed analysis paralysis. Procrastination in the name of reducing risk actually increases risk.[53]

The flipside of waiting too long is jumping in too soon before enough of the context is known. We need to be very cautious about acting on our presuppositions. "Going with your gut" does not mean that you are driven by capricious and fickle visceral passions that drive you in one direction one moment and then in another direction the next. There is a vast difference between understanding enough about the context to be discerning, intuitive, and insightful, and hurtling headstrong into decisions that, on the surface, seem mission oriented but in actuality fall short of producing promised or hoped for deliverables because of incomplete or nonexistent connections within the context.

Foxes and Puppy Dogs

I know leaders who pride themselves on how many decisions they make quickly. But their employees tell me the leader's decisions lack focus on achieving the organization's mission by making appropriate connections between the players in the context. These leaders are like the fox, first jumping over an obstacle and getting nowhere and then climbing up a hill, only to have to run down and around again. Because of factors within the context that the leader has not learned enough about to take into proper consideration, his/her initiatives are doomed to fail. Sometimes the failure is realized quickly, but the leader stubbornly will keep pursuing the initiative until it slowly fades from recollection through painful expiration. Often, the decisions include promises made to partner organizations that never can be fulfilled yet set up false expectations. The challenge for organizations is that while their leader foxes are going through their learning curves (assuming they can learn anything), they drag into their lair so many people and they interrupt so many process resources that the mission gets sidetracked and crippled.

Other leaders act like puppy dogs with their noses to the ground, going in this direction after an initiative and then in that direction after another, as they are enticed by every different scent they come across. Mature dogs are trained to hunt specific game and in specific ways. If the mission is to retrieve pheasants, they are disciplined to not be sidetracked by the scent of rabbits. Leaders who are properly oriented to and focused on the organizational mission look for opportunities to fulfill it rather than straying around the context, chasing fruitless initiatives.

The Well of Ambiguity
A Reservoir for Data Collection and Analysis

Rather than jumping to conclusions with frenetic puppy dog energy and being overwhelmed by all the sights, sounds, and complexities within the context, or feeling paralyzed by its unknowns, leaders need strategies to negotiate it. I use a tool I call the "Well of Ambiguity" (WOA) to pace my decisions when I am in the process of dissecting the context to determine informed, strategic initiatives. While conducting research and analysis, I often come across information that does not directly relate to what I am focused on at the moment, but which seems to have value within the context. I siphon this information into the WOA for future reference, research, and analysis, which allows me to move forward with the information related to the decision at hand. By placing information in the WOA, I am not distracted from the task at hand, and I avoid being sidetracked by information that seems mission focused but is not practical to act upon at this time. My goal is to maintain my focus to avoid making decisions today that are inconsistent with the ones I have to make tomorrow in pursuit of the long-range strategic mission.

The "Well of Ambiguity" (WOA) is not a copout, but a device where I store information that requires clarity before I am certain it is useful for the long-term strategic mission and goals I am tasked to achieve. Periodically, I dip into the WOA to examine and reanalyze the ambiguous information. Sometimes I notice patterns in this information that I can segregate into pools of related material that I continue to store and analyze in relation to the context in which my mission must unfold. This ambiguous yet coalescing information does not impede my ability to move forward on current issues.

Three-dimensional leaders know that there probably are two or three very good and more than one so-called "best" way to do almost anything, so they nudge subordinates to pull a straw or flip a coin to choose one of those "best" ways to keep the process moving forward. If it becomes apparent that the method is not working to accomplish the desired results, I back out of the process or strategy to pursue another method. The reason you can confidently go forward to pursue one avenue or another is because the difference in outcomes between pursuing one "best" way versus another way often are too miniscule to measure. Once you have analyzed enough to narrow your options down to two or three methods, rather than devote too much time in further study that may not make the choice any clearer, act—move forward, but be alert to emerging information that will determine if you should keep going as planned or if some adjustment is necessary. Choosing also spares the emotional agony and conflict that could result over indecision or endless haggling over options.

SMART is the concept many leaders use to determine if ideas and initiatives are suitable and valid for their organizations. SMART means specific, measurable, adaptable, realistic, and trackable. Initiatives must be smart in relation to the organization's core mission. They must have specific outcomes that can be tracked and measured by the management-information system (MIS) that captures and provides data on the organization's employees' activities. Initiatives that meet these tests are "realistic" in relation to the actual mission and can be undertaken within the organizations core operational success dynamics (COSD).

Core mission SMART initiatives are those related to the organization's front-end work. They are related to what employees do within the context, such as client acquisition, patient intake, service provision, manufacturing, repairs, sales, and pick-ups and deliveries. Being a front-end-focused leader helps to keep your fingers on the pulse of the main reason the organization exists and to make decisions compatible with it. Ideas are siphoned from the Well of Ambiguity (WOA) and analyzed to be acted upon. They only become initiatives when the details can be worked out SMARTly, by specific, measurable, adaptable, realistic processes that can be tracked with data-management systems.

One-, Two-, and Three-Dimensional Responses to Data

Three-dimensional leaders are astute to glean relevant data from the context. One and two-dimensional leaders tend not to respond well to data if they don't know the people who are providing it. I-D's operate based upon who they know and not what must be learned to manage effectively. I-D's tend to reject great and useful information because they are unfamiliar with the source. If I-D's do not know you, they can't objectively analyze what you are providing or saying. If II-D's know you, it does not matter if your ideas are unrelated to the reality of the mission within the context, the leader is prone to respond to you. Thus I- and II-D's and their misguided associates are like the blind leading the blind. This is a great tragedy for organizations stymied by I-D's. Leaders need an objective ten-thousand-foot perspective to view all data in relation to the mission and context in which it must unfold. Objectivity is needed that disassociates one from the emotional connection felt with others with whom we have camaraderie but who may not be mission focused.

At one of John Maxwell's Maximum Impact leadership conferences, Don Soderquist, Senior Vice Chairman of Wal-Mart, related how he and Sam Walton went to visit a competitor's store. Their typical strategy was to get into the store and then split up to scout it. When they convened outside to compare notes, Soderquist said that all he saw was how dirty the store was and how disheveled its shelves were. Sam, however, was excited about a jewelry display layout he saw. Walton said it was the most attractive display he had seen, and he had taken notes so he could make all the similar displays in his stores look like that. Soderquist says he learned from that experience that valuable information can come from a crummy source. From that point on he began scoping out the competition to see how he can improve what Wal-Mart does rather than to see how poorly another shop was doing things.

Don Soderquist joined Wal-Mart in 1980 and is renowned as a driving force behind Wal-Mart's rise to become the largest company in the world. Soderquist became known as the "Keeper of the Culture" after Sam Walton died. Sam taught his leaders to locate good information and act upon it, regardless of the source. Not all the information available to Sam Walton was quantifiable. Some of it came in the form of suggestions from employees based upon their empirical experiences. Once the information is acted upon, however, it should contribute to improving quantifiable outcomes, such as cleanliness, neatness, customer satisfaction, and sales and profitability.

Changes in the way people work must be accompanied by changes in how data is input, collected, and possibly analyzed. It may be important to make decisions in ways that will generate data that is as consistent as possible with the current data being analyzed. The changes may interrupt or sever data consistency so that patterns and trends cannot be determined. If you cannot tell the impact your decisions are having on data outcomes in relation to how you were doing before, you don't know how effective they are. You will lose historical continuity that helps determine where the synergies are and what specifically needs to be adjusted to improve performance or obtain productivity from your resources in the context in which they are deployed. Your change might have thrown out the proverbial baby with the bathwater. When organizations too often change what data is collected and the way it was collected, any analysis becomes murky at best. Because "mission matters most," the focus of data tracking is to determine what key service providers accomplish, which is the organization's chief competitive advantage. If you lose sight of this, you have lost your way.

Leaders who understand the mission, the nature of the work that fulfills it, and the data that captures its synergies provide information that makes fluid possibilities for their organizations rather than trapping them in "either/or thinking." One- and two-dimensional leaders do not understand how to achieve balance in the context. They lock themselves in to believing that you have to work in the extreme realm of "we either can do this or that, but we can't do both." Jim Collins has said that great organizations understand they can do both things. They can make products better and cheaper and make deliveries timely and cost effective. III-D's do not allow their organizations to get trapped in the "either/or" but lead them to function in the fluidity of the "*and* and *and.*"

Once processes are broken down into the actions, activities, and behaviors that contribute to them, the organization gets a handle on how to count the meaningful steps. We must be careful, however, not to count things merely because they can be counted. Don Giek of DGG Consulting says,

> Counting trivial or meaningless things, such as the actions that contribute to typing a letter, will make managers appear to be foolish and petty in the eyes of employees. One wants employees focused on the number of letters typed and transactions mailed with appropriate information attached to them, as opposed to the number of papers handled and keystrokes used. Only when a manager or supervisor is in the process of trying to improve or document the performance of an extremely incompetent person should such measurements be viewed as meaningful.[54]

Meaningful action is based upon relevant data. Keep in mind that in the middle of a true crisis, a sure path to defeat is to think you can be passive and survive by doing nothing. Tara L. Brooks-Smith, an office manager with the New York State Department of Labor, says her husband had a sergeant in the army who would say, "You respond to a combat crisis by taking immediate action to get things moving in the proper direction!" His mantra was "immediate action is the unhesitating application of the proper remedy to reduce stoppage without further investigation of the cause!" Before action is taken, however, make sure you are treating the right symptoms.

Action for delivering first aid for combat wounds is conducted according to the following process steps: bleeding, breathing, shock, and wounds. The process to save a patient calls for treating those things that will cause death first. If the patient is not breathing, he or she will suffer brain damage and will die within a few minutes. Once breathing, the patient still can bleed to death in about twenty minutes—depending upon the nature of a wound. So once the patient is breathing, it next is imperative to stop the bleeding. Use a tourniquet if necessary, which cuts off circulation, resulting in amputation of what is below the bandage, but stopping the loss of blood saves the patient's life. Next the patient must be treated for shock to ensure that blood flows with vital oxygen and nutrients to organs and limbs. Shock is a significant cause of death of the critically ill. Finally, wounds are treated to prevent bacterial infection from killing the patient, who has survived the other traumas above.

Each symptom above is treated following examination that provides data that the remedy is needed. Placing a tourniquet where not needed, say above the knee to treat a severe foot or ankle wound, for example, means amputation of the knee and all that is below it. The tourniquet should be as close to the wound as possible to prevent unnecessary loss of limbs. It is imperative that you are treating the right symptom, less the cure truly become worse than the disease or injury. The same is true when prescribing remedies to fix organizational problems.

Calm Competence Overcomes Crisis

Many leaders think that by creating a crisis, they can generate productive action. Just as one must be systematic to treat battlefield injuries, going about addressing organizational issues requires sane and methodical strategy. Creating a crisis mentality can lead to people reacting emotionally rather than strategically. People tend to make poor decisions when they are tired, ill, and feeling overly pressured. The leader who creates a crisis mode of operation places undue stress on his/her decision makers, which often leads to poor outcomes. The same is true of bosses who feel they have to overstate things to get people to act upon initiatives.

By contrast, one of my mottos is "underpromise and over-deliver." If I think I actually can hit eighty-nine percent, but the organizational standard is sixty-five percent, I talk about the sixty-five, because my experience is that is what people will feel comfortable dealing with. I make and implement plans that will facilitate hitting the eighty-nine if all things go well. Since, however, all things rarely go well, we'll still tend to exceed the sixty-five, so everyone is happy. I've worked with too many I-D leaders who learn enough to be dangerous and rush to make predictions and pronouncements about outcomes that depend upon too many variables for them to be a sure thing as stated.

Usually these leaders state a premature time frame, hoping to be the first to provide the "good news," thinking that gives them more stature as a leader. What often happens, however, is the leader later tasks a subordinate to explain why his/her pronouncement never came about as predicted. You can state what you believe is possible without scaring off the timid, while also leaving plenty of room to inspire those who dare to dream big dreams and who are willing to work hard to accomplish them.

The Stockdale Paradox
Having Faith and Dealing with Facts

Admiral Stockdale, who was a prisoner of war for eight years in Vietnam, following being shot down as a navy pilot, cautions about imprudent optimism. His advice when confronted by seemingly insurmountable odds is, "You not only organize for resistance, you organize to prevail." According to Stockdale,

The optimist who said, "We're going to be out by Christmas" ... and then, "We're going to be out by Easter," died of a broken heart. This is a very important lesson. You must never confuse faith that you will prevail in the end—which you can never afford to lose—with the discipline to confront the most brutal facts of your current reality, whatever that might be. You can't afford to lose faith. While going forward, you must exercise the discipline to confront the most brutal facts of your current reality. Focus on the few things that will have the greatest impact. This requires stripping away all lies and clutter, false promises, and hopes. [55]

A clear and accurate view of the context is necessary to deal appropriately with ambiguity to bring from it structure that accomplishes the mission. III-D's are disciplined people who attract disciplined people who together engage in disciplined MRC thought and undertake well-coordinated disciplined MRC actions to pursue organizational objectives over the long haul.

Inculcating your workforce with MRC concepts is foundational to them exercising good process to succeed in their contexts. Successful process requires consistent attention to the details that achieve the desired end. If indeed good process leads to good outcomes, then success can be obtained by getting a team to reach its potential by performing each of its process steps with a repeated high level of mission-oriented quality and consistency. Doing the right mission-focused things, in the right mission-focused ways, for the right mission-focused reasons gives an organization the best opportunity to achieve the right outcomes and success. Setting up your data collection appropriately to determine how your resources are accomplishing the mission is essential for understanding what your internal and external contexts reveal about how you have done and how you are doing in relation to what you are tasked to achieve. Data appropriately captured and gleaned provides actionable information about what your organization needs to do next to accomplish goals.

Context Determines Strategy and
How to Define Success

Success can mean different things to different teams and organizations. For Joe Sluzska at the Albany Housing Coalition, success initially meant pursuing a strategy to stay solvent and maintaining enough properties to house existing clients and finding residences for those he could not. With the initial crisis behind, success for the Coalition now means moving forward into a strategy that includes affordable ownership options for them.

For sports teams that are in a rebuilding phase, a 500 season can be considered success. For a team that has come in second the previous year, nothing short of a championship is success. If the same team has lost several key players, however, achieving what it accomplished last year would be considered success. The contextual starting point is a chief determinant of what should be considered mission success. The American free enterprise system provides hope that each day presents new opportunities to negotiate the context, regardless of your starting point.

When organizations require intervention, their strategies need to include accountability. Federal government intervention in the airline, auto manufacturing, and in the financial industries changes the context for those companies, because the entity that provides a significant investment gets some say or control over how an organization is administered, led, and run. Consider what transpired during 1979 and 1980, when the federal government loaned the Chrysler Corporation 1.2 billion dollars to avert bankruptcy. There was intense congressional scrutiny of Chrysler that involved months of hearings that resulted in Lee Iacocca personally putting his livelihood on the line and agreeing to an annual salary of just $1.00 (that's right, one dollar!) until he could repay the loan.

Even so, Chrysler was held to a strict repayment schedule, had to submit a new business plan, and cooperated with fiscal oversight. Furthermore, the agreement called for limits on all executive salaries and required union concessions, all of which remained in force until Chrysler repaid its obligation. In 2001 the federal government assisted the airline industry that struggled near bankruptcy just after the attacks on the New York City World Trade Center on 9/11/2001. Assistance was contingent upon approval of those companies' restructuring plans, caps on executive pay, and fiscal oversight. This type of scrutiny should accompany any requested government intervention in private business dealings.

When companies are publicly traded, their leaders' jobs are to create shareholder value. Investors provide resources in exchange for stock to assist businesses to implement plans to provide goods and services that customers are willing to pay for at a price that makes a profit for the seller and the investor. Corporations fulfill their missions by efficiently acquiring and deploying resources to achieve success within the context. A company's assets minus its liabilities, divided by the number of shares of stock it has on the market, can provide a baseline value of each of those shares.

Stock investments of private citizens and organizations are overseen by the U.S. Securities and Exchange Commission (SEC). According to its Web site, the SEC's "mission ... is

> to protect investors, maintain fair, orderly, and efficient markets, and facilitate capital formation. As more and more first-time investors turn to the markets to help secure their futures, pay for homes, and send children to college, our investor protection mission is more compelling than ever. As our nation's securities exchanges mature into global for-profit competitors, there is even greater need for sound market regulation. And the common interest of all Americans in a growing economy that produces jobs, improves our standard of living, and protects the value of our savings means that all of the SEC's actions must be taken with an eye toward promoting the capital formation that is necessary to sustain economic growth."[56]

Thus SEC rules and regulations are part of the context that honorable publicly traded corporations must negotiate. Honorable corporations are headed up by honorable, mission-focused people. In my opinion, since the CEO of a publicly traded company is paid a salary to create shareholder value, if the company is in financial trouble, and the value of its shares decline beyond a certain point, say ten percent, the leader's income should decline accordingly. The salary and bonuses of a CEO of a publicly traded company should track the value of its shares. The leader's income, in part, should be a reflection of that shareholder value or stock performance. This does not overcome the challenge that there always may be I-D corporate leaders who will attempt to artificially inflate stock values to make themselves look good and increase their own income. SEC oversight is designed to police this type of activity.

While there are reasons other than company performance that can influence stock values, such as the activities of speculators and short sellers that can drive up and lower prices, the determination of the leader to pursue MRC-focused strategies remains the most significant variable in the organization's long-term health and success as an investment vehicle. Board members will serve their corporations and its investors well by holding CEOs accountable to achieve MRC principles.

I believe it is conscientious for a leader who earns tens of millions of dollars to take less to assist a company to survive. For example, if a leader's salary and bonus package includes that he can withdraw a hundred million dollars from a struggling company, I believe it is a selfless and moral act for him or her to forgo $83 million to squeak by on $17 million. This gives the company the opportunity to plough tens of millions of dollars back in to operations to pay for thousands of salaries for employees to continue paying their mortgages, making car payments, and putting their children through school, providing the company has the hopes of making a profit from their labor.

Large sums of money and other benefits, known as golden parachutes, do have a legitimate place in corporate strategy. Many corporations guarantee large golden parachutes to their chief executives to offset the risk that they will be without jobs if the company is purchased, acquired by a hostile takeover, or dismantled by corporate raiders. Such arrangements make it more attractive for people to assume the risks of taking on leadership roles within companies. Corporations also provide lucrative guarantees to their executives to make a takeover less attractive, since potential new owners immediately would have to pay out large sums of money to the chief executives of a corporation they have succeeded in acquiring.

Contracts for golden parachutes, however, should be written to link their reward to the actual personal performance of the executives. This could prevent executives from being motivated to see the companies that hire them underperform, so the stock prices drop, making a takeover more likely, so they can cash out. Executives should be motivated to keep their companies performing as well as possible, because, generally speaking, the healthier a company is the less likely it is to be sold or acquired for the wrong reasons.

Because no organization is perfect at negotiating its context, there is a continual need for the leadership displayed by Lee Iacocca, who oversaw the Chrysler Corporation through its crisis during the late 1970s and early 1980s. To protect investors, the SEC also must show leadership and be vigilant about its mission and deploy its resources appropriately to negotiate the context of the global economy to ensure it provides appropriate oversight to secure publicly traded capital. The SEC's role also should include ensuring that speculators do not escape with artificial profits that victimize investors by leaving corporations vulnerable to juggle fluctuating stock values. Corporations should not be allowed to gouge consumers by taking undue advantage of the inflationary price fluctuations created by speculators and short sellers.

Quality corporate earnings result from profits from operations. Stable returns on capital, equity, and investment result from organizations pursuing the missions that give them competitive advantage in the marketplace. This is achieved when leaders effectively and efficiently pursue strategies that deploy resources within a changing context. Ultimately, leaders position their organizations for success when they train and provide potential for their people to fulfill their job roles and responsibilities. According to *Smartbrief on Leadership,* an online newsletter, Harvard Business School research by Assistant Professor Zynep Ton linked "increased spending on staffing and increased profits" because people fulfill behind-the-scenes tasks, such as ensuring that stock [or product] was on the sales floor and not in the storeroom, returning unsold items and keeping display shelves tidy."[57] People provide potential. This has been true in the past, and it will be true in the future.

Chapter Thirty-three
The Future Tri-Dimensional Leader

Change and Out-of-the-Box Achievement (OO-B Achievers)

I believe that what often is attributed to intuition on behalf of a leader actually is the outcome of study, reflection, and practice that provides foresight to understand the context in which the mission unfolds and how to deploy resources to effectively negotiate it. For those of you who "think outside of the box," much of what you envision has not been done before or has not been done in a particular way before. Thus others think that the achievement "came out of the blue" of intuition. But what the out-of-box thinker (OO-B-thinker, pronounced "Ooh-Bee-thinker") achieves results from studied practice at making connections within the context. Albert Einstein did not invent or create the elements of $E=MC^2$. His genius was seeing the patterns and making the connections between the elements that were there in the context. Einstein knew there was more there than what was realized. He pressed beyond those boundaries not to create a new reality but to discover the connections in the reality that already were there but were unrealized. OO-B achievers do the same.

I used to file VA compensation and disability claims and won on behalf of a veteran what at that time was the largest retroactive settlement in state history and perhaps in the nation and paid lump sum entitlements from 1954 to 1994. Years of study and practice tutored me to think of each case as a legal context, the components of which were like puzzle pieces, which consisted of the client's military history, medical diagnostic and prognostic status, and the likelihood of employability within the job market. I would turn the puzzle to view the context of the case from different perspectives to see if various angles revealed connections between its elements.

When I discussed the parameters of that claim with others, the objections they raised as to why it could not be won provided me with information about what must be overcome to win it. I generally, however, only spoke once or twice to someone who was a naysayer because I did not want to get discouraged from pursuing what had not been done before. I did make sure, however, that I completely understood the naysayer's perspective regarding exactly why the case that originally had been denied in the 1950s could not be overturned in the 1990s. Even when I found encouragement from other industry experts, they could provide little direct advice about what to do next, because I was in uncharted territory, and their past experience had limited relevance to what I was trying to achieve and where I had to go.

The Five Factors of OO-B

So to encourage those of you who are destined as OO-B-thinkers to become OO-B achievers who will accomplish what has not been done before, I advise you to do and be aware of the following:

1. Listen and learn from all, but be discouraged by none.

2. When people tell you why something cannot be done, realize that they also are telling you what to overcome if you are to achieve it.

3. Seek out experts, but realize that their advice and input only can take you so far. They often provide great historical analysis that helps you review the map of the known existing world and its waterways, forests, valleys, and mountains. Their analysis helps you to better understand the context of information, processes, and materials that have brought the world to what it has achieved so far. You will have to use this information as a launching pad to build the future vehicle that will take you into the uncharted areas in which you are destined to succeed.

4. Be prepared to go it alone, because as congenial, good hearted, and encouraging as others may try to be, they do not see what you see; they do not feel what you feel; they do not think what you think; and they, therefore, cannot go where you are going—even though they may wish to accompany you.

5. The fifth factor of OO-B is the most significant and involves learning how to learn so that contextual transference occurs through the process described below.

Learning how to learn is essential to being an OO-B thinker. Sometimes someone will ask me how I am progressing on a project, and I'll say, "I am not making much progress yet, because with this particular task I am in the process of learning how to learn. I am trying to figure out what the dynamics and parameters of it are, and once I figure that out, then I will know in what direction to focus my research to get to a place where I can have actionable information with which to work and move forward."

Information stored and categorized properly in the "Well of Ambiguity" (WOA), once segregated into pools of related material, is added to, takes shape, and becomes its own body of knowledge. Once identified as such, related patterns can continue to emerge from other information within the context to become tributaries that feed into this new amalgamation. As it takes shape and solidifies, it becomes actionable as its own strategic entity. Contextual transference has occurred.

Contextual Transference

"Contextual transference" is thoroughly understanding your context and making connections that lead to new applications of that existing information. What exists, however, needs to be relevantly associated or connected to reveal its new future potential. This is my theory of why so many inventions come from unlikely sources. The biologist Mendel started out as a priest. The telephone's inventor, Alexander Graham Bell, was a speech therapist. The ballpoint pen was invented by leather tanner John Loud. The airplane was pioneered by bicycle shop owners Wilbur and Orville Wright. The astronomer who discovered Halley's Comet, Edmund Halley, invented the diving bell. Each of these people, while pursuing their primary field of study, siphoned ideas from their context that they pooled, analyzed, and transferred to apply to another field.

OO-B achievers accomplish contextual transference by realizing that information is a resource. While all the information may not directly apply to fulfilling their current mission, OO-B's categorize what they siphon from their contexts and store it for future access. When they collate or pool enough of a particular type of information so that patterns begin to take shape, OO-B's organize it into separate and distinct bodies of research. As they pursue this, they learn more, are able to classify preliminary results, and define information for further and more specific study.

OO-B's do not impose what they currently know upon the developing informational patterns. Instead, they allow the emerging prototypes to challenge what they currently know. They allow it to speak for itself as they objectively examine this new empirical data and phenomena without bias. Thus, they allow it to guide them into channels where it becomes its own waterways leading to the future, emerging state of the way things soon will be.

Innovation is the Point OO-B

The reason why OO-B thinking is so important is because it leads to innovation, and innovation is the calling card of many successful businesses and organizations. Innovation secures the future of industry from auto manufacturing to breakfast, and snack food products. If a company ignores innovative trends in product design, materials and fabric and upholstery processing, and dietary supplements, its products will not stay on the cutting edge of "what customers want now." Companies that fail to innovate lose their relevancy in the marketplace. One-dimensional leaders kill innovation. Remember that whatever I-D's do not know they fear, and whatever they fear they kill. Two-dimensional leaders tend not to recognize, appreciate, or take advantage of innovation because they fail to see its relevance within the context.

Auto manufacturers today are making the same mistakes they made in the 1970s, ignoring emerging trends related to fuel prices. The global economic meltdown means that people will become more frugal. Negotiating the context of consumerism that is efficiency and economy minded means providing product designs that are not big, oversized, and pretentious to glitter and shine like "bling." (Bling is a street term for costume jewelry.) Fuel efficient cars with conveniences and safety features that previously only adorned luxury vehicles is innovation that will provide a healthy future for auto makers.

Globalization Makes "OO-B Achievement" More Efficient

Globalization is the concept that thoughts and ideas are transferred rapidly into worldwide significance. Because common people, regardless of location, can communicate through the World Wide Web, kids all over the world, including Yugoslavia, Australia, Africa, America, and China, can dress alike in the latest fads because they globally are connected to the same information. Web services like Facebook and YouTube provide worldwide social networking and access to what takes place in students' computer rooms, so opportunity abounds for the cross-pollination of ideas and contextual transference.

Wikipedia[58] is an example of how information can be compiled from collaborative people who are willing to function in the "high-right quadrant" to contribute what can be categorized, verified, shared and made available to feed curiosity and spur productive achievement. Many organizations have developed intranet wikis that allow people from diverse divisions to facilitate the intersecting of ideas into new fusions that will yield future innovations. Hence, because of the World Wide Web, globalization makes contextual transference more efficient.

People who are destined to be OO-B-achievers now can obtain and categorize greater amounts of information more rapidly than ever before. The Web allows OO-B's to find others who are passionate about the same theories and postulates. Global teams connected through the Web provide amazing synergies that can increase the productivity of ideas and reduce the cycle time for them to take shape. This can shorten the learning curves for those ideas to evolve into products and services. The leaders of tomorrow include those who will harness these Web tool synergies to propel their organizations to the front-end of learning and achievement.

Conclusion

Highly effective leadership focuses upon the three operational dimensions of mission, resources, and context. Three-dimensional leaders comprehend all three elements to negotiate a favorable set of circumstances so employees can succeed at their jobs, which ultimately is what makes the organization successful. One-dimensional leadership is all about "me," the leader, and not the mission. Two-dimensional leaders function within one or two of the three operational elements. More often than not, II-D leaders fail to perceive the context and how available resources must be deployed to fulfill the mission within it. To grow as a three-dimensional leader, a simple question to ask your followers is, "What can I do to make it easier for you to succeed at our mission?"

Since "mission matters most," the leader's focus upon it makes all the difference in organizational performance. When a leader has a clear sense of the core mission for which the organization exists, he/she discerns how to deploy resources to fulfill it. Rather than dream up initiatives that are designed to bring attention to themselves as leaders, three-dimensional leaders train, trust, and time how they empower people resources so they assimilate the context to negotiate accomplishing the mission. Delegation that allows others to take initiative and obtain the credit for doing so provides the synergy that makes the collective outcomes much greater and more powerful than the sum of the individual parts. Three-dimensional leaders achieve resource integration and coordination that provides quadruple wins for the organization and its employees, its partners, and its clients.

Leaders must solve problems and make daily decisions consistent with the organization's long-range mission, vision, and values. III-D's will not undermine them just to get something done today. Effectively negotiating the context means first understanding the mission; second, what resources are available to accomplish it; and third, into what arena, forum, or set of circumstances are the resources to be deployed to accomplish it. When you understand your context, you know how and in what way to deploy your resources to fulfill a mission.

The reason franchising your core cultural values and operational success dynamics is so important to your internal context is because you want what is being accomplished to succeed you. None of us will be around forever. Stick your fist into a fish tank full of water and then pull it out. There is no hole or vacancy from where you have withdrawn your hand. That is how life will go on after each of us is gone. Is it not better for us to work in a way that allows our organizations to succeed after we've moved on? Three-dimensional leaders prove they are great leaders by how well their teams perform in their absence. That's the legacy I want to leave. That's a three-dimensional legacy worth working for.

Endnotes

1   Einstein, Albert. *Essays in Science.* Covici-Friede, Inc.: 2004. pg. 7.

2   Hybels, Bill. *Courageous Leadership.* Zondervan: Grand Rapids, 2002. pg. 31.

3   Lencioni, Patrick. *The Five Dysfunctions of a Team: A Leadership Fable.* Jossey-Bass: 2002. pg. vii.

4   Collins, Jim. *Good To Great: Why Some Companies Make the Leap and Others Don't.* Harper Collins: 2001. pgs. 131–133.

5   *The Leadership Challenge, 3rd Edition.* Jossey-Bass A. Wiley Imprint.

6   BNET Business Network Market Wire April 2006, http://findarticles.com/p/articles/mi_pwwi/is_200604/ai_n16136133

7   http://www.engr.uky.edu/alumni/hod/boyd_jo.html

8   Collins, Jim. *Good To Great: Why Some Companies Make the Leap and Others Don't.* Harper Collins: 2001. pg. 14.

9   Collins, Jim. *Good To Great: Why Some Companies Make the Leap and Others Don't.* Harper Collins: 2001. pg. 181–182.

10 Siklos, Richard. "The Math Whiz vs. The Media Moguls in a Battle for Millions." *The New York Times.* April 3, 2006. "Amid the flash of the Internet bubble, Henry C. Yuen, the chairman and chief executive of Gemstar-TV Guide International, did things his way." http://www.nytimes.com/2006/04/03/business/03yuen.html

11 Hybels, Bill. *Courageous Leadership.* Zondervan: Grand Rapids, 2002. pg. 62.

12 Pope, Alexander. *Selected Poetry and Prose, Second Edition.* "An Essay on Criticism, Part II, Line 215." Introduction by William K. Wimsatt. Holt, Rinehart, and Winston, Inc.: 1972. pg. 73.

13 Radice, Betty. *Who's Who in the Ancient World: A Handbook to the Survivors of the Greek and Roman Classics.* Penguin Books: New York: 1973. pg. 163.

14 *Organizational Behavior.* Irwin/McGraw-Hill: 1998. pg. 652.

15 *Organizational Behavior.* Irwin/McGraw-Hill: 1998. pg. 302–303.

16 Ohmae, Kenichi, Director. *The Mind of the Strategist: The Art of Japanese Business.* McKinsey & Company: Tokyo, 1982. pg. 216–218.

17 http://corporate.servicemaster.com/overview_objectives.asp

18 http://corporate.servicemaster.com/careers.asp

19 Julian, Larry S. *God Is My CEO: Following God's Principles in a Bottom-line World.* Adams Media: 2002. pgs. 14–17.

20 Sun Tzu. *On the Art of War.* Translated from the Chinese by Lionel Giles, M.A. (1910) VI. "Weak Points and Strong," pg. 27. http://www.chinapage.com/sunzi-e.html#01#01

21 www.nyfb.org

22 Davis, Keith, and Newstrom, John W. *Human Relations at Work: The Dynamics of Organizational Behavior, 3rd Edition.* McGraw-Hill: 1967. Figure 7.2, pgs. 117–118.

23 *The Army Leadership Manual.* FM 22–100, section 2–59, says, "Culture is a group's shared set of beliefs, values, and assumptions about what's important."

24 *The Manager-as-Mediator* Seminar Resource Manual, for instruction in Managerial Mediation, developed by Daniel Dana, Ph.D. MTI Publications (hereafter cited as Managerial Mediation): 1994.

25 The Thomas-Kilman CMI appears on page 246.

26 *Managerial Mediation.* pg. 5.

27 *Managerial Mediation.* pg. 6.

28 Goldsmith, Marshall. Marshall@MarshallGoldsmith.com. Marshall Goldsmith Library Web site/Forbes.com

29 Hopkins, Michael S. "The Antiheroic Leadership Style- 4 New Rules." *INC Magazine,* June 2003 issue.

30 Hybels, Bill. *Courageous Leadership.* Zondervan: Grand Rapids, 2002. pgs. 121–130.

31 Hybels, Bill. *Courageous Leadership.* Zondervan: Grand Rapids, 2002. pg. 130.

32 Hybels, Bill. *Courageous Leadership.* Zondervan: Grand Rapids, 2002. pgs. 139–159.

33 Lencioni, Patrick. *The Five Dysfunctions of a Team: A Leadership Fable.* Jossey-Bass, A Wiley Company: 2002. pg. vii.

34 Lencioni, Patrick. *The Five Dysfunctions of a Team: A Leadership Fable.* Jossey-Bass, A Wiley Company: 2002. pg. viii.

35 http://www.boonepickens.com/thoughts/default.asp

36 Copyright © 2002 by CPP, Inc. All rights reserved. Further reproduction is prohibited without the Publisher's written consent.

37 http://www.mph.ufl.edu/events/seminar/Tuckman1965DevelopmentalSequence.pdf

38 New International Version of the Bible, Matthew 7:12

39 Hybels, Bill. *Courageous Leadership.* Zondervan: Grand Rapids, 2002. pgs. 170–171.

40 Sowell, Thomas. *Basic Economics, A Citizen's Guide to the Economy, Revised and Expanded Edition.* Thomas Sowell: 2004. pgs. 129.

41 Sowell, Thomas. *Basic Economics, A Citizen's Guide to the Economy, Revised and Expanded Edition.* Thomas Sowell: 2004. pgs. 127–128.

42 Sun Tzu. *On The Art of War: The Oldest Military Treatise in the World.* Trans. Lionel Giles, M.A.:1910. http://www.china-page.com/sunzi-e.html#01#01

43 Sun Tzu. *On The Art of War: The Oldest Military Treatise in the World.* Trans. Lionel Giles, M.A.:1910. http://www.china-page.com/sunzi-e.html#01#01

44 Collins, Jim. *Good To Great: Why Some Companies Make the Leap and Others Don't.* Harper Collins: 2001. pgs. 97.

45 Bill Minchin is the Executive Pastor of Grace Fellowship Church (GFC) in Latham, New York.

46 Rex Keener is the Senior Pastor of Grace Fellowship Church (GFC) in Latham, New York.

47 Sun Tzu. *On the Art of War II.* Attack by Stratagem, 17. (3) http://www.chinapage.com/sunzi-e.html#01#01

48 The acrostic for Core Operational Success Dynamic is COSD and is pronounced "cos-dee."

49 *Movers and Shakers: The 100 Most Influential Figures in Modern Business.* Bloomsbury: Cambridge, 2003. pg. 66.

50 Hill, Charles, and Hill, W.L. *Strategic Management Theory: An Integrated Approach, 4th Edition.* Houghton Mifflin Company: Boston, 1998. pgs. 7–8.

51 *Strategic Management Theory.* Houghton Mifflin: 1998. pgs. 384.

52 Kotler, Philip. *Marketing Management, Analysis, Planning, Implementation and Control.* Prentice Hall. pg. 770.

53 Amos 3:3, King James Bible

54 Powell, Colin. "Lesson Fifteen of his Leadership Primer, Lesson 15. A Leadership Primer from General (Ret.) Colin

Powell, Secretary of State, by Oren Harari. http://www. chally.com/enews/powell.

55 Conversation with Don Giek, DGG Consulting. March 2007.

56 Collins, Jim. *Good To Great: Why Some Companies Make the Leap and Others Don't.* Harper Collins: 2001. pg. page 85. Collin's interview with Admiral Stockdale, pgs. 83–87.

57 http://www.sec.gov/about/whatwedo.shtml

58 http://blogs.ft.com/management/2008/10/02/retailers-should-not-skimp-on-staffing-in-downturn/

59 According to http://en.wikipedia.org/wiki/Wiki, a wiki is a page or collection of Web pages designed to enable anyone who accesses it to contribute or modify content, using a simplified markup language.[1][2] Wikis are often used to create collaborative websites and to power community websites. The collaborative encyclopedia Wikipedia is one of the best-known wikis.[2] Wikis are used in business to provide intranets and Knowledge Management systems. Ward Cunningham, developer of the first wiki software, WikiWikiWeb, originally described it as "the simplest online database that could possibly work."[3]

listen|imagine|view|experience

AUDIO BOOK DOWNLOAD INCLUDED WITH THIS BOOK!

In your hands you hold a complete digital entertainment package. Besides purchasing the paper version of this book, this book includes a free download of the audio version of this book. Simply use the code listed below when visiting our website. Once downloaded to your computer, you can listen to the book through your computer's speakers, burn it to an audio CD or save the file to your portable music device (such as Apple's popular iPod) and listen on the go!

How to get your free audio book digital download:

1. Visit www.tatepublishing.com and click on the e|LIVE logo on the home page.
2. Enter the following coupon code:
   80dd-9643-7cd3-5beb-f950-0f74-5f7d-4971.
   Download the audio book from your e|LIVE digital locker and begin enjoying your new digital entertainment package today!